THERESA MORITZ & ALBER

The World's Most Dangerous Woman: A New Biography of Emma Goldman

Subway Books
Vancouver, Toronto

ISBN 0-9681660-7-5

Printed on acid-free paper

Canadian Cataloguing in Publication Data

Moritz, Theresa, 1948–

The world's most dangerous woman: a new biography of
Emma Goldman

Includes bibliographical references and index.
ISBN 0-9681660-7-5

1. Goldman, Emma, 1869–1940. 2. Anarchists–United States–
Biography. I. Moritz, A.F. II. Title.

HX843.7.G65M67 2000   335'.83'092   C00-901176-5

Orders:
Customer Order Department
University of Toronto Press
5201 Dufferin Street
Toronto, Ontario M3H 5T8
Canada

Toll-free ordering from Canada or the US:
Telephone 1-800-565-9523
Fax 1-800-221-9985
Email:
utpbooks@gpu.utcc.utoronto.ca

To L. Susan Brown, Regina Cochrane,
Maria Lester, and Bob Melcombe,
the "anarchs", and to all who keep alive
the spirit of Emma Goldman

Contents

THE WORLD'S MOST DANGEROUS WOMAN:
A NEW BIOGRAPHY OF EMMA GOLDMAN

1

A Veritable Fury Unchained

In the last quarter of her tumultuous life, the anarchist and feminist Emma Goldman—enemy of all government and champion of free love, who plagued generations of Babbitts and imperialists—spent three extended periods living and working in Canada: from 15 October 1926 to 20 February 1928, from 10 December 1933 to 3 May 1935 (during which time she made a three-month tour of the United States), and from 17 April 1939 to 14 May 1940, the day of her death. Already fifty-seven when she arrived in 1926, she nevertheless was frantically active during all but the last three months of her almost four years in the Dominion; only a paralyzing stroke in February 1940 could stop her constant speaking, writing and organizing. In her day, Goldman was denounced famously as "the most dangerous woman in America", but the scope of her activities was so truly international that detractors might have stigmatized her just as easily as the "most dangerous woman in the world". Her years in Canada seem to us to illustrate this point.

Her three Canadian residences were the direct result of her attempts to find a field for anarchist activities after the First World War, in face of Russian communism and international reactionary politics. They can also be seen as an outgrowth of her successful activity in Canada much earlier, when her fame and influence were at their height. In the period 1906 to 1908 she made several visits to Canada, which until now have been virtually unknown to her biographers altogether. She played a significant part in the introduction of the May Day workers' holiday and in other causes.

Goldman's Canadian years have until now been passed over lightly by scholars, radical thinkers, and popular historians, no doubt in part because they do not fit the US emphasis that is naturally standard to American biographical portraits. Neglect of her Canadian experience may also be explained by reliance on Goldman's 1931 autobiography, *Living My Life*, which of course could capture only the first of her three stays. In English-language, single-volume biographies (Richard Drinnon's *Rebel in Paradise*, Candace Falk's *Love, Anarchy, and Emma Goldman*, John Chalberg's *Emma Goldman: American Individualist*, and less substantial ones by Alix Kates Shulman, Marian J. Morton, and B.N. Ganguli), the three years and eight months of Goldman's life in Canada receive only a handful of pages. The only Canadian incident these biographies treat in some detail is Goldman's death. Falk, who concentrates on Goldman's love affairs, describes liaisons which took place in Canada but her life in the country remains otherwise unexplored. Insofar as the biographies recite some of Goldman's Canadian activities, they offer brief summaries and add little to one another's accounts. The Canadian experience appears insubstantial even in the work of Alice Wexler, who retells Goldman's life in two volumes, one of which, *Emma Goldman in Exile*, is devoted solely to the period after 1919, when she was expelled from the United States. Yet Goldman spent about twenty per cent of these twenty years in Canada.

Other recent sources that provide impressions of Goldman also neglect her Canadian experience. For example, E.L. Doctorow's portrayal of her in *Ragtime* concentrates on her New York era. John Reed's *Ten Days That Shook the World* shows her only in the context of revolutionary Russia. Warren Beatty's 1981 film version of Reed's book, *Reds*, featured Maureen Stapleton's Academy Award-winning portrayal of Goldman as disillusioned and weary, thus repeating the assessment of her current in the United States since soon after her 1919 deportation: that she was a self-marginalized and ineffective if noble idealist, and that by the 1920s her era had passed. Even the Canadian playwright Carol Bolt's *Red Emma* concentrates on her glory days around the turn of the century.

In Canada, and especially in Toronto, Goldman does continue to be remembered and even to have an effect. A faction of the city's remaining anarchist community, small but active, has made her the namesake of its drop-in centre and book shop, Who's Emma, in Kensington Market, not far from the location of her 1926–28 apartments on Spadina Avenue. Prominent members of the city's journalistic and cultural communities continue to find it necessary to mention her, usually as a measure of the city's narrow past, against which she stands out colourfully. A typical example is James Lemon's *Toronto Since 1918* (1985): "Quiet, Orange, British Toronto could not nourish ... an Emma Goldman who ... was told by a Toronto librarian: 'No, we do not censor books, we simply do not get them.'"[1] Lemon's anecdote is from Goldman's autobiography and is repeated in Richard

Drinnon's biography, from which it is repeated again in a 1983 Toronto *Star* column by Robert Fulford, "Emma Goldman Saw Toronto Harshly", written on the occasion of the paperback reissue of Drinnon's book. Interesting as it is, this oft-repeated incident only symbolizes the fact that Goldman's life in Canada has been narrated largely in terms of a very few items, passed from hand to hand without further inquiry.

As an anarchist, Goldman believed in involving herself in local affairs wherever she happened to be living. On these grounds alone—as an examination of her method—the Canadian years are worthy of study. But her Canadian experience was also rich in incident and makes up a distinct phase of her life, with its own characteristic elements and significance. This book concentrates on her Canadian years, drawing on the voluminous documentary evidence available in her correspondence and other records, but treats them in the context of her entire life, with emphasis on her important activities between the three extended Canadian stays, most notably the writing of her autobiography in France in 1928–31, and her participation in the Spanish Civil War in 1936–38. In addition, the summary of her life prior to 1926 contains a full account of her activities in Canada during her several visits in 1906–08.

The frustrated yet indomitable intensity of Goldman's efforts during the 1925–40 period, and especially in Canada, illuminate many modern and contemporary issues: issues of idealism versus compromise, of ageing and "living beyond one's time", of the nature of personal fulfilment, of how our social system controls access to public life and permits or denies effective participation. Also, the role Canada played in her later life points beyond the perennial criticism of Canadian political insularity and inertia to a related but universal and far more interesting problem.

The Canada of the 1920s and 1930s foreshadowed the present worldwide scramble to mount the hierarchical ladder of control, wealth, and prestige, workers and masses yearning to identify with the "haves", to deny self-comfortingly that they are the victims of class war. Just as today, capitalism and the democratic governments in the 1920s and 1930s were creating mechanisms to spread wealth and attach more persons to the status quo through economic self-interest. By these (and other) means, much of the impetus was taken out of radicalism. Goldman struggled to find ways to oppose such trends, which have since become so widespread that effective radical politics can often seem impossible. What could shake the general conviction in most nations that there is no creditable mode of social organization beyond the present one? Today it is easy to recognize the plight of shrinking social idealism caught in ever-thickening conformity, but difficult to know what to do. Goldman's Canadian years are in part the story of how prophetically she lived, understood, criticized and fought this problem, which was then coming into existence in its current form, but which few noticed.

Goldman was a person of action, not primarily a thinker and writer. Her resolution of such questions would have come through achieved results, not through a written theory and programme. This biography gives equal weight to the private evidences of her inner life and the interlace in her character between social action and the personal realms of sexuality, love, sensual and aesthetic response, and the play of the feelings. One of the distinguishing elements of Goldman's anarchism was the broad notion that within each person there is a close interdependence of public and private selves and that this unity is of key importance for effective social action. For her, the individual conceived in full psychological, sensual, and spiritual complexity was the grounding of a radical anti-authoritarian social vision. Important throughout her life, this idea gains force and definition in her Canadian years when, cut off from an effective political movement, she sought fulfilment—and defence against near manic-depressive swings of emotion from hope to despair—in the realms of personal relationships and the reimagining of an anarchism for the future.

Since her political and social goals did not become reality, and her anarchistic ideals and movement have long been in abeyance, Goldman might be seen to have failed. In Canada, she moved, struggled, and finally died under muffling restrictions. Moreover, she was unable either to establish a fully satisfactory erotic and romantic life or to make public even to her own comrades such love relationships as she did achieve, for fear of the deleterious consequences on her political work. And yet, as few other historical figures do, she allows those who encounter her story to see that rarely questioned social arrangements can and must be questioned, and that human beings are capable, if not of total freedom and angelic energy, then at least of much greater freedom and energy than most ever permit themselves. She provides not an intellectual solution but an example of unfailing effort towards liberation. To paraphrase an observation on Samuel Johnson by W. Jackson Bate, one of the first effects Goldman has on us is that we find ourselves catching, by contagion, something of her courage. This is especially true of her repeated struggle in Canada to create the conditions necessary for free action.

Born 27 June 1869 in the Jewish quarter of Kovno (present-day Kaunas, Lithuania), Emma Goldman was the first child of Abraham Goldman and Taube Bienowitch. Kovno had been a part of the Russian empire since the partitioning of Poland in 1795, and increasingly restrictive imperial treat-ment of Jews greatly influenced Goldman's young life, as did the troubled personal history of her parents. Abraham, a native of Kovno, was Taube's second husband. The daughter of a physician, Taube brought to their mar-riage two daughters and a considerable inheritance, which Abraham lost in an unsuccessful investment before Emma was born. Abraham's repeated business reverses and enforced moves in search of work, his dependence on his wife's family for jobs and money, his desire for sons, and his violent temper all played parts in his increasingly bitter struggles with Emma.

Emma wanted an education, but in Abraham's view she did not require one to be a good wife and mother. Besides, the family needed her earnings, first from sewing done at home and then in a corset factory in St Petersburg, whose crowded ghetto drew the Goldmans in 1881 after periods in Popelan and Königsberg. Emma wanted love, but Abraham arranged a marriage for her and beat her when she refused the match. What little information she gives in her autobiography about her early life conveys her interpretation that her passionate independence, her hatred of traditional marriage and organized religion, and her condemnation of the limits placed on women by society had been forged by her childhood in Russia. She recounts a conversation with one of her first mentors in the United States, the anar-chist lecturer and newspaper editor Johann Most, soon after they met: "He was now more convinced than ever, he told me, that it was the influence of my childhood that had made me what I was."[2] On fire with the revolution-ary dreams of St Petersburg's nihilists, she finally extorted permission from her parents to emigrate to the United States with her half-sister Helena in December 1885. She threatened to throw herself into the River Neve if her father tried to keep her at home.

The United States appeared to her at first as a disheartening duplicate of her confined life in St Petersburg. Family expectations weighed heavily on her: her father and mother arrived in autumn 1886 in Rochester, New York, where the sisters had settled near the eldest of Taube's daughters, Lena. Goldman felt cut off by language and culture from the larger English-speak-ing society and confined in the Russian Jewish immigrant community. Almost at once she resumed grinding factory work, but now under condi-tions more oppressive than those she had known in St Petersburg: she quit her first factory job, making ulsters at Garson, Meyer and Company, after being refused a raise on her starting pay of $2.50 a week. Finally, she was disappointed in love. Her 1887 marriage to a fellow Russian Jew, Jacob Kersner, urged on her by her family, ended in divorce in less than a year; a brief reconciliation lasted an even shorter time before she made a final break in August 1889 and left Rochester for New York City. By now, she was determined to devote herself to the cause of anarchism. Goldman repeated throughout her life, in word and in deed, that the event that inspired her commitment was the execution on 11 November 1887 of four Chicago anarchists convicted in the so-called Haymarket bombing. On 4 May 1886, the fourth day of a general strike, seven Chicago policemen were killed and scores of citizens injured by a bomb thrown at the end of a rally at which eight anarchists, including the four men later hanged, had spoken. On her first evening in New York, Goldman attended a lecture by Johann Most, in whose newspaper, *Die Freiheit*, she had followed the Haymarket story while living in Rochester.

Her escort to Most's lecture that first night in New York was Alexander Berkman, called Sasha by friends, like herself a recent immigrant from Russia. Berkman would become the most important person in her life: her lover, editor, collaborator, co-conspirator. For both of them, life in the early years in New York was a tragicomic hybrid of looking for work, sometimes running small businesses and sometimes doing piecework for the garment trade, and campaigning for anarchism, largely under the direction of Most, who recognized Goldman's potential as a lecturer and sent her on her first speaking tour in January 1890. In early 1892, Berkman became outraged by violence against striking workers at the Carnegie Steel plant in Homestead, Pennsylvania, and set out to assassinate Carnegie's chairman, Henry Clay Frick, in hopes of fomenting a broad workers' revolution in the United States. He forced his way into Frick's office on 23 July and wounded him seriously but not fatally; workingmen in Frick's office held Berkman for police. Berkman was sentenced to twenty-two years in prison, and Goldman, remorseful that she had not been arrested with him, devoted herself to overturning the conviction, reducing the sentence, and even organizing an escape attempt. Soon after, she herself served a year in Blackwell's Island Penitentiary for a speech at a New York demonstration. She said the state "could have rendered me no greater service",[3] for she emerged with a new way to support herself, nursing, and a new fearlessness about what she might face in campaigning for anarchism. She spent 1895 in Vienna studying midwifery, and on this and two subsequent trips to Europe she became friendly with most of the major European anarchists and radicals. Her friendship with Peter Kropotkin, the most influential anarchist thinker and writer of the nineteenth century, was especially vital to her development.

On her return, Goldman began to speak extensively throughout North America. In the days with Most, she had spoken in Yiddish and German, but now she began to reach out to a wider audience in English. She became convinced that only an arousal of revolutionary sentiment in the broad US population would bring about actual social change. Her topics expanded beyond workers' issues to include ones which had become important to her through her work as a nurse and midwife to tenement women: birth control, women's rights, education.

Her increasing success, which paralleled a promising recovery in the anarchist movement, was cut short in 1901 when President William McKinley was assassinated by Leon Czolgosz, who identified himself as an anarchist and said he had been inspired by Emma Goldman. While in the Midwest on a lecture tour, she learned from newspapers that she was being sought throughout the country, and she surrendered to Chicago police, who questioned her for several days before releasing her. Goldman consistently denied any connection with Czolgosz, although she spoke and wrote sympathetically of him then and throughout her life; but the press relentlessly linked her to the president's assassination, and she soon found that this was even more damaging than the previous link to Berkman's attack on Frick. Turned out of rented rooms, refused work, distrusted by demoralized anarchist organizations, she found herself reduced to living under an assumed name and remaining apart from the cause which had become the centre of her existence.

She found her way back into public life gradually over the next four years. One of the spurs was a law passed in 1903 by which aliens could be kept out of the United States if they espoused anarchism. She found an audience in attacking this measure on the plea that free speech was in jeopardy from such attempts to exclude people on the basis of their beliefs. Although she was routinely denied access to halls and lodging, often arrested, and once jailed after being convicted of illegally disseminating birth control information, Goldman nevertheless, by 1906, had resumed the sort of active touring that had been the core of her life before the assassination. She frequently took the stage not to speak on anarchism (although she welcomed any opportunity given by questioners to voice her beliefs) but rather to champion causes such as birth control, the modern European drama, and free speech. The frustration of cancelled rallies, and the desire to reach a wider audience, led her in 1905 to begin a monthly magazine, *Mother Earth*, which she managed to keep going for twelve years, until her arrest for conspiring against the draft once the United States entered the First World War. Her partner in the venture, soon after its beginning, was Berkman, who was released from prison on 18 May 1906 after serving fourteen years.

Goldman added Canada to her lecture circuit when she began extending her trips outside the New York City area to raise money for *Mother Earth*. She first crossed to Toronto in March 1906, during a tour with her comrade Max Baginsky (he lecturing in German, she in English) to Cleveland, Buffalo, then Toronto, and on to Rochester, Syracuse and Utica. In the April 1906 issue of *Mother Earth*, she and Baginsky wrote that "the monarchical authorities of Canada were more hospitable and much freer than those of our free Republic. Not a sign of an officer at any of the meetings." The city of "gray sky, rain, storms" reminded them of a witticism of Heine's about a certain German university town: "Dogs on the street . . . implore strangers to kick them, so that they may have some change from the awful monotony and dullness."[4]

Some time early in 1906 she also visited Montreal. In 1908 the Montreal *Gazette*, reporting a lecture she had just given in the city, vividly recalled her earlier appearance: "Emma Goldman was attired in similar simple raiment to that she wore when two years ago on the Champ de Mars, she addressed the big gathering that was dispersed by the police. . . ." This suggests Goldman may have participated in a 1906 May Day celebration. The French-language daily *La Presse* described the 1906 May Day events in detail and reported a disturbance. About 1,000 workers, after a day of meetings at a downtown site, marched through city streets carrying banners and torches and singing revolutionary hymns such as the "International" and "La Marseillaise". As the demonstrators were moving up rue Saint-Denis toward the Champ de Mars, they passed in front of Laval University at Montreal, where they began shouting "Long live anarchism" and "Down with the clergy" and insulting the priests and their middle-class pupils. The police of the local station—Post 4—intervened to prevent violence. As a result, in May 1907 the city allowed a rally at the Champ de Mars only on the stipulation that no mass march would occur. Goldman did not visit Montreal in 1907 but she again visited Toronto in March of that year: "I addressed here three meetings, and not a policeman in sight! In Toronto they seem to employ the police at dangerous street crossings, for the protection of children and cripples, while our 'finest' are protecting the gambling resorts in Wall Street and suppressing free speech. I suggest that we raise a fund to send our free democratic police to school in Toronto."[5] She then went to Detroit before travelling to Winnipeg for six days of lecturing, 10–16 April.

In *Mother Earth*, and later in her autobiography, Goldman mentioned that at this time North American newspapers, including those in Toronto and Winnipeg, had begun to report her meetings fairly. She cited an editorial from the Winnipeg *Tribune* as a model for "our Eastern journalists":

> Emma Goldman has been accused of abusing freedom of speech in Winnipeg, and Anarchism has been denounced as a system that advocates murder. As a matter of fact, Emma Goldman indulged, while in Winnipeg, in no dangerous rant and made no statement that deserved more than moderate criticism of its wisdom or logic. Also, as a matter of fact, the man who claims that Anarchism teaches bomb-throwing and violence doesn't know what he is talking about. Anarchism is an ideal doctrine that is now, and always will be, utterly impracticable. Some of the gentlest and most gifted men of the world believe in it. The fact alone that Tolstoi is an Anarchist is conclusive proof that it teaches no violence.
>
> We all have a right to laugh at Anarchy as a wild dream. We all have a right to agree or disagree with the teachings of Emma Goldman. But we should not make ourselves ridiculous by criticizing a lecturer for things that she did not say, nor by denouncing as violent and bloody a doctrine that preaches the opposite of violence.[6]

When she arrived on Wednesday, 10 April 1907, Winnipeg, then a city of about 45,000, was coated in snow and showed "not a sign", she said, "of life or warmth". But the greetings of comrades and her enthusiastic reception by large audiences soon gave the lie to this impression. She commented in *Mother Earth* that people from "every nook of the world gather in Winnipeg, the land of promise", only to find the same oppression, greed, and robbery they fled. Yet the true promise of the city, she wrote, lay "in all these nations coming together, to look one another in the face, to learn for the first time the real force that makes for wealth. Men and women knowing one another and clasping hands for one common purpose, human brotherhood and solidarity. Yes, Winnipeg is the place of promise. It is the fertile soil of growth, life and ideas."[7]

At the invitation of the anarchist branch of the Winnipeg Radical Club, founded only two years earlier, she delivered five lectures at the Rupert Street Trades Hall: "Misconceptions of Anarchism", "The Spirit of Revolt in Modern Drama", "Direct Action vs. Legislation", "Crimes of Parents and Educators", and "The Position of the Jews in Russia". Her account of the trip in *Mother Earth* implies that she must also have delivered other talks, perhaps in Yiddish. She found that in Winnipeg the priests "who infest the streets and [street]cars of Montreal are not as numerous . . . but the horrors of their creed are as dominant here as there . . . still holding the

Canadian people in power, befogging their minds as in ages past." But the atmosphere among immigrants, workers, and radicals seemed to her warm and vital. She had eager audiences every evening and twice on Sunday and a "beautiful social gathering that united two hundred men, women and children in one family of comrades, and people constantly coming and going during the day, all anxious to learn".[8]

The day after her arrival and before her first lecture, the *Tribune* published a front-page story, based on an interview, which included a summary of her political life and beliefs and described her as "a small woman with a soft voice and ready smile but withal of seriousness quite fitting to one who preaches a gospel so new that it has not yet advanced beyond the stage of persecution and unbelief so violent that law and anarchy, as each is understood, represent the very antipodes of human thought and action". The following day the rival *Manitoba Free Press*, reporting her initial lecture on anarchism, ran the headline "She Abuses Our Freedom of Speech" and editorialized on her ideas, claiming that anarchism's principles "justify murder" and anarchists intended "to destroy society by the agency of the bomb". Although milder, the *Telegram* now also found it necessary to warn against Goldman, taking the line that she was "sowing seeds of discontent" but that "where British institutions flourish the weeds of anarchism have little chance to grow. . . ." The *Tribune* editorial, which Goldman quoted many years later in *Living My Life*, was a follow-up to this coverage. The *Tribune*'s account of her first talk was headed "Lecture Not Sensational" (using *sensational* in the common meaning of the day, *sensationalistic*), and it scolded its competitors: "The morning papers evidently expected a shock and when they didn't get it their nerves gave way and left them in hysterics."[9]

None of her remaining four lectures was covered in the dailies, but the city's labour weekly, the *Voice*, reported and pondered her lectures on the spirit of revolt in modern drama ("splendid") and on direct action versus legislation, which it saw as an argument in favour of militant anarchism and against socialism. She criticized organized labour, urging more frequent, harder, and longer strikes, building towards a general strike. Local socialists such as John Mortimer and L.T. English took issue with her at this lecture, the latter rising to read the Socialist Party platform as a counter-argument. The *Voice* commented that her doctrine did not appeal "to people who recognize that they are responsible for the government and who could be the government if they would",[10] a remark meant of course to promote law-abiding socialist and labour action but one that rather misses the point of anarchism.

In June 1907, Goldman was again in Canada, coming to Calgary after lectures in Portland and other northwestern US cities. On Monday 17 June, the Calgary *Daily Herald* carried a detailed report, complete with a photograph of a stern Goldman with a heavy book clasped to her chest, on her lecture the previous evening. "Some Misconceptions of Anarchism" had crowded Alexander Hall "to the limit of its capacity" with an audience including "almost every Russian in the city". "The entertainment concluded at 10:30", the reporter wrote. "This remarkable woman had been talking very vehemently for two hours and twenty minutes, and her words poured out at the rate of fully 120 words a minute. Yet she did not seem to be in the least fatigued, and shook the Russian contingent severally by the hand." To this familiar lecture, which combined the background and principles of anarchism with a fiery call to anti-capitalist and anti-government direct action, she managed to add some pungent comments for her largely immigrant audience on the national culture in which they found themselves: "'Canadians,' she stated, 'were like the Scotch. They wanted a lamppost struck in between their ribs before they woke up.'"[11]

Goldman's next visit to Canada had more sinister implications for her future. In August and early autumn 1907, Goldman spoke at an anarchist conference in Amsterdam, toured major cities of the Continent, and in October crossed to England, lecturing in London on "The Labor Struggles in America". There she learned that in the United States Jacob Kersner's citizenship status was being investigated and would undoubtedly be revoked as a means of denying Goldman's claim to citizenship-by-marriage and so barring her from re-entry under the 1903 aliens law. With the help of a longtime friend, Rudolf Rocker, the leader of London's Jewish anarchists and a major anarchist author, she was hidden in a suburban house and then helped to Liverpool, where she sailed for Montreal instead of New York. She outflanked the watch that had been set for her by entering the United States in a Pullman coach travelling from Montreal to New York. Canadian immigration authorities, she reported in her autobiography, "proved less inquisitive than the American".[12]

Despite her worries, she returned to Canada several times in 1908, including an eventful visit to Montreal in February. Coverage began on 14 February when the Montreal *Star* reported a lecture by her under the headline "Miss Emma Goldman Explains Anarchism". She also spoke on Sunday 16 February, to unionists at the Montreal Labour Exchange, the city's headquarters for international unions, in a meeting organized by the pioneer Montreal socialist Albert St Martin. In her *Mother Earth* account of the visit, Goldman alluded to her familiarity with the city, which "proved unusually wide awake this time". She jibed at the Montreal press for sounding the "alarm of horror" when she scheduled a meeting on a Sunday; the scandal was even greater, she wrote, because the meeting was "attended by Canadians" and she was even offered "a vote of thanks". The Montreal newspaper *La Patrie* challenged those responsible for permitting such a dangerous event. It later claimed to have been told by the authorities that they had not known the purpose of Goldman's lecture. Goldman's presence rankled with social and religious conservatives and seemed especially sinister in that May Day was approaching again. On 29 February, a letter in the Catholic newspaper *La Croix*, signed "Un Magistrat", expressed outrage (and inaccurate information): "The public authorities, without any intervention, have allowed a self-proclaimed anarchist, a veritable Fury unchained, expelled from the United States, named Emma Goldman, Russian by birth, to come and fulminate publicly at the Labour Temple, meeting place of the socialists of this city, who have unrolled their red banners for the occasion." Writing on 18 March, "Un Magistrat" again warned *La Croix*'s readers against Goldman-inspired workers "spreading the gospel of socialism", citing a 22 February *Star* article reporting on "La Loge Goldman", an anarchist organization founded in the Saint-Laurent neighborhood. On 30 April 1908 a writer in *L'Action Sociale*, a conservative Quebec City newspaper, accused Goldman of having originated or inspired May Day celebrations in Montreal.[13]

After Montreal, Goldman travelled to Toronto, staying with a comrade named Simons at 65 Gerrard Street East, lecturing under the auspices of the Free Thinkers' Society, and also delivering at least one lecture in German at the Finnish Hall on the subject of how modern feminism had failed to free women. The Toronto *Evening Telegram* for 19 February carried an extensive interview in which she recounted her life, aphoristically described some of anarchism's principles, and stated that "there is no happiness in Toronto",[14] pointing to the collections then being taken up in the city at a time of economic recession for relief of the poor.

On Thursday 20 February, Goldman lectured in London, Ontario, on the revolutionary influence of modern drama, an event reported the following day by the London *Free Press* under the headline "Anarchist Looks on Darker Side / Ideas Born of Misbegotten Genius Crowd Lecture of Female Agitator". The writer's reaction was a mixture of shock, rejection, and admiration that Goldman, possessed of "a spirit that is nothing short of fanaticism", was able to "move an audience to the wildest pitch of excitement and then to relieve the tension with laughter". She declared at the end of the lecture that the spirit of revolution "has permeated every mind, and will not keep silent until you have smashed the institutions of hypocrisy and lies, and stand true". She then asked for questions, answering one by saying that the idea Jesus Christ was "a supernatural being . . . is only good for the foolish-minded". The article concluded: "Nothing was too sacred to be held up to ridicule and everything, including people and press, was made the subject of a laugh."[15]

As the year progressed, however, the campaign to bar Goldman from the United States began to preoccupy her. What's more, she was encountering ever-stiffening opposition to her appearances from local and state authorities throughout the United States. In spring 1908, after her trip to Montreal, Toronto, and London, she cut short a series of meetings in Winnipeg, to which she travelled from Minneapolis by train, arriving on the morning of 31 March and proceeding to the home of local anarchist leader, Samuel Prasow, at 452 Manitoba Avenue, where she was to stay. According to a report sent to the State Department by John E. Jones, the US consul at Winnipeg, six days later Goldman "unexpectedly left . . . in an effort to evade the Immigration Authorities".[16] A separate US government surveillance directed by the chief immigration inspector at Winnipeg, Walter E. Carr, resulted in a highly detailed nine-page report to John H. Clark, the US immigration commissioner at Montreal ("I have the honor to report that almost constant watch was kept by this office on the movements of this woman from the time of her arrival in Winnipeg to the time of her departure therefrom"). According to Carr, Goldman was scheduled to remain until Wednesday 8 April, lecture on that date, then go on to Calgary, Vancouver, and Victoria, but "information was received that her real intention was to proceed south to Minneapolis on Monday the 6th, returning by the route used in coming, and therefore she was kept under constant surveillance all day Monday, the 6th." The Americans patiently observed her leave the Prasow house with her baggage, go to the home of a Mrs Cramer at 670 Burrows Avenue, travel from there to the Canadian Pacific Railway station "about 5:25 P.M." and take the train south, arriving at Emerson, Manitoba, where according to a Winnipeg *Telegram* story, she registered at the Anglo-American Hotel as Mrs J.E. Kaisnie of Minneapolis.[17] On 7 April, she walked across the border to Noyes, Minnesota, where she was detained by US customs officials and questioned about her right to enter the country.

Her early decampment, however, may have been due in part to a third government initiative, co-ordinated harassment from local Winnipeg and Dominion authorities. Reporting in December to federal immigration official Frank Oliver on Goldman's visit, Superintendent of Immigration W.D. Scott stated that Goldman had been forced to leave the city by Winnipeg police harassment. A letter by Winnipeg mayor J.H. Ashdown, along with newspaper reports, tend to support this. Ashdown wrote to Oliver on 8 April 1908, "We have a very large foreign population in this city. . . . Many of these people have had trouble in their own country with their Governments and have come to the new land to get away from it, but have all the undesirable elements in their character that created the trouble for them before. They are just the crowd for Emma Goldman or persons of her character to sow the seeds which are bound to cause most undesirable growths in the future."[18] Ashdown was unmoved by the 1907 Winnipeg *Tribune* editorial urging intelligent tolerance towards Goldman and anarchism. He took exactly the opposite view about the nature of the city's immigrant populations. Carr, the US immigration inspector, reported that Goldman "gave five lectures . . . to good sized audiences, and, there being no demonstration of any kind at any of the meetings, the Canadian authorities did not in any way interfere".[19]

What had so flustered the mayor that he perhaps appealed to the federal government and activated his police force? Goldman's first lecture, on the day of her arrival, 31 March, packed the Trades Hall with about 1,000 persons. She defined anarchism, compared the social conditions of the day unfavorably with those advocated by anarchists, and declared that change could not be brought about "with kid gloves and pink teas, a revolution must come, and it would depend entirely on the mental attitude of the world whether it should be peaceful or bloody." The *Tribune* paraphrased some of her message to Winnipegers: she "quoted statistics to show that by working two hours and forty minutes a day for fifteen years the individual would do his share toward the labor necessary to provide for the necessities of the world. The balance of the time could be devoted to sport, recreation, study, science, literature or art."[20]

After spending 1 April with comrades, Goldman returned to the stage the following night with "Trade Unionism's Relation to Anarchy", praising organized labour insofar as it opposed capitalism, and arguing in detail that no "good union man" could belong to the armed services since the military was maintained not to defend against outside enemies but rather to repress the working class and kill strikers. She held discussions in Winnipeg in which she tried to persuade dissatisfied urban transport employees that they should strike for an eight-hour work day. On 3 April, she spoke on "Why Direct Action is the Logical Method of Anarchy". The *Tribune*'s very brief account of this lecture shows how many pieties she could affront in a single evening. "Miss Emma Goldman addressed a slightly diminished audience last night on the subject of 'direct action.' She stigmatised all negotiation on the part of working men with their employers as wrong. If they wanted to strike they should walk right out of the works, without warning." In the discussion section she managed to bring out that no "really intelligent man" believed in the divinity of Christ, and that the church and state have no business interfering in relations between the sexes: "Why should a man and a woman . . . have to go through a ridiculous ceremony mumbled by a priest or preacher before they can live together? If they love and love purely, that is sufficient." In the *Telegram*'s paraphrase, she said that some people "took up Christianity as a profession, others as a money-making scheme, and a great many more because they just didn't know any better". The newspaper reported that after her address her ideas were rebutted briefly by "representatives of the revolutionary socialists, free-thinkers, trade unionists" and that "Emma followed in the argument, applying the squelching process to her predecessors. The meeting closed at 11:30 o'clock."[21]

On 4 April, Goldman attended a reception in her honour at the Trades Hall, and the next afternoon, Sunday, spoke on women's emancipation and in the evening on "The Revolutionary Spirit in Modern Drama". The latter lecture was reported in great detail by Carr to Clark. Goldman dealt in thumbnail fashion with specific works by Tolstoy, Gorky, Ibsen, Shaw, and others, summarizing plots or crucial scenes and interpreting them to bring out aspects of revolutionary struggle; for example, Gerhardt Hauptmann's *The Weavers* "gives us the greatest revolutionary thought with reference to the economic struggle. He shows hunger and poverty, wealth and gluttony, in their worst contrast." After the limit of endurance has been passed, the sufferer "will become mighty in his wrath and in the fight for his very existence will shrink from nothing".[22]

On 8 April the *Tribune* reported on the events of the preceding two days, and even interviewed Goldman at Noyes, much to the disgust of Carr: "Every effort was made to keep the matter out of the public press, but unfortunately the express messenger on the train from which she was removed gained information as to the holding of Miss Goldman for examination and reported same in Minneapolis, whereupon the papers at that place wired to Winnipeg for accounts of the affair."[23] The *Tribune* reporter dispatched to Noyes discovered that she had been detained on the evening of 6 April by the border immigration inspector, who had been notified to do so. He had examined the proof of citizenship she presented, a copy of her father's naturalization papers plus her statement that she was married to an American citizen. The inspector declared himself unable to determine if these were adequate, and wired for two other inspectors, including Carr, who arrived the following day. Sitting as a board chaired by Carr, they considered the matter, awaiting a wire from Rochester verifying her father's naturalization. They apparently felt the reply made it impossible to detain Goldman further or refuse her re-entry from Canada, so she boarded the evening train to Minneapolis on 7 April.

According to a *Tribune* report datelined Emerson, "It is hinted here . . . that Miss Goldman left Winnipeg because she realized she had thrown herself open to prosecution under the Lord's Day Act" by charging admission at one of her Sunday lectures. This may have been the grounds of the police harassment mentioned by the Canadian immigration official, Scott, but Goldman herself gave a different account. The newspaper quoted her as claiming that she had agreed to speak to a Winnipeg dramatic society but had been forced to leave when the organizers of a scheduled appearance in Salt Lake City, Utah, moved the date forward. As to the US authorities, she was careful to mollify them, stating that the officials "were just careful with me because I'm an anarchist." She went so far as to accept explicitly their claim that a board of three was necessary due to the nature of her papers. The *Tribune* writer, however, clearly believed that city and local authorities had forced her out and that the American immigration men were acting on definite orders from Washington. "Those who are in touch with the officials say that it was very evident that they desired to keep Miss Goldman on the Canadian side of the line, if possible."[24]

The *Telegram* published a story on 8 April adding little to the *Tribune*'s coverage, but kept Goldman's presence in Winnipeg alive for two more days. On 9 April it reported a resolution condemning Goldman by the local branch of the Women's Christian Temperance Union: "be it resolved that individually we deeply deplore the fact that a person of such a character and reputation has been allowed freedom of speech in our city, believing that such appeals particularly to those who are as yet scarcely Canadianized are detrimental to the best interests of both state and individual." Then on 10 April the *Telegram* published, under the headline "Reds Have a Firm Grip in the States", a story that recalled the reporting of Goldman's difficulties at the border: "The determined effort of the American authorities to prevent Emma Goldman, the female anarchist, returning to the States after her campaign in Winnipeg is in line with the resolution of the Roosevelt administration to expel the reds from all part of the States or imprison their leaders." The two-column article, datelined Washington as though it were a news story, in fact was an anti-anarchist editorial: "It is an unpleasant thing to publish, but the facts are . . . that anarchy apparently has obtained a much greater hold in the United States than any one was prepared for

[and] is better organized than the government had any reason to believe". The paper endorsed in admiring tones the US efforts to root out radicals. It lamented that authorities could not do more against an anarchist network that possessed "a system of communication, signs, grips, passwords and ciphers".[25]

One Winnipeg resident on whom Goldman made a lasting impression was J.F.B. Livesay, a reporter for the Winnipeg *Telegram*. He was the father of the poet Dorothy Livesay, born the following year. In her memoirs, Dorothy Livesay recalled that her father had been sent to cover a Goldman lecture on Maxim Gorky. The speaker's "knowledge of Russian literature and her admiration for his heroes—Ibsen and Shaw—must have impressed him so much that when twenty years later he heard she was to give a lecture series in Toronto he decided my education needed expanding".[26] He arranged to take his daughter to one of the anarchist's literary talks, an event which played a key role in the young poet's intellectual and political development. What either Dorothy Livesay or perhaps her father recalled as a lecture on Gorky was in fact "The Revolutionary Spirit in Modern Drama", in which Gorky, Ibsen, and Shaw, among others, were dealt with at some length.

Although in her autobiography Goldman reported the Noyes border incident as a triumph, in which she demonstrated that she was exempt from the 1903 anti-anarchist immigration law because of the number of years she had lived in the US and was "an American citizen by marriage", the New York *Herald* reported the incident as proof that the Department of Commerce and Labor, which regulated immigration, "wanted to deport Emma Goldman".[27] Nevertheless, Goldman appeared in Canada twice more during 1908.

She returned to Winnipeg on 24 November and again gave a series of extremely well attended lectures at the Trades Hall. On this trip she was accompanied into Canada for the first time by Dr Ben Reitman, the colourful figure whom she had met in Chicago in early March and who became her lover and tour manager during her most successful years as a lecturer. A physician specializing in gynecology, Reitman had spent many years as a philosophical vagabond when the romanticism of the "open road" and a certain interpretation of Goldman's favourite poet, Walt Whitman, had wide appeal; on establishing himself in Chicago, he founded a mutual aid and education society for wanderers, the Brotherhood Welfare Association, called the "Hobo College", which had tried to come to Goldman's aid with the offer of its premises when Chicago authorities were closing all venues to her. When they arrived in Winnipeg, the *Tribune* devoted a long interview article to Goldman, in which she aired basic beliefs. One was the need of workers to prepare themselves for freedom through self-education by reading authors such as Emerson. She voiced her criticisms of socialism, which sought centralization whereas anarchism desired decentralization. Socialism, basing itself on belief in the power of the majority, enabled the majority to subvert the rights of minorities, which was only another form of tyranny; under socialism, she continued, everyone would have to accept conditions dictated by the majority or "go out of existence".[28] These remarks were in preparation for a 1 December debate with J.D. Houston, the local Socialist Party candidate for Parliament in the most recent federal election, a debate perhaps occasioned by her impromptu sparring with socialists during her April 1907 visit and the argumentative interest taken in her then by the socialist *Voice*.

This event was to be held in Selkirk Hall, which was owned by the local Baptist congregation of the Rev A.A. Holzer, a fact that occasioned a contention among Baptists. G.J. Lee, the Baptist trustee and as such the only person empowered to let the hall, turned the key over to Ben Reitman on the morning of the event. The *Tribune* reported that, in a church meeting to debate Lee's decision, the majority had been opposed, but quoted one "businessman" as rising to say, "I thought you Baptists stood for freedom of speech". Holzer sent a letter to the editor denying this report, stating that "the church is like one man" in opposing Lee's decision. The congregation, the *Tribune* reported, had "pleaded" with Reitman to persuade Goldman not to criticize churches and religion. "Dr. Reitman replied in a very sympathetic way and said that anarchists recognized that the religious organizations are endeavoring to achieve good and that they, the anarchists, had the same worthy aim though differing with the churches in many respects as to what constituted good." When the meeting opened, however, Reitman, who introduced the speakers, declared that they were appearing in the church despite opposition and said, as paraphrased by the newspaper, "The church . . . has had its swing for over two thousand years and has not made good. Anarchism should be given a chance."[29]

Goldman threw further light on the incident in *Mother Earth*: "An amusing feature of the debate was a Jewish convert to Christianity, now minister of the Baptist church which holds its services in the hall rented for the debate. When this soul baiter learned that I was to speak in 'his' church, he called the wrath of his Lord and the police on my head". When the police refused to intervene, offered to pay Goldman her expenses and cover her loss—$130—if she would desist. "Much as *Mother Earth* needs cash, we refused the offer, as we thought the baptized Reverend needed a lesson."[30]

The debate went off as planned, attended mainly by anarchists, socialists, and members of labour organizations, but with a "fair sprinkling of businessmen anxious to see the fun", the *Tribune* reported. Alas, there was "no disturbance of any kind, the Anarchists and Socialists were given the hall without a murmur and then the speeches were all as mild and inoffensive as anyone, no matter what his convictions were, could desire." Clad in a princess gown of black silk, Goldman seemed to the writer like a lady out for a social function: "It was only when she began to speak that her power could be seen." While Houston defended the notion of action within the political system, saying that if socialists could get enough members elected they would be able to make capital bow, Goldman stated that socialism's victory would result in tyranny and thus the destruction of its own announced aims. In *Mother Earth* she called Houston honest for admitting that he knew little of anarchism—or indeed socialism. "He is very young in the Socialist movement, and therefore also knows little of the workings of that party. Else he would realize that, though as yet they have but little power, they have already become arbitrary, despotic, and compromising on every step."[31]

On 14 December, Goldman and Reitman, on a tour of the Pacific northwest, were arrested in Bellingham, Washington, and placed in jail as a way of preventing a scheduled lecture. Brought before a judge who set a $5,000 bail, they found help in a local lawyer who volunteered legal service and another man who posted the bond, whereupon Bellingham authorities put them on a train for Vancouver. At Blaine, Washington, the crossing point to Vancouver, Goldman was stopped for a day by an apologetic Canadian immigration inspector, who explained that he had learned from American newspaper accounts that she was "a very dangerous person" and that he had to appeal to Ottawa before permitting her to enter the country. Recalling this event in *Living My life*, Goldman wrote that the decision of "monarchical Canada" not to bar her made "the American democracy" look ridiculous. In Vancouver, she completed several speaking dates without incident; she felt relieved to be there, "after the democratic bulldozing we had received in our own free country".[32]

Goldman was planning to accept anarchist invitations to travel to Australia, but the obvious intentions of American immigration authorities to try to exclude her made her postpone the trip. Then in April 1909 the federal court at Buffalo did indeed invalidate Jacob Kersner's citizenship; this action meant that Goldman's claim by marriage might no longer be honoured, that if she left US soil she might not be able to return. She was so concerned about the possibility of being denied re-entry that she cancelled the Australian lecture tour in January 1909, and stayed in the US until her expulsion in 1919.

Her greatest successes ever on the lecture circuit were thanks to Ben Reitman. With his flair for publicity and promotion, Reitman orchestrated extensive North American winter tours. Of the 1909 one, Goldman wrote, "Now with Ben as my manager my work was lifted out of its former narrow confines. On this tour I visited thirty-seven cities in twenty-five States, among them many places where anarchism had never been discussed before. I lectured one hundred and twenty times to vast audiences, of which twenty-five thousand paid admission. . . . [T]en thousand pieces of literature were sold and five thousand distributed free."[33] Reitman, whom she considered the grand passion of her life, for a time was the answer not only to her need for effective assistance but also to her longing for passion and love, frustrated since 1906 when Berkman had declined to resume their relationship after his release from prison. Yet Reitman was a womanizer and a heedless self-promoter; on one occasion he even stole from the lecture proceeds. Perhaps most damning of all, he seemed to her a coward in the face of violence and threats, which often greeted them on the road. He was distrusted by everyone else in Goldman's circle, even the assistant editor of *Mother Earth*, M. Eleanor Fitzgerald, whom he had been instrumental in bringing to New York. Eleanor, or "Fitzi" as she usually was addressed, became a trusted co-worker and Berkman's lover. This romantic tangle at the magazine was one of many strains that caused Goldman and Reitman to separate frequently over the twelve years of their relationship.

In the years before the First World War, Goldman published two books based on lectures and her articles in *Mother Earth*: *Anarchism and Other Essays* (1911) and *The Social Significance of the Modern Drama* (1914). But these subjects took second place to a campaign against any participation in military activity when war broke out in Europe. When the United States entered the war, Goldman and Berkman formed a No-Conscription League, which offered counselling to draft resisters. Arrested together in June 1917, they were convicted of violating the new Selective Service Act, under which it was an offence to induce young men not to register for the draft. During the appeal process, Goldman spent almost two years in the Missouri State Penitentiary in Jefferson City, while Berkman was incarcerated at Atlanta, Georgia.

After the US Supreme Court's refusal to hear a final appeal, proceedings were begun to deport them under the terms of the 1918 Immigration Act. While in prison, Goldman and Berkman welcomed news of the Russian Revolution and its implications for the anarchist cause; Berkman did not fight the deportation order, partly because of the rumour that the deportees would be sent to Russia. Goldman received legal advice that she could contest the order successfully on the grounds of her marriage to Kersner. In addition, she was offered a second marriage by the radical Harry Kelly for the purpose of preventing her expulsion, and many friends urged her to take this course; but she refused, partly because of her philosophical opposition to marriage, partly because she too hoped to participate in the new Russian socialist society. She and Berkman would go into exile together. They left the United States on 21 December 1919 on a ship carrying 249 deportees. In the crowd seeing them off was Leon Malmed, whose passion for Goldman would help draw her to Canada seven years later.

For Goldman and Berkman, the next two years were ones of disenchantment with their new home and of self-imposed withdrawal from the Bolshevik leaders of revolutionary Russia. Despite the enthusiasms of her 1918 publication from prison, *The Truth about the Bolsheviki*, Goldman worried even before she arrived that she would find no acceptable role within any state government, even one which had proclaimed its sympathies for anarchism. She and Berkman spent their first several months in a fact-finding tour, which convinced them that an absolutist state authority was the fact behind the Bolshevik façade of tolerance. Within a year, they met with Lenin to protest the arrests of a growing number of anarchists. They were disturbed to find their challenges deflected, first by compliments, then by the chilling announcement that there could be no freedom of speech in a revolutionary period.

Berkman, who was more inclined than Goldman to accept violence as a necessary part of social change, had at first trusted the Bolshevik assurances that the period of violence would be brief. But he and Goldman were united in dismay at the brutal suppression of the Kronstadt sailors' revolt in March 1921. From that point on, they wished nothing more than to escape, believing that any help they might give to the suffering anarchists of Russia would be more effective if attempted from outside the country. Accepted as delegates to an international anarchist conference in Germany, they left Russia in December 1921.

They could escape the territory of Russia but not the influence of the Bolshevik revolution, whose friends and supporters were able to shout down their publications and speeches and to harry them with the accusation that they were serving the cause of enemies on the right. Goldman and Berkman entered Latvia from Russia, intent on attending the German conference, only to learn that they would not be allowed to enter Germany or to remain in Latvia. Their hopes were raised when they obtained visas for

Sweden, only to be dashed when radical publications in Europe and the United States refused their articles about conditions in Russia. The mainstream New York *World* in April 1922 printed Goldman's first attacks in the campaign against the Russian communists she would wage through the rest of her life.

Warned by the Swedish government against any further such public criticism of Russia, Goldman and Berkman worked desperately to find another place to settle. By late 1922 they had managed to gain admission to Germany and were in Berlin. Both were beginning to write books about their experiences in Russia, since they were largely cut off from any other effective means of voicing their opposition to what was happening in their native land. The one meeting that Goldman succeeded in organizing in Berlin was broken up by hundreds of communist demonstrators. Their books, Goldman's *My Disillusionment in Russia* (1922) and Berkman's *The Bolshevik Myth* (1925), brought down even more calumny from Russian communists and their sympathizers round the world. Adding to Goldman's frustration was the difficult history of her text. When she received copies, she discovered that the publisher, who had not sent her proofs, had accidentally omitted the final twelve chapters. These were published in 1924 as a separate volume, *My Further Disillusionment in Russia*. Finally, in 1925, C.W. Daniel in Britain printed a complete one-volume version, thanks to a $250 donation from Dr Michael Cohn, an old anarchist comrade and now a well-to-do Brooklyn physician. In the midst of these difficulties, Goldman decided to go to England, where she hoped to be able to return unimpeded to the lecture stage. Her decision meant parting from Berkman, who could not obtain entry to Britain and had to remain behind.

2

Inseparably Allied with the Future

Goldman arrived in London in November 1924, back in an English-speaking country for the first time in five years. She was happy for the chance not only to work for anarchism in the United Kingdom but also to do so in English and thereby reach a world audience. Furthering this intention, in spring 1925 Goldman put aside ideology and quietly made plans to marry James Colton, a sixty-five-year-old Welsh coal miner, veteran anarchist, and widower, a man without formal education, who had supported himself in the mines from the age of eight, still worked there, and was often hard pressed. "He had given the greater part of his life to active service in our ranks", she wrote in *Living My Life*, "and with much pride he told me that, like myself, he had become an anarchist as a result of the judicial murder of our Chicago martyrs. With no chance for an education, he had picked up much knowledge and a clear understanding of social problems. He devoted his native ability as a speaker to the cause and he contributed to the propagation of anarchism from his meagre earnings."[1] Goldman paid his fare to and from London and compensated him for the loss of two and a half days' work; she made the official registry date her birthday, 27 June, although the civil ceremony was performed earlier.

Both Goldman and Colton understood the marriage was a device to enable Goldman to work on behalf of the movement. In a letter to her American friend Ben Capes, Goldman explained: "Next Saturday I will be fifty-six years of age—an old woman in years if not in heart and spirit. It is alright to be young in heart and spirit if one can apply both. In my case it is only a hindrance. I have energy and spirit enough for ten but what are they when there is no field, no way of expression?"[2] Colton wrote to Berkman that the marriage "will rank with me as a Memory of how two fighters Thwarted the Powers that Be. . . . i had a Comrades Duty to Perform, to hit back at our Enemie for the Cruel treatment Meted out to you and Emma and for that i am Thankful."[3]

Writing two weeks afterward to Max Nettlau, the historian of anarchism, Goldman interpreted the marriage and the British citizenship she would gain thereby as a step towards full entry into English life: "I had to do it in order to be able to do real work here. . . . I am hoping fervently I may succeed in building up a movement which I can only do if I throw myself into the work with all the intensity of my being. . . . How can one be so strange in the land as I am here. And the English are so difficult to reach, to arouse out of their thick skin. But I mean to try very hard, I can tell you. The need of doing something vital drove me to the step which for personal reasons I could never have gotten myself to take, it was always so disgusting to me."[4]

Yet it was not only access to English life but also other benefits of British citizenship—in particular, entry to other English-speaking countries, including Canada—which lay behind Goldman's decision to marry. To her niece Stella Ballantine, Goldman explained the marriage this way: "You will know that my scope of activities has been enlarged. Canada, and Australia and New Zealand are now open to me and I can easily get to France, Belgium, Switzerland and Holland if need be. It means a terrible lot to me after years of cramped uncertainty, so you may congratulate me."[5]

But in England, the lack of an active, coherent anarchist movement, the strength of post-war anti-radical reaction, and relentless pressure from the Russian communists and their English sympathizers, all hemmed her in and made her feel that her time, now in short supply, was wasting. Summer 1925 passed in largely unsuccessful attempts to ignite anarchist feeling and support radical causes: a pattern of heavy slogging for little progress that became her familiar English round. She attempted to organize lecture series and tours, as she had done in North America, but experienced difficulties in attracting adequate audiences. Her talks on the drama—mainly the Russian dramatists but also Eugene O'Neill and others—barely paid her enough to live. Her attempts to arouse interest and raise money for political prisoners and hungry children in Russia met with no success; she complained of the difficulty of getting together a committee of English people who constantly put holidays and business before political action.

Nonetheless, she was multifariously active. She involved herself in a publicity campaign to lift the lord chamberlain's ban on O'Neill's *Desire Under the Elms*, and had the pleasure of meeting Paul Robeson, who was appearing in *The Emperor Jones*. But London, she said, was barren of friends, and England was barren of anarchists, with the exception of Bristol, where she visited and lectured for several weeks in the summer and again in the autumn. The most promising events of the summer were an offer from a book publisher seeking "some of my reminiscences to cover a period of ten years or more"[6] and the subsequent thoughts and correspondence with friends about the possibility of a true autobiography.

Soon Goldman began to question her decision to make England her base. Her change of mind was a gradual one, and perhaps was never finally complete; even as she departed for Canada a year and a half later, she thought she would have to return to England by March 1927, and was corresponding with the veteran British anarchist William C. Owen in the hope of finding at least one compatible comrade with whom to begin re-building English anarchism. At this time, however, her dominant insight was the one that she expressed to her friend and fellow anarchist Angelica Balabanoff, in exile on the Continent: "I feel the tragedy deeply that both you and I should be outcasts from tragic Russia and from the people, for whom we might be able to do much. I feel very much of an alien, being robbed of America and Russia. I know, I will never feel at home here, in fact, nowhere!" She was, she wrote to her New York friend and lawyer Harry Weinberger, "trying to gain grounds here and earn my living", but by early November she was informing Berkman that she didn't "intend to continue in England unless I can get enough lecture dates to keep me going." She found herself wavering between determination and hopelessness: "The struggle here to adjust myself and to make a living", she wrote to G.P. Wiksell, "has sometimes seemed beyond my strength. Still I am hopeful that eventually I will become sufficiently known in this country to continue the work arbitrarily stopped" in the United States in 1919.[7]

The English political situation, she knew, limited the chances, and her own unremitting idealism played against her as well. The prestige of the Russian revolution with British labourites and liberals, and the fierce ha-tred of it by English conservatives, left Goldman a mere anomaly with nowhere to stand: an enemy of the Bolsheviks but on grounds of advanced radical thought and love of political freedom rather than reaction. "My situation is really a desperate one," she wrote to Berkman. "The Tories have taken a stand against the Communists, in France they are being hounded, the Pope comes out against them. And here I am doing the same. It is no wonder that everybody refuses to join me. It really [means] working hand in glove with the *Reactionarie* [sic]. On the other hand I know I must go ahead and that our position is of a different nature."[8] Just as in Europe, criticizing the Bolsheviks as betrayers of the Russian revolution and call-ing the Russian state the enemy of the people had no resonance. Even in the British socialist press she found publishing so much as a letter–to–the–

editor against summary imprisonments and other abuses in Russia to be difficult.

Reactionaries pointed to her as an example of radicalism acknowledging its own failure; leftists saw her as proof that those who accused the Bolsheviks of tyranny were tools of capitalism. Despite his respect for her, Bertrand Russell, for example, was among the latter. Because he could not believe that an ideal state free of government was likely within the twentieth century, he found it necessary to support the revolutionary government in Russia and not contribute to lowering its prestige by joining Goldman's campaign. It seemed at times that the Bolsheviks had converted the entire radical world against her. She told an American anarchist friend, Joseph Ishill, about her visit to the "venerable" Mrs T.J. Cobden-Sanderson, widow of the craft printer and book designer. She was a former associate of Kropotkin's in anti-tzarist activity, and had asked, "Miss Goldman, are you with Churchill and the Tories?" Goldman wrote that she "went out to her, talked for two hours. In the end the good lady said she could do nothing as it would only be working in the hands of the Tories. This was the excuse of all the Labour people in England. . . ." She regarded the incident as typical of English progressivism. "Goodness, these people talk of bourgeois ideas, they are themselves ultra bourgeois and middle class, the whole Independent Labour Party is nothing else."[9]

Goldman knew, however, that she would be similarly squeezed between Bolshevism and reaction in many places throughout the world. Michael Cohn told her that "the US government might [now] overlook your anarchism, since your series of articles in the New York *World* against Bolshevism has made a rather favorable impression upon the powers that be". She herself was determined to go forward in service of truth as she saw it, making necessary distinctions, whoever might be unable or unwilling to understand them. "For I have learned through tears and blood", she wrote to Ben Reitman, "that the intrinsic human value . . . is the capacity to stand out against friend and foe, to be inseparably allied with the future".[10]

The first hint that Goldman was laying plans to come to Canada appears in a note to her, written probably in October 1925, by a London friend, Ted Switz: "I'm almost certain that British subjects going to the Dominions require passports. . . ." This ambiguous (and erroneous) sentence indicates that Goldman had been making inquiries, likely spurred by a long letter from Rudolf Rocker, written on 1 October from Toronto, where he and his wife Milly—one of Goldman's most intimate friends—were stopping during a lecture tour he was making for German and Yiddish anarchist groups across North America. In this and subsequent ones, Rocker described his warm reception in Canada, especially in Toronto, gave Goldman the names of Canadian comrades, and explained how these people had enabled his tour by organizing and assuring the success of his Yiddish meetings. The Rockers apparently told Toronto anarchists that Goldman was able and eager to travel to Canada and then passed along the Canadians' enthusiasm. The next evidence of her planning a Canadian trip comes 19 January 1926, in a letter from a US friend: "Canada: Mum's the word. Hope you do it."[11] The inference is that she had been asking correspondents to keep the idea secret; this later grows explicit and obsessive. But as the plans firmed up, Goldman began to speak somewhat more openly to selected friends. This openness paralleled the renewal of her romantic relationship with Leon Malmed, who had bid her farewell at the pier when she was deported in 1919. Malmed was an anarchist from Albany, New York, whom she had first met in 1906; a delicatessen (and, later, hosiery shop) owner, he had represented *Mother Earth* and arranged lectures for Goldman in upstate New York, and had sent her packages of food, which she remembered as vital to her survival, during her incarceration in the Missouri Penitentiary. In 1915, Malmed had accompanied her and Ben Reitman on a tour to the West Coast. In her letters of 1926 and later to Malmed, Goldman implies that on this tour, and especially in Los Angeles, they had enjoyed a brief, romantic and perhaps sexual involvement. She had written to him sporadically throughout her exile, with tardy response or none, even though her own letters had expressed a nostalgic passion, a longing for home and former days. She seemed to be awaiting any sign from him to reignite the relationship. From Germany in September 1923, for example, she had proclaimed passionately, "Oh Leon, dearest Leon. I am so hungry for some one who knew my life, my work, my devotion to our cause. Of all the people I long for you most. You really must come over, if only to bring with you a breath of that past . . . my spirit cries out in rebellion against the cruel circumstance that has thrown me overboard and made me so utterly useless".[12] Silence in reply to such expressions soon caused Goldman to become resentful towards Malmed, but she never dismissed him from her thoughts.

Now, however, Malmed was growing restive in his confinement to business and family routine (he was married with children), and began to think more about Goldman. In the first half of 1925, after his prolonged coolness, he tentatively began to explore the promise of her earlier protestations by sending her messages through her New York City friend and comrade W.S. Van Valkenburg, editor of the anarchist magazine *Road to Freedom*. In June, she wrote querulously to "Van" that "I am not writing him [Malmed] because he rarely replys [*sic*] to my letters".[13] Apparently Malmed was ashamed of his sad history as a correspondent. His gingerly third-party approach to Goldman continued until he finally achieved a breakthrough as the result of a 5 January 1926 letter from Van Valkenburg to Goldman: Malmed had kept him up an entire night and into the following morning, Van Valkenburg wrote, pouring out his admiration for her. One of Malmed's chief topics had been his fear of giving up his letters from her: she was now thinking seriously enough about her autobiography to have begun gathering research materials, a task in which Van Valkenburg was helpful, and he must have asked Malmed for the loan of letters.

On 19 January 1926 from Nice in France, where she was staying with Frank Harris the anti-prudery controversialist and his wife Nellie, Goldman responded to Van Valkenburg's go-between efforts by writing Malmed a long letter that may be said to announce and define the next phase of her life. In it, she makes explicit reference to her desire to come to Canada and also of her fear that the trip may be prevented, which signals her increasing investment in it: "There is a possibility that I may make a tour in Canada this year. Please do not mention it to anybody because it is not certain and it must be kept quiet until I am there." The hopes that were developing behind these sentences are made more explicit in another letter to Malmed, in February, from Paris: "if my Canadian tour would come off it would solve many problems. I am sure I could put life into our movement, even in America though I would be in Canada. And I could raise enough money to secure me for a few years when I would want to write my autobiography. . . ."[14] Canada was coming to seem the key for revivifying anarchism in the English-speaking world, re-establishing her own political relevance, solving the endless problem of earning her bread, and providing the means to write her life-story.

Canada's proximity to the United States also held out the promise of renewed friendships and family ties. And now, suddenly, it also offered another chance at romantic love, an opportunity to act on Goldman's belated understanding of life's fleeting sensual and aesthetic pleasures. Then, too, Malmed was being measured as a source of some of the funds necessary for the Canadian adventure. For all these reasons, Canada and Malmed came to be associated, even united in her thought. In February, from Paris, she wrote: "Dearest Leon, it will be wonderful to meet you again. I wonder if you know what the seven years [since deportation] have meant to me. The agony of spirit, the hunger of heart, the lonelyness [*sic*], the utter, utter despair. . . . It will be a miracle to meet the few friends I have and whom I love, and my own flesh and blood who have stuck to me through thick and

thin. But I dare not hope too much. I could not bear the bitter disappointment if I failed to get into Canada. So let us keep quiet for the present."[15]

For all its promise, though, Canada was also becoming one part of a
torturing polarity for Goldman. She saw in Europe, especially in France, a
fresh and living responsiveness to the energy and substance of life, whereas
the Anglo-Saxon world of North America and England represented restrictive and depressing carefulness, moralism, and materialism. Throughout
this period she constantly expressed a deeply felt need to work politically
in an English-speaking country: the United States was preferable though
impossible. On the one hand, the English language was now her soil. On
the other, she felt a superior attraction to the French "gift of abandone"
(*abandone* was a frequent misspelling of hers). In her January letter to Malmed
from Nice she wrote of the French: "I know of no people who drink the
goblet of life with such joy and intensity . . . , who have such sense of beauty
and leisure even if they belong to the exploited class. One can not live for
very long in France without being infected by that wonderful spirit of life, of
joy, of forgetfulness. And they are right. Unless one grasps every second
and makes it mean much in one's life one has nothing, is cheated out of
every moment." No one, she commented, knew this so well as she, because
for thirty years she had "begrudged every minute of joy and contempla-
tion" as self-appointed carrier of the world's burdens. This joyless and
bloated sense of responsibility she associated particularly with the seven
years since deportation and more particularly with England but also with
the United States, which she now saw as still more money-blighted and
routinized than England. "It is true that [in Europe] the masses do not have
as much material comforts as they have in America, I mean those who
work. But on the other hand they have more of the precious element which
alone makes life worth living, they have much more freedom of spirit, capacity for enjoyment, the gift of abandone which in America the poor never
had and the rich in their mad chase for wealth have lost. Yes, there is much
more personal freedom in England and France than there ever was in the
States." Again, the following summer, she wrote in a letter to William C.
Owen, "The 'safety first principle' is another very Anglo Saxon trait, isn't
it? The Latin people live every moment [and] are therefore capable of living
'dangerously.'" She could separate herself from the hustling masses by
remembering that she too, if never a devotee of pleasure, could claim a
dangerous life, a life lived "all out". "But you and I dear comrade", she
congratulated Owen and herself, "will not convince the average mind,
average habits, their happyness [*sic*] consists in what Nietzsche called 'the
desperate scramble of flies for a small place on the window pane'. . . ."[16]

She recognized that she too had become one-sided. She protested to Malmed that since deportation her dedication to work instead of a more balanced life had helped no one and embittered her, but that she did not regret the past. "Only I have been made to realize that one must learn to invite one's own soul, that one can get nothing out of life unless one learns to live each moment. I am trying to do it during my visit here [in Nice]".[17] From this point forward a quest for the Dionysiac passion of the moment was an important motivation in all Goldman's decisions, giving a heightened colour to what had long been her strongest belief: that anarchist political action, without losing any of its communal and altruistic basis, must derive its value from the fulfilment, which is to say the pleasure, it provides each person.

Perhaps this was, for Goldman, the ultimate implication of the fact that anarchism founds human society on freedom from regimentation, coercion, and hierarchical control. Certainly it led her to an awareness, which surfaces at times in her late writings, of how hard it will be for anarchist education, or propaganda, to make headway against a capitalist society more and more able to spread pleasures throughout the population—and more and more aware of the value of doing so. Seduction, where possible, is more effective than police, and the vast illusion of choice will convince many that they have freedom. From Canada, ten years later, she wrote in her essay "Was My Life Worth Living?": "The hundred-percenter easily swallows syndicated information and factory-made ideas and beliefs. He thrives on the wisdom given him over the radio and cheap magazines by corporations whose philanthropic aim is selling America out. He accepts the standards of conduct and art in the same breath with the advertising of chewing gum, toothpaste, and shoe polish. Even songs are turned out like buttons, or automobile tires—all cast from the same mold."[18]

Such "hundred-per-cent Americans" (a catch phrase of the time, a legacy from the Red Scare) were not an elite as traditionally understood. They were instead an immense percentage of the population that, being fairly well off or hoping to become so, put all its faith in the American system *in statu quo*. Divorced from the real sources and forms of pleasure, the new middle-class masses were becoming, due to the sense of liberty their comforts and illusions gave them, freedom's most troubling new opponent.

After leaving the Harrises', where she completed and posted a 5,000-word character sketch of Johann Most for H.L. Mencken at the *American Mercury*, Goldman spent a few weeks in Paris and then returned to London, where she had to find less expensive lodgings. In late March she lectured again for the comrades in Bristol, writing to Mencken from there: "To arouse the Britishers is worse than carrying water, chopping wood and going hungry all of which I had to do while in Russia. Really, it is the most heart breaking task I have yet confronted. I suppose centuries of restraint have paralysed the emotional springs of the British people. They dare not respond to anything new for fear their whole ancient habits will crumple."[19]

Goldman's isolation and precarious circumstances are poignantly evidenced in her excitement over Mencken's acceptance of her piece on Most. "And I got $200 for it", she wrote to friends. "The first real, honest to God money I made in ages. Believe me, I was excited, and cheered too. Heavens I needed both. . . . [M]y lectures have been so wretchedly attended they drive me to despair."[20] A few days later, in early April, she had determined that with her British passport she needed no visa to enter Canada, and had settled with Rocker that he would work with Canadian and American anarchists not only to arrange lectures but also to raise money for her expenses. Through Harry Weinberger she determined that the two-volume edition of *My Disillusionment in Russia* published by Doubleday, Page in New York was out–of–print, and reclaimed the Canadian rights so that she would be able to hawk the one-volume British edition in Canada.

At this point Goldman's Canadian plans were for a lecture tour, in which she would visit at least Montreal, Toronto, and Winnipeg. In April, Michael Cohn, who had inserted himself unasked as the trip's chief fundraising co–ordinator, wrote that he had contacted Ben Capes in Chicago "to help me raise the initial $1,000 necessary for your tour, assuring him that the money will be promptly returned from the profits realized by your lectures. I do not think he will have any difficulty in raising the necessary amount as I personally will advance a goodly part of it." She planned to pay back all loans out of tour proceeds. In May, Cohn wrote that he had not yet received any money toward the $1,000, but that Rocker had led him to expect $300 from "Albany comrades" (presumably Malmed), $100 from Capes, and $150 from an old comrade, Yudin (actually, Judin) in Cleveland. "I suppose I will have to come in for the balance", he wrote, adding that he had not yet heard from Toronto or any other Canadian city.[21]

She spent much of March, April, and early May in research on Russian dramatists and their mid-nineteenth-century intellectual background in Russian radicalism; the material was intended for a book on the subject and would also be used for her upcoming lecturing. Plans for Canada seemed trouble-free, but her dread at possibly being barred from Canada was intensified by further frustrations in England. One of these was her inability to arouse interest in the plight of Russian female political prisoners and starving children. The closest she ever came to stirring British activity was a series of meetings and letters with Lady Astor, who was an American, originally Nancy Langhorne of Danville, Virginia, and the first woman to sit in the House of Commons. Lady Astor introduced Goldman to the head of the Save the Children Fund, and received from Goldman a lengthy, detailed list of female anarchists held in Russia for political reasons, often without charge or legal process. Goldman sought Lady Astor's financial support to write a book about starving Russian children and apparently received encouragement, but soon was enquiring urgently: "What about the book on destitute children? Do you want me to go ahead with it? You see, if part of it is to be ready for you to take to America, I will have to begin right away."[22]

In the end, one of Goldman's causes interfered with the other. In the wake of the great general strike of that spring, Lady Astor told her that conditions among working people in Britain precluded her attention to Russia in the near future. The general strike was another of Goldman's English frustrations. It had begun as a strike in the coal industry, in which many of Goldman's anarchist comrades were employed. When the Trades Union Congress supported the miners, the strike spread to railways, iron and steel, construction, and printing. Frantically, Goldman sought a way to participate, but she was unable to find anyone in London anarchist ranks willing and able to help her write, print, and distribute a manifesto. Through John Turner, a veteran anarchist and prominent unionist, she approached the strike leadership. Turner thought that this action would rehabilitate her with the pro-communist trade unions and "demonstrate that anarchists not merely theorized, but were ready for practical work and were ready for any emergency".[23] But she was rebuffed.

She now felt that no accommodation to British politics was possible. Before the nine-day strike had even concluded, she left England, travelling by air to France. She had made no arrangements for a place to live in England the following autumn, nor had she arranged lectures or any other means of livelihood. Her sights were now entirely set on Canada. She arrived in France confident that arrangements for the Canadian experiment were proceeding smoothly. Her principal worry was not whether there would be funds enough, or lecture dates enough, but rather whether Canada would bar her landing, under pressure from US authorities. In the meantime, the south of France was cheaper than London and promised relief from colds and neuralgic ailments. She would live for a while with Berkman, and enjoy the pleasant company of some of her acquaintances among the era's well-to-do liberals and dilettantish bohemians who supported and dabbled in advanced artistic and political activities. Most of all, though, she was determined to go on learning how to live each moment. She felt free to spend the time, because of her growing confidence that her Canadian tour would open a more hopeful future.

She and Berkman rented a small cottage, which they called Bon Esprit, on a hill near the then unknown and unspoiled fishing village of St Tropez. There she carried on a full schedule of working and worrying—worrying that her newfound sybaritism had become her chief occupation. Her description of the summer at Bon Esprit became an almost standardized yet always heartfelt feature of her correspondence. She wrote to one American friend in September: "We have the sea, the mountains, can see as far as the white tops of the Italian Alps, acres upon acres of vineyards and of pine woods. And we were most fortunate in finding a cottage away from the village on a hill where we have been quite private and with all the gorgeous beauty spread before us. For weeks and weeks, Sasha and I were like drunk, we could not get enough of the marvels, you see it is the first time in my life to have such a summer, and the first time in S's since he left his home in Russia as a boy." Visitors included Kathleen Millay, sister of the poet Edna Millay; Margaret Anderson, the editor of the *Little Review*, and the arts patron and society figure Peggy Guggenheim and her husband Lawrence Vail. Goldman reported on one occasion drinking and dancing at the St Tropez hotel until midnight, then being driven by Guggenheim and Vail to Nice. "The trip along the fascinating country during the night was marvelous. We returned yesterday about eleven in the morning. It was glorious." She complained that "[t]he only trouble with this place is it is too beautiful and too enchanting to work, one wants to loaf",[24] but she soon got down to a strict schedule of work, over and above her voluminous correspondence, her chores as housekeeper, and her diligent acquisition of "swimming and floating" skills. She wrote a manuscript on "The Origin and Development of the Russian Drama"; eventually retitled *Foremost Russian Dramatists*, it was never published once her British publisher failed to bring it out in 1926 as planned. She also prepared a companion piece to the Most sketch on the American anarchist Voltairine de Cleyre (Mencken eventually rejected it), wrote an article on the British general strike, and provided a congratulatory essay for the London anarchist paper *Freedom* on the occasion of its fortieth anniversary. In addition, she did her best to assist in various crises, including the imprisonment for murder of a friend, the anarchist Sholem Schwartzbard, a generous, gentle man, much loved among the comrades, who had fled Russia and was now settled in Paris, where his watchmaker's shop served as a drop-in meeting place and sometimes a free hostelry for impoverished radicals. In May he shot to death Simon

Petlura, who during the chaotic 1919–21 period had led Ukrainian nationalist forces and carried out pogroms in which, by Goldman's estimate,
100,000 Jews had died. Goldman engaged in a worldwide correspondence
to help raise funds for Schwarzbard's defence, even though under the direction of his lawyers he intended to avoid mentioning his anarchist beliefs. And then, too, with a view towards writing her autobiography, she
was continuing to make contacts with admirers such as Theodore Dreiser,
solicit funds from friends such as Kathleen Millay and Peggy Guggenheim,
and beg the loan of her letters from former correspondents.

Meanwhile, her thoughts were full of the trip to Canada. On 24 May, she
wrote to Malmed that she now felt she was "really going" due to his and
Cohn's guarantee of the bulk of the initial expense. Her letter showed plainly
the many different vectors in Goldman's emotions and affairs that had
begun to converge on Malmed. She not only pressed him for conspiratorial
secrecy to keep knowledge of her plans from the public and the authorities,
but also prodded him on the money front: she "must know early in June"
whether the whole required sum had been raised. She told him her projected sailing date, 23 September, and speculated on how he might come to
be with her. Should he meet the ship in Montreal or arrive later for an
extended stay there or in Toronto? She imagined how he would be able to
take off "a few weeks or even a month" from his business to stay with her,
how he would listen to her talk about all that had happened to her since
she had left America, "things that have left so many painful scars on my
soul".[25]

Most important, the 24 May letter defined her resolution regarding the
search for the field of activity that had been denied her by her deportation
and subsequent experiences: the totalitarian debacle of the Russian Revolution, the severe anti-radical reaction throughout continental Europe, and
the steely dullness and immobility of the British political scene. The need
for a new arena had now become an insistent theme of her life and would
remain so until the end. She told Malmed she would be "heart-broken"
should the Canadian tour not take place because she now had to admit the
failure of her desperate struggle to "gain a footing" in England. Her letters
that summer were full of the feebleness of British anarchists ("as to our own
comrades there are none in England, least of all in London"), the nonrevolutionary character of British trade unionism and liberalism, and the
safety-first attitude of the Anglo-Saxon world. In Canada, though, she felt
certain she would have "successful meetings", a phrase which condensed
her hope for an easier living, accumulation of savings for the projected two-
year task of her autobiography, wider personal influence, and successful

propaganda and fundraising for Russian political prisoners.

By mid-July, she was prodding her phlegmatic lover, who (Cohn had reported) had not yet contributed his share of the expenses. So she asked him to send the money directly to her, guessing that he did not want to deal with Cohn, that the two men were competing for her friendship. Later in the month, Cohn wrote that he had received two $100 contributions. Her preparations were quietly advancing; she had begun to give out a Canadian address, 683 Spadina Avenue, Toronto, the home of a comrade, Joseph Cleman. In late July, her friend Albert Boni, of the New York publishers Albert and Charles Boni, was already writing to her at that address. Malmed, however, remained silent. "I don't know why I am writing you when you never reply to my letters",[26] Goldman raged at him on 7 August; months had passed, and she had expected that after he had written, his first letter in several years, he never would again keep her waiting. There was good reason for her increased annoyance. "[S]ince Wed. [4 August] I have been so paralyzed I have not been able to do anything", she wrote Malmed. "The cause for it is a cable from Michael Cohn to the effect that 'the tour is cancelled, letter follows'. Can you imagine what that means to me. For eight months I have been clinging to the C. project as a drowning man clings to a straw."[27] Cohn's high-handed conduct galvanized Goldman to begin organizing, pleading, cajoling, and knocking heads together to salvage the scheme, which had been left too trustingly to others while she had worked "like possessed" on her book about the Russian dramatists and delighted in southern France. She pressed Malmed urgently for his $300, and revealed that she was seeking money from her nephew Saxe Commins (son of Goldman's half-sister Lena and an influential writer and editor) and from another American who is "not far from us" (this was Henry G. Alsberg, a friend who had intelligently reviewed Goldman's *My Disillusionment in Russia* in the New York *Post*). Each was solicited for $300.

On Wednesday 11 August, a week after Cohn's wire, Goldman also wrote to her old friend and follower Ben Capes, asking for his contribution to be paid directly to her, and expressing the cold, reasoned and lasting fury towards Cohn that the original flare of her dismay had burnt down to: "what I could not forgive is the impudence of the man in cancelling my tour. The outrage of the power of money is that those who own it believe they can buy your soul and decide your destiny. Well, Cohn will not decide mine." Goldman was drawing to herself all the lines of communication she had allowed to go through Cohn. Other letters on this same day went to Malmed and to her anarchist contact in Toronto, Joe Desser, a leading activist in the city's Jewish anarchist and labour communities, who was to become one of her most faithful Canadian friends and helpers. Her letter to Malmed implored him to cable his contribution immediately; of Cohn, she stated that she conceded him the right to back out but not to cancel her tour. To Desser, she recalled that Cohn had also failed in a commitment to Rudolf Rocker regarding Rocker's recent trip to Canada and the United States, forcing the anarchist thinker to borrow from his wife Milly's family at the last minute. She informed Desser that she was determined to go through with the original plan on her own, provided that the Canadian comrades would fulfil their agreement, which was simply to organize meetings and lectures before Jewish audiences, mainly in Yiddish. "I have never in my life given up anything I have undertaken to do as long as it depended on my efforts. No difficulty has ever meant anything in my way."[28]

On 14 August, she finally wrote directly to Cohn, summarizing his correspondence to remind him of a hopeful letter he had sent 23 July, which gave no sign of impending difficulty, and then a "despairing" letter of 2 August, which had arrived after the fateful 4 August cable. Reading his cable had been "like being hit on the head by a heavy object", she said. She reproached him for knowingly leaving her facing a winter with no means of support and no lodgings, for he was aware that she had put all her efforts into Canada and not made arrangements to return to England and schedule lectures there. She mocked his suggestion that she should postpone until the following autumn: her intentions were becoming widely known and would surely come to the ear of American authorities and be blocked. "No," she summed up, "I must test whether I can enter C. If I can it will give me a larger field than what I have now, if not, I must know it as soon as possible and then give up all hope of propaganda, do as most of our comrades did who began life with me, engage in some pursuits that would give me a living and set me free once for all from ever having to appeal to comrades more successful in life than I, materially. . . ."[29]

This letter reached Cohn where he was vacationing at the Green Acre Inn, in Eliot, Maine. From there on 1 September he mailed a counterblast, stating "your insinuations and Billingsgate abuse was beneath my dignity to reply to" and that "of course" his "tour cancelled" cable meant only "as far as I am concerned".[30] He went on to argue that he had received responses "only" from Toronto and Winnipeg, none from Montreal. As Goldman reminded him accurately in a later letter, those involved in the tour, including Cohn himself, had agreed that the Canadian ticket-buyers, mainly poor workers and shopkeepers, were not being asked to advance any money and that they had been enjoined to avoid correspondence, fund raising, and other activity that might draw unwanted attention. Cohn also complained that Goldman expected him to advance her $1,200, an untruth, for she merely had accepted his self-appointment as collector of funds and his offer to make up any shortfall, which would have been $475 according to Goldman's calculation, and could possibly have been reduced to zero if Cohn had been diligent. Within four weeks, Goldman had managed to raise the whole amount with no contribution from Cohn, though he did forward to her, with his riposte, $225 that had been sent him by comrades. After receiving Cohn's response, Goldman rebutted on 14 September, "only because I want you to see how uncalled for is the blame you place upon the Canadian comrades, and which really is a mere excuse for your having broken your word".[31] She made a detailed recapitulation of the plans and agreements that she, Cohn, Rudolf Rocker, Canadian contacts, Malmed, and others had made, and did careful arithmetic, supported by existing earlier correspondence, to disprove his assertions.

But her attention by then had shifted to more substantial issues. Cohn had come to her to seem an example of a dilettantism that well-heeled radical sympathisers could not be free of, and she contrasts him brutally with herself. "For many, many years now you have lived a life of ease . . . in a position to go and come. . . . How could you feel what it means to have been torn out by one's roots from the soil which I have ploughed in blood and tears. To be thrown out into the world without means, without security, without the possibility of even earning one's living, without the possibility of being of service to what one loves more than life, one's ideal?" Goldman praised Cohn's previous generosity but pointed out that he was remote from the movement, which had been secondary to him for years. With her, on the contrary, "the movement and our ideas have been my life and my only interests. . . ." She replied angrily to a passage from his letter of self-justification, in which he had quoted her back to herself: "You say ironically 'if your life depends upon Canada, go'. Now that is gracious of you I must say. But I do want to call your attention to the fact that your point of view on 'life' and mine are so different that you are not likely to grasp the meaning of what I said. . . . [N]either man, child or material considerations have played any part, my ideal was the only raison d'etre in my whole life and the work for it the deepest urge."[32]

On 1 September, Goldman responded by letter to a cable from Malmed promising immediate dispatch of funds; on 5 September she was thanking him, praising "your spirit which has impelled you to do what Cohn has unfortunately failed to do, to carry out the plan which may decide my whole future". It is a likely inference that with Cohn out of the picture Malmed not only acted quickly but provided more than the $300 he had originally promised. The month was filled with correspondence to friends in the United States regarding funds, and arrangements for accommodation in Montreal. She found it necessary to postpone sailing from 23 September to 7 October, but by 26 September she was in Paris preparing to leave. From there she wrote to Malmed to give him a Montreal address for her—c/o Meyer Bernstein, 2376a Waverly Street—and her schedule: she would arrive on the Canadian Pacific steamship *Minnedosa*, which was to land at Quebec on 13 October; she would be in Montreal on the fifteenth. "So you have a car", Goldman had written to Malmed earlier in the month; "maybe you will come to C. with it and give me a ride. Are you quite efficient as a chauffeur?"[33] Besides such badinage, she was reminding Malmed and others—such as her friend the New York journalist Don Levine, who was planning to drive to Montreal to meet her—to be sure to address her aboard the *Minnedosa* by her married name, Mrs Emma Colton: another precaution.

Her trip to Canada was about to begin. She had succeeded where well-placed and well-to-do professional men had dragged their feet or given up; she had succeeded despite an unexpected, last-minute catastrophe. While waiting to sail, she made use of her few days in Paris. On Monday 27 September, she had a protracted luncheon conversation with her admirer, Theodore Dreiser, who suggested she write an autobiography, not knowing she already intended to do so, and promised to seek a $5,000 advance for her from a publisher. He wrote to her shortly afterward of his "deep appreciation of the dignity and purity and force of your spirit. You are— and will remain—a great force."[34] As she boarded the *Minnedosa* at Lisbon on Thursday 7 October for the six-day crossing, she had succeeded in opening up a new country for her activities and had taken the first positive steps towards writing the story of her life.

3

If Only I Had Known It Would Be So Easy

From Quebec City on Friday 15 October 1926, Goldman wrote to Leon Malmed that the "legal business" of entry to Canada had not taken five minutes. "If only I had known it would be so easy I would have enjoyed my trip. . . ." She meant to "strain every nerve"[1] to make her stay productive, and immediately began worrying about the lack of a competent assistant to organize meetings and propaganda among English-speakers. Determined as she was to regain a foothold in an English-speaking country, she recognized the difficulty that the French-speaking and religiously conservative character of Montreal placed in her way. She wrote in the *Road to Freedom*, "Montreal is essentially a French city, 75 per cent of the million population are French, body and soul under the dominion of the Catholic Church, and as far removed from the cultural efforts and life of the English speaking part of the city as if they lived thousands of miles away."[2] On 17 October, she was settled at 150 Prud'homme Avenue, the home of Louis and Lena Shlakman, with whom she was to lodge.

There was immediate press interest in her arrival. Don Levine, who met her in Montreal, stimulated it issuing a publicity release. He had also arranged for her to write a series of paying articles, which she began immediately, for US newspapers. The Shlakman house was too far from downtown to allow convenient meetings with the many journalists now demanding to see her, so on 20 October she took advantage of the offer to stay with Max Zahler at 334 De L'Epee Street, Outremont.

The New York *World* and *New York Times* reported her presence in Canada, and another newspaper, which she must have clipped with amusement, announced "Noted Anarchist Brings Along British Husband, Loves America, Russia". No one else made the error that she was travelling with James Colton, but a standard feature of press coverage was to jibe at her marriage as a proof of her supposed ideological inconsistency and "mellowing". She refuted these characterizations in clear terms, telling one reporter: "Yes, I married. What about it? It doesn't mean that I have changed my views. Since the State pokes its nose into private lives it becomes more comfortable to make the gesture than not. The ceremony can never make any difference in two lives."[3] Other frequent themes were that times had caught up with her and her positions (feminism, birth control, modern literature as exemplified by Ibsen, Strindberg, and Tolstoy), rendering them less than radical; that she had some positive words to say about the United States and only negative ones for Bolshevik Russia, a fact that was likely to occasion attacks from North American communists; and that she openly wished to return to the United States, if only for a brief trip. On this point, her cautious hopes were fuelled early in her Montreal visit by contacts with American friends. She received a letter from H.L. Mencken, full of praise for her manuscript on the Russian drama. On 20–21 October, Goldman had several visitors from the US, including W.S. Van Valkenburg. A few days later, Goldman wrote Don Levine that she had been absolutely certain in England that a return to the US was impossible, but "since you were here my mind keeps reverting to the damned thing and hoping against hope that it may yet be possible".[4] During what turned into a seventeen-month Canadian residence for Goldman, Levine and Van Valkenburg, along with her lawyer, Harry Weinberger, responded by working, at times vigorously, to gain Goldman's readmission.

Her exaltation at glimpsing a return to the States, and the influence on public issues she might regain, suffered a troubling setback when she had to give up her private room at the Zahler home and return to the Shlakmans' after Max Zahler's wife got back from a trip. Not only was she inconveniently far from the city centre and the press, she also lacked independence and privacy, which represented the restrictiveness of family and community expectations from which, as a young woman, she had worked so hard to escape. Already from France she had written to Malmed that "I shall most likely have to put up with [i.e., lodge with, but the inadvertent pun is meaningful] some Jewish comrades, not that I like to do it, I have lived so long away from them and independent. . . , but it is because of the expense in hotels and also because I do not wish to hurt them". Lack of privacy at the Shlakman home spoiled Malmed's initial visit, which came near the end of her first full week in Canada. On another occasion, the whole house was roused and annoyed by a 3 a.m. telephone call from Texas from Ben Capes—just the sort of thing she enjoyed. A call from Malmed himself soon after his visit was ruined by the fact that it had waked the Shlakmans' daughter, who slept in the room with the telephone. "I wanted so wildly to talk to you, to tell you how depressed and lonely I felt yesterday knowing that you had gone and that I remained alone in this city, an alien among comrades."[5] Her frustration spilled over into complaints about every detail of her days in Montreal. Her living conditions were restrictive, the anarchists disorganized, Yiddish meetings ill-attended, and there was no one competent to arrange English meetings. Soon she was actively seeking a Montreal room of her own: it had to be quite inexpensive yet have a telephone, a difficult combination to find. Meanwhile, in her cramped quarters she prepared her lectures, carried on a vituperative correspondence with the New York communist periodical *New Masses* about a possible debate on the Russian Revolution with the communist leader and writer Scott Nearing, shot off letters to many friends, kept up her intense epistolary affair with Malmed, and wrote the series of articles Levine had arranged. And then there were her Montreal friends. In addition to Max and Gertrude Zahler and Louis and Lena Shlakman, there were Hannaniah Meyer Caiserman and his wife Sara, and Meyer and Rose Bernstein. Many of these people were only on the fringes of what Lena Shlakman many years later described as "a small anarchist group, mostly Jewish garment workers".[6] Their beliefs tended to be broadly liberal or socialist, and their interest was in Goldman herself.

Max Zahler was in 1926 the most prosperous of the lot: his Pure Food Stores Ltd operated thirty-nine Stop and Shop grocers in Montreal and environs and had offices and a wholesale store at 10 Ontario Street West. While in Montreal, Goldman used this office and Zahler's secretarial service for some of her correspondence. Meyer Bernstein, conversely, was in the hospitality industry, and at this time was manager of the Silver Café. His wife Rose was one of Goldman's most faithful Montreal helpers. When Goldman arrived in Montreal, the Bernsteins lived at 2376a Waverley, an address which soon became 5634 Waverley in one of the city's not infrequent street renumberings. Lena Shlakman, born in Vilna in 1872, was originally an immigrant to New York City, where she met and married her fellow immigrant Louis Shlakman, a ladies' tailor and lifelong social democrat sympathetic to his wife's anarchism. The two had come to Montreal in 1901 and resided there thirty-six years, at various times playing host to Rocker and Berkman as well as Goldman, who, Lena said, "had a strong character, too strong for some, but honest and fine". It seems certain the Goldman had known the Shlakmans at least since her 1906 and 1908 visits to Montreal, perhaps even from their years in New York. In 1926, Louis Shlakman was employed by Simons' Ladies Wear. Later he founded a cooperative contracting shop with a man named Kars, a now shadowy individual who does not figure in Goldman's accounts of Montreal but whom Lena Shlakman designated the "head of the Montreal anarchist group".[7] H.M. Caiserman, whose business was the Knit-to-Fit Manufacturing Company, was a representative example of the politically radical component of the Canadian Jewish community. Born in Rumania in 1884, he arrived in Montreal in 1904 a convinced syndicalist of the radical anarcho-socialist stamp. Disembarking at Halifax, he recalled, he was taken by immigration authorities into a small examination room where he saw scratchings in Yiddish on the wall: "Your horrors are now beginning", "You will soon wish yourself dead", and "Give up all hope". In Montreal he found much poverty and prejudice, but also a thriving Jewish intellectual community typified by a number of Yiddish periodicals, which had been scarce in Rumania. He was an enthusiastic visitor to Elstein's Bookstore, on Ontario Street near Zahler's offices, where the proprietor, a socialist and social-justice activist, encouraged an atmosphere of political debate. Israel Medres, a prominent writer for the *Canadian Jewish Chronicle*, recalled the intellectual stimulation of the literature displayed and the conversations held at Elstein's and other Jewish bookstores along St Catherine Street between Main and Ontario. "The Jewish immigrant stood in wonderment before such discussion. To him it was a puzzle that in the great America, where there is so much freedom and worldly goods for all, there should be the need for allotting such an important place to such extreme theories as anarchism." He continued, "The task of the lecturer [was] to explain . . . that in the course of time a technique would be evolved which will revolutionize human progress. . . ."[8] Caiserman became the founder, in 1919, of the Canadian Jewish Congress, and after it lapsed, led its revival in 1933 to develop responses to the darkening situation in Europe. Over the years he was a mainspring of the Jewish Immigrant Aid Society, the action committee of the Labour Zionist (Poale Zion) movement, the Jewish Public Library, the J.L. Peretz schools, and the Jewish Authors' Association (he was himself a poet in three languages as well as an enthusiastic promoter of Jewish-Canadian writers). In 1926, the Caisermans lived on St Urbain Street. This residence, and their subsequent ones on Esplanade, St Joseph, and Maplewood, were centres of discussions and social events until Caiserman's death in 1950. This indefatigable man maintained a steady friendship with Goldman despite his shift, under the influence of the socialist Zionist leader Leon Chazanovitch, to a combination of Zionism and state-based socialism essentially at odds with Goldman's beliefs.

As Goldman reached Canada, her intention was to travel, lecture, and live for an extended period in Montreal, Toronto, and Winnipeg, and from those cities to attempt to reach smaller centres and the Pacific coast. When her ship touched at Quebec City her most recent experience of the country was eighteen years past. Much had changed. How much did Goldman know of the Canada she now was entering? Her almost immediate dissatisfaction with Montreal and her Montreal comrades raises this question, as does the absence of specific information about Canada in her papers and writings. Were her hopes for a freer field of action well grounded?

Her decision can seem incongruous. She despaired of England but was coming to a land still largely British in culture and political attitudes. Yet Canada was also similar to the United States in many respects. Since the 1880s, the Canadian government had encouraged, under the influence of industrialists, a flow of central and southern European immigrants to provide workers for the growing if still underdeveloped industrial system. This in turn had led to a resentment of foreigners similar to, if milder than, that expressed in the US Red Scare of 1917–32, which had led to Goldman's and Berkman's 1919 expulsion. Such resentment was redoubled by the radical political ideas found in immigrant populations and the participation of some immigrants in the labour unrest after the First World War. The Winnipeg General Strike of 1919 was ended on the promise of a royal commission to investigate industrial relations and the situation of labour, which found that "ostentatious display of wealth"[9] was a main cause of post-war dissatisfaction. A more substantial outcome of the strike, however, was the rushed-through measure by Mackenzie King's Liberal government creating the loosely defined crime of sedition under Section 98 of the Criminal Code. The new law was used to arrest and charge labour leaders after the 1922 strike against the British Empire Steel Corporation, which resulted when the company suddenly imposed a wage cut of 37.5 per cent on its 12,000 Nova Scotia workers.

Canadian industrialists and their supporters in government had frankly sought immigrant industrial workers to exert downward pressure on wages. Such recruits were thought unlikely to organize or gain any political power. Prominent among those who came were the Jews of Russia and the states of the faltering Austro-Hungarian Empire. The Jewish census of Canada, only 2,393 in 1881, was 6,414 in 1891, 16,401 in 1901, 74,654 in 1911, and 125,197 in 1921. After this the effects of restrictions on eastern European immigration began to be felt, but the Jewish population continued to grow, reaching 155,766 in 1931. These figures were far from insignificant in a total national population that stood at 8,788,000 in 1921 and 10,377,000 in 1931.

Jewish immigrants were thus a major component of immigration to

Canada 1880–1940, that is, the period that formed the Canada Goldman first encountered in 1906 and the times corresponding to her later Canadian trips. Most Jewish immigrants settled in large cities; presuming that social characteristics of Jews arriving in Canada 1899–1910 were similar to those arriving during the same period in the United States, for whom survey information exists, then about 75 per cent of them were tradesmen, shopkeepers, craftsmen, and skilled workers, about 12 per cent unskilled workers, and only about 13 per cent agricultural labourers, peasants, and servants.[10] By the 1920s they formed vital and colourful sections in the major cities, especially Montreal, Toronto, and Winnipeg, strongly influencing the local environment. Some Jewish immigrants had brought with them, to the dismay of many Canadian leaders, radical notions of labour organization, human rights, and social reconstruction. "An influx of Jews", wrote the Toronto *Evening Telegram* in 1924, "puts a worm next the kernel of every fair city where they get hold. These people . . . engage in the wars of no country, but flit from one to another . . . following up the wind the smell of lucre."[11]

Thus, in the Canada where Goldman arrived in 1926, the dominant society was likely to be inert if not hostile towards her and her ideas, in the style of England; and its attitude towards the working class and workers' political self-consciousness was likely to be repressive, with a tincture of suspicion regarding "foreign" elements, as in the United States. Yet this last factor actually recommended Canada to Goldman rather than discouraging her. Canada was now more like the United States than it had been in 1906–08. It exhibited more sharply the conflicts with which she was concerned. Its urban industrial and garment workers, shop owners, and labourers were those whose causes she had championed, through anarchism, connecting them to a call for universal human liberation. If she had to live on the margins, and speak from and for the margins, she knew that in Canada margins now existed of sufficient scope to welcome and perhaps support her.

As to the demoralization of anarchists, of which she was soon complaining in Montreal, this was no different from what she found elsewhere, and could be traced to the same causes. There were the effective measures against radicals taken by governments after 1914. And there was fierce competition from other radical strains possessing various attractions. Communism offered the success of the Russian Revolution and the Soviet Union; socialist labour, the promise of working within the system rather than always painfully against it; Poale Zion, the opportunity to combine radical socialism with the seemingly incompatible nationalist Zionism. What Goldman had to discover was whether there was enough potential for radicalism in Canada, a big enough population open to anarchism at least in principle, that she could work there. Her trip was designed to show her what only experiment could discover. But she had not acquainted herself specifically with Canadian issues and did not arrive ready to address the situation of Canadians or Canadian labour. Nor had she written lectures or planned other activities in which she oriented her own international and philosophical concerns, such as the menace of Bolshevism or the theory of anarchism, directly to local conditions. Her approach to Canada perhaps contained more hope and less preparation for sustained engagement than would have been ideal.

Goldman gave only two English-language lectures in Montreal. The first was held on 31 October at His Majesty's Theatre. In the *Road to Freedom*, Goldman credited William Fraser, "a very broadminded and altogether splendid spirited Scotchman at the head of" the People's Forum of Montreal, with the impulse and organizational skill that led to this appearance in such a prominent venue. Although she prized the experience for the publicity it drew, she was disappointed with the turnout, saying that the meeting was "heartbreaking, an empty house"[12]; in the *Road to Freedom*'s account, W.S. Van Valkenburg estimated the audience at 700 to 800. The Montreal English press reported the lecture *con brio* and showed no sign of judging that the crowd was less than satisfactory. If the newspapers were dissatisfied, it was only because the insults, perhaps even brickbats, they had forecast on Goldman's arrival failed to fly between communists and anarchists. In interviews given 20–21 October to such newspapers as the Montreal *Star* and *Gazette*, the Toronto *Evening Telegram*, and the New York *World* and the *New York Times*, Goldman lambasted the Soviets ("a Russian dictatorship which added to the many evils of Czardom a great many evils of the communist state"), signalling the theme of her first Canadian lecture and of her entire stay. But all was decorum during Goldman's address on "The Recent Crises in Russia". The *Star* reported that police protection, which Goldman had scorned in an earlier interview, "was not needed, even had she been willing to receive it", and the *Gazette* commented, "If there were red-hot Communists who listened to her denunciations of absolute dictatorship and utter failure of democracy, they did so without protest. If there were pro-Bolsheviks who heard her speak of the 'delusion and snare' and saying that the workers in Russia are 'abject slaves' under Soviet iron rule, they did not lift their voices in contradiction." The afternoon lecture was followed by respectful dialogue—much of it in Goldman's fluent Russian, the *Star* noted—between audience and speaker until the meeting chairman, the Rev. T.A. Bourke, "had to call a halt through the lateness of the hour".[13]

Goldman gave a historical account of the Russian Revolution down to the situation in late 1926, which she characterized as a power struggle between followers of Stalin and those of the exiled Trotsky. But her lecture's main purpose lay elsewhere. Her goal was to imply and support her own anarchist position through an analysis of the threat Russian communism posed to radicalism. Her analysis amounted to an almost prophetic account of the nature and effects of modern state propaganda, which came to be more widely understood after the Second World War. Goldman was early into the field in recognizing that modern centralized states were able to present themselves as so massive, impressive and total that they could convince most individuals of the futility or destructiveness, or even the non-existence, of any method of social participation other than through the existing political system and economy.

In her lecture, Goldman strongly emphasized the degree of centralization—the degree of democracy's absence—in Russia. Trotsky had been exiled in 1923 for even a pallid approach to democracy, his idea that workers, supposedly the makers of revolution, be given more say in determining new industrial directions. She tried to show her listeners the absolute incompatibility between, on the one hand, post-revolutionary Russia and, on the other, their revolutionary hope (if they were anarchists or radicals) or their belief in political betterment (if they were liberals and communist sympathizers). She documented the horrors of Bolshevik rule: concentration of power in a tiny elite, formation of a ruthless and efficient secret police, forced sixteen-hour work days, night-work for women, teachers' salaries unpaid during the second half of 1926, rising cost-of-living, low and falling wages, massive unemployment, many impoverished women and children living in the streets, systematic elimination of leaders of the original revolution who had come from other radical movements such as the Mensheviks and anarchists, persecution and imprisonment even of those who refused to espouse a political opinion. These facts were the groundwork for her attempt to expose the way in which Moscow was destroying world radicalism. Russia, she said, deliberately put up a false front of democracy to delude workers and enlist them in its cause. "But if revolution is a mere exchange of governments, a mere exchange of fetishes, like an icon for a Lenin, then a revolution is not only useless. It is criminal."[14] Its success in deluding people and drawing them to itself was enlisting idealistic persons in the cause of tyranny and emptying the ranks of truly revolutionary and libertarian movements.

In this first English lecture in Canada, Goldman emphasized an idea she had long held, one which was to grow in importance in her later thought. She paid tribute to the men and women of the intelligentsia who, she said, had suffered persecution in the struggle for freedom and equality for a hundred years. They had made the revolution. Early in the address she used the same phrase, "made the revolution", with regard to the workers. As the next fourteen years progressed, she became ever more critical of the masses and the proletariat and invested more and more hope in artists and intellectuals. Presumably, she hoped that they would see through the self-presentation of modern social systems, whether capitalist or socialist, and would have the courage to stand opposed.

Goldman's probing for a new constituency points to her fear that she was failing again to reinvigorate her traditional anarchist supporters and to catalyze action around her sense that anarchism had a role to play despite its beleaguered position. "[T]he ideal to which I have dedicated my life seems further away than when I began my work", she wrote to Malmed from Montreal on 11 November. "No doubt it is my stand on Russia that is killing my chances with the Jews [from whom she had hoped for large attendance and donations at her meetings]. . . . But . . . it would mean a complete betrayal of our unfortunate comrades who [are] languishing in the prisons of Russia not to speak in their behalf." And on 20 November 1926 she declared to a US supporter that "the reason for the failure [of her lectures] is my stand on Russia. Moscow has impressed such a terrible lie upon the world . . . although many of our friends are opposed to the things done in the name of the Russian revolution they yet seem to feel that it would be best to ignore Russia. . . ."[15] As had happened during the First World War, she was being pressured to suppress truth for expediency and was dismissed when she refused to do so. The problem for Goldman was not only that Moscow had succeeded in deluding radicals the world over that the Russian Revolution was a true social advance and Russia a true workers' democracy, but also that it had managed to present as fact its contention that no other radicalism, progressivism, or revolutionary theory was practicable.

In Russia first, and again later during her experience of the reactionary twenties and thirties in the western democracies, Goldman had perceived the newly developing form of control by the state. The threat of significant dissidence could be obviated by masking just enough abuses, and handing out just enough benefits (often adapting socialist proposals and demands), that despair and unrest would never catch fire. But quite a lot of tyranny could be exercised, quite a lot of impoverishment imposed, because the vast and dispersed nature of modern populations, and their dependence on modern communications for a sense of their nation, always allowed the system to produce overwhelmingly large numbers of misinformed, contented and politically inert people. The modern state's vastness induced despair in dissenting individuals and groups. Each person faced a stark decision: whether to agree to the narrow range of accepted values and alternatives, work and argue within that framework, and in return be allowed to participate, or to stand by an alternative sense of social good and be powerless, deprived of the public half of human existence. Leninist Russia, Goldman saw, was a chief creator of this method of social control as a consciously directed and exploited technique (rather than simply as a situation tending to occur in mass societies as soon as wealth is used to buy off the masses). Goldman outlined a third position, opposed both to communist totalitarianism and to the reactionary conservatism of the democracies. Anarchism was the diametrical opposite of both these abusive ideologies, both of which tried to present anarchists as in league with the other. Anarchism was in fact at one pole, that of freedom, and they were together at the opposite pole.

On the same day as Goldman's first English lecture in Montreal, the Communist Party held a memorial meeting at the city's Prince Arthur Hall to mark the death of Eugene V. Debs, the prominent American labour and socialist leader, who had been a great admirer of Goldman and a sceptic and critic with regard to Bolshevism. In fact, in the *Road to Freedom* both Goldman and Van Valkenburg claimed that the timing of this memorial for Debs had been a form of Bolshevik interference. Michael Buhay, founder of the local Communist Party and a prominent Montreal political figure from the 1910s through the 1940s, denounced socialists and, the *Gazette* reported, "also found time to denounce Emma Goldman whom he termed 'one of those beauties of socialism who is now the darling of the capitalist press and the bourgeoisie, because of her lying attacks against the Soviet republic'".[16] This article throws an incidental light on a difficulty that the communists and anarchists alike experienced as a result of being based in ethnic communities. The reporter at Buhay's meeting commented, "Due to the rather polyglot nature of the large audience, the applause was confined to the scattered groups who understood the speakers in the various languages." As a riposte to the communist attempt to seize the fallen mantle of the great socialist leader, Goldman herself organized a Montreal Debs memorial lecture for 6 November to be offered to the city's Jewish and anarchist communities.

Two days after her 31 October lecture, Goldman canvassed the event's frustrations in a letter to Malmed. A blunder in the printing of the Yiddish handbill had announced the wrong date. The Montreal comrades had decided to set a $2 admission. She went on, "Worse than the poor meeting is the [w]rangle among the comrades", for one of them was now abusing the others for consenting to charge such a restrictive price: "The same spirit among the comrades as in the past."[17] She would be glad, she said, when she could move on.

In this letter she provided a glimpse of an average Goldman day. She was writing in mid-afternoon after having stayed up until 3 a.m. working on the fourth of the articles for the US newspapers, as arranged by Levine. Then she had slept briefly and resumed working on other lectures. This was followed by letter-writing: the one to Malmed was among several she composed that afternoon, pouring out her distress.

There would be only one other English lecture and seven in Yiddish arranged for her in the city. Publicly she had come to champion anarchism and raise needed funds, but privately she had come for the sake of Leon Malmed. The two agendas conflicted particularly in the matter of housing. She was so desperate for privacy to be alone with Malmed, especially after the frustration of his first Montreal visit when she had had no place to share with him, that she took an apartment alone. This did not end the conflict, for she reported that the "comrades think I am crazy and terribly extravagant, and I think so myself". On Saturday 6 November, she wrote to Malmed that for $65 a week and $5 to have the all-important telephone installed she had rented rooms in the Arlington Apartments, 654 Union Avenue. On 8 November she moved in and Leon visited her between 13 and 16 November. Also, they spent at least some time away from Montreal. The sexual intimacy which Goldman had been seeking seems to have begun not in Montreal but in the nearby resort town of Napierville, whose name remained for months afterward in Goldman's correspondence a touchstone for a peerless memory. In letters that followed Malmed home to Albany beginning 17 November, Goldman exclaimed over their new closeness: "since you listened to the music of my soul—since you have felt the elemental force of my being—since you dissolved into me and I in you—you will understand my Leon that there is something more expressive than words. It is by means of this *some*thing that I speak to you." The next day she wrote him that "something fresh and new" had come into her life after she had "given up all hopes". She added: "In me it is the awakening of spring, only more wonderful than that because of what the maturity, the experience, and the art of life has taught me. Yes, I want our love to be a true work of art." And on the following day: "I feel like a Sarah, to whom a son came in old age. Not that I feel old, indeed, I never felt younger, never gladder than I do now, for my lover loves me and he finds me beautiful, and I can give him ecstatic joy."[18]

Yet even as she praised the joys of their love, Goldman began to chide Malmed. Why, she asked, did he allow fears of being recognized by Toronto anarchists to cause him to hesitate about visiting her there? Did he scruple to declare himself her lover? Already in the first few days after the consummation of their affair, she was discovering, to judge by her responses to Leon's letters, that her physical presence had not worked the transformation in him—from careful shopkeeper to Dionysiac hero—that she had urged from Europe. Now, she said, she wanted to see more commitment to the anarchist movement and to her. In her 8 November letter rebutting the Montreal comrades' charges that she was crazy and extravagant to take an apartment, she expressed her own views thus: "I have always found that only extravagant and 'crazy' people know the meaning and mystery of life and love. Only they know how to live dangerously and drink the cup of life with all its bitter sweetness to the last drop. This is why they are so vital and retain their youth, their capacity for great love and great deeds."[19]

During Goldman's last ten days in Montreal, her assessment of the first leg of her Canadian trip became decidedly negative. She was disappointed at how her meetings were organized and publicized. She criticized what she found to be the lack of spirit and of true concern for social issues. She complained consistently of poor attendance. When she did achieve good attendance, as for instance at her 6 November Debs memorial lecture, she found reason for bitter complaint in the relative failure of the fundraising; the meeting earned only $28 for political prisoners. "That is all the memory of the sweet soul Debs meant to the Jews of this city."[20] She echoed the same note when writing contemplatively of a 11 November meeting, the thirty-ninth anniversary of the Haymarket executions, "the heroic death which was my birth". She wrote: "My heart is full of sadness. In all the years of passionate belief in our ideal and in complete devotion to it what have I achieved? Not a hundred people who are sufficiently interested to hear me, no new life, or the least sign of growth."[21]

Two small bright spots stood out in the otherwise dismal assessment of Montreal. First was the women's group that she managed to found, as an entity separate from herself, to conduct ongoing fundraising for anarchists imprisoned in Russia. In late December, she wrote from Toronto that it was organized and successful; she called it the high point of her Montreal trip. In February 1928, she was able to report that the club had raised $500 for Russian political prisoners, meaning that a scant six weeks in Montreal had produced better results than her two years in England. Second was the banquet in her honour scheduled for 22 November, a few days before departure for Toronto. At first, she was disappointed at the extreme slowness with which subscriptions came in. In the end, however, forty people attended. She wrote to Malmed the night of the banquet that "I was determined to move the people and I did".[22] She reported that she raised $311.65 from twenty-five contributors, mostly women, who gave $25 each.

Still, the disappointments of Montreal had outweighed its successes. Especially troubling was its seeming confirmation of anarchist demoralization and the futility imposed on her own efforts: "our comrades", she observed, "have lost all interest in the grave social problems of our times".[23] What would she find in Toronto? In early November, Fred Jacobs, the drama critic of the Toronto *Mail and Empire*, to whom she had written for help in finding a venue for her drama lectures, wrote that he had failed to locate an organization, among the many that professed interest, bold enough to sponsor her. "The tendency of Toronto", he commented, "is to be a very conservative city. The wealthy organizations have that policy, and the poorer ones are afraid to risk criticism. . . . [W]e have two evening papers here [the *Daily Star* and the *Evening Telegram*] that go quite beyond the bounds of decency when they attack people and things of which they disapprove, and they both are out to protect the stupid and standardised form of respectability. They make clubs, even of liberal-minded people, hesitate before they invite abuse and before they take under their wing a person whom the editors would regard as a disruptor." About a week later, Jacobs continued in another letter: "It would have been pleasant for me to be able to report that Canadians are as liberal and tolerant as you hoped. However, that is one respect in which we resemble our over-grown cousins across the line. . . ."[24] After only a month in Canada, Goldman started to wonder if she would not have to begin prospecting all over again for the better field of activity she sought. She confessed in a letter, "I do not know how long I shall remain in Canada. I had planned it should be until March. But if the rest of Canada will be like Montreal, it will not be worth while."[25]

4

Toronto, Autumn and Winter 1926–27

When Goldman arrived at Toronto's Union Station on Friday 26 November, she was met by a "warm-hearted and eager" crowd and taken to the Prince George Hotel, 91 York Street, in a car owned by Julius Seltzer. "[H]ere I found the beautiful pink roses of my own Leon", she wrote to Malmed later that night, "and Desser gave me your letter. I was happy beyond words and deeply moved." She was also met by interested reporters. Her first interview came almost the moment she reached her hotel, where she found a Toronto *Daily Star* man, Robert C. Reade, and kept her friends waiting in another room while she talked with him. Afterwards, she and the others again squeezed into Seltzer's car and went off to a restaurant for what Goldman called her formal introduction to the group. In *Road to Freedom* she recalled the presence of "Desser, the Langbords, Simkin, [the] Steinbergs, Gurian, Judkin [and] a radiant creature in a lovely Spanish shawl, Maria Tiboldo", a daughter of Italian American anarchists who, unbeknownst to Goldman, spoke no Yiddish but "sat there for several hours, just happy in the thought of being with dear comrades". The very next morning, Goldman was up early to speak to a female reporter from another newspaper. She wrote to Leon that she hoped the flurry of press interest might mean something: "I think the *Star* will help much with my meetings."[1] And indeed the next day's *Star* carried a two-column feature on the first page of the second section, to which readers were directed by a large picture and cutline immediately under the day's front page banner. The caption introduced her as "The Most Complete Individualist . . . famous exponent of individualism and dramatic literature", and the story itself emphasized her peaceful beliefs; a subhead proclaimed she was "Pacifist And Wants No Bloodshed Only Freedom From Accepted Ideas". Reade had written: "She is still an 'anarchist', but there is no danger that while she is here she will throw any bombs other than intellectual ones." The famous radical who exuded such security showed in her dress "no subjection to the tyranny of fashion. Her hair is unbobbed. Her skirt drops nearly to her shoe tops. . . . She is a short, plump woman, well advanced in middle life." The Toronto *Evening Telegram* disagreed; in a wide-ranging interview published 1 December, it noted that "Miss Goldman's hair is bobbed, and in every way she is extremely modern."[2]

Goldman used the *Star* interview to address the issue of the communist seizure of all radical ground. She strongly denied that her repudiation of Leninism was a break with her former ideals. She was still a rebel against all authority, she said, but she was an emancipator of minds even more than of bodies. "She wants to rid the world of Main Street as well as of Mussolini", the *Star* paraphrased, "not by assassination, but by lectures on dramatic literature, which to her is the most dynamic of human creations." Reade told her she was not the "fire-eating Emma Goldman" he had expected. Her response was a bit of revisionist autobiography that expressed the recent direction of her thought: "Although I was interested in economics I was always more interested in literature." She had never, she reminded him, followed Marxism or socialism but had always "believed in appeals to . . . the individual rather than the mass".[3] Goldman later praised Reade as "the most intelligent and best-informed reporter I have met in a long while and himself more of an Anarchist than he realizes".[4] She was delighted with his culture and acumen generally, and his knowledge of anarchism and the thought of Bakunin in particular. In the course of her stay, this delight was to ripen into a friendship with the newspaperman and his wife, both of whom became "sponsors" of Goldman, as she called them. Mrs Reade helped organize one of Goldman's courses of drama lectures, and Goldman often dined with the couple in their home at 72 Avenue Road. One of the first Rhodes scholars from the University of Toronto, Reade had returned from Oxford in 1922 to become an outstanding member of a group of young, intelligent, and literate reporters at the *Star*, where he first worked for the Monday-to-Saturday paper but was soon transferred to the *Star Weekly*, the famous Saturday supplement that also had a freestanding existence on newsstands across Canada and abroad. Indeed he became one of its two or three most prominent staff members.

As the first few busy days in Toronto proceeded, friends filled her nights with conviviality. Looking back over her first lecture season in March 1927, she described the circle's activities to her *Road to Freedom* readers in these terms: "Sunday the 28th of November all the comrades forgathered in the Langbords['] house to a huge repast. This marked the beginning of the process to stuff me for slaughter. The comrades evidently thought I had been starved not only for activities during my exile of seven years but also for food. They vied with one another who is to do the feeding best. And so like an old time Yeshive bocher (Talmud student) I was given kast (board) each day in a different home."[5]

As in Montreal, she found herself in a Jewish immigrant group that cherished radical or progressive views in the midst of their larger community, many of whose members involved themselves in political issues via labour unions. In 1926 Toronto was undergoing a sustained spurt of immigration-fueled growth. The population tripled between 1901 and 1931; from 1921 to 1931 alone it increased from 522,000 to 631,000. In 1931, Toronto was home to nearly a third of Canada's Jews, or about 45,000, representing 7.2 per cent of the city's population (the next largest ethnic group was Italian, 2.1 per cent). Their homes, businesses, and labour and fraternal organizations were centred on Spadina Avenue between Dundas and Front streets, where a thriving garment industry arose, bearing witness to the skills and backgrounds of a large proportion of Toronto Jews.

In 1907, when the Jewish population was still only a few thousand persons, a Toronto branch of the Arbeiter Ring (Workmen's, or Workers', Circle) was established. The Circle originated in New York in 1900 and grew to be the world's largest Yiddish social organization. Its anarchist wing may well have provided the impetus for Goldman's 1907–08 appearances in Toronto. In the 1920s, the Circle, with its associated Women's Circle, was the centre of political and social activity for most of Goldman's anarchist colleagues. The group, nonpolitical in itself, was formed of several usually compatible elements: a purely fraternal component, a group of socialists, a smaller band of anarchists (perhaps never more than about forty persons), and until 1922 a group of communists. In 1922, at the Arbeiter Ring's national convention, held at the King Edward Hotel in Toronto, the communists were expelled to prevent their taking over the organization, an action that cost the Toronto Arbeiter Ring an estimated thousand members. But this still lay far in the future when, in 1913, the Circle along with the Socialist Farband and number of garment industry unions cooperated to form the Labour Lyceum as a hub for Yiddish-speaking workers. For this purpose, a pair of adjacent houses was purchased—346–348 Spadina Avenue, at the southwest corner of Spadina and St Andrew, two blocks north of Dundas. The anarchists were extremely active in both the Lyceum and the Workmen's Circle; the anarchist group's central figure, Joe Desser, was president of the Toronto Labour Lyceum Association in the 1926–28 period when Goldman was living in Toronto. Over the years, down to the 1950s, the

Workmen's Circle directors included, at various times, many of Goldman's friends, such as Joe and Sophie Desser, Julius and Marion Seltzer, Maurice and Becky Langbord, Louis Judkin, and I.N. Steinberg. In 1926, Goldman found some of the anarchists engaged in intensive local activity in the Workmen's Circle anarchist branch called Free Society, and in labour unions, and in the Toronto Peretz Schule. Goldman supported many of these activities. In addition to scheduled public lectures she sometimes addressed the Workmen's Circle itself at the Lyceum, adapting some of her standard topics, such as "The Relation between the Workers and the Intelligentsia". In early spring 1927, she spoke to the pupils of the Peretz Schule, reciting Olive Schreiner's allegorical poem "A Dream of Wild Bees" and interpreting it to bring out "the need of an ideal in life".[6] But at various times during her stay, the others' preoccupation with union issues, and with Arbeiter Ring initiatives such as the founding of a summer camp, left her frustrated and fuming that they were scarcely anarchists at all.

Who were these men and women who, despite work and financial difficulty few can now imagine, nevertheless devoted themselves consistently to political, social, and intellectual endeavours with an energy that finds scant parallel among citizens today? They ran from business- and factory-owners to tradespeople and shopkeepers to workers. In the 1930s, for example, Ahrne Thorne (Thorenberg), who in 1940 moved to New York and eventually became the distinguished editor of the radical newspaper *Fraye Arbeter Shtime*, worked as a machine operator in the Dominion Knitting Mills factory where Julius Seltzer was vice-president; the two discovered their mutual anarchism when the employee began discussing the works of the anarchist theorist Rudolf Rocker during a talk on the factory floor. Many of the Toronto anarchists had previous connections with Goldman in other places.

Joe Desser was in many ways typical of them. Born in Poland in 1885, thus sixteen years younger than Goldman, he had been a yeshiva student in his youth, but had fled to London with his older brother in 1902 rather than be inducted into the Polish army. In London, he learned tailoring, lost his religion, became radicalized, and met Goldman's future Toronto colleagues Maurice Langbord and Morris Simkin. Indeed, as they were part of the Arbeter Fraynd (Liberated Worker) group surrounding Rocker, they must have encountered Goldman in London in 1907. Desser came to Toronto in 1908 and was a founder of the Workmen's Circle anarchist branch (Branch 339), the Fraye Gezelschaft (Free Society). In the late 1930s an employee of the Hirschorn Garment Co., Desser would rise early for work, attend political meetings or study groups in the evening, and return late; he spent Saturdays and Sundays selling the radical newspaper *Fraye Arbeter Shtime* at the Labour Lyceum and in other Workmen's Circle activities. His home at 759 Bathurst Street was itself an anarchist centre; Rocker, whom Desser worshipped, was a guest there when lecturing in Toronto, and Goldman stayed at the address briefly in 1934 before locating an apartment. Desser's daughter Millie, a high school senior in 1934–35, acted as Goldman's typist-secretary in those years and again in 1939–40. Another was Morris Simkin, a printer, the owner of Automatic Printing Press at 169 Queen Street East, while Alex B. ("Sasha") Gurian worked as a barber, with residence and shop at 285 College Street. Joseph Cleman too was a hair dresser, with home and business at 683 Spadina Avenue, above which Goldman lodged for a time.

Maurice (sometimes "Morris") Langbord and his wife Becky (Rebecca) were two of Goldman's most faithful helpers, but also prominent among those who frustrated her by their diversion to activities not specifically anarchist. Founding members of the Workmen's Circle and its anarchist branch, they were also busy contributors to Peretz Schule and summer camp. Langbord, who had also helped found the Toronto hod-carriers' union, established a successful business, Canadian Wrecking and Construction (later, Wrecking and Salvage); his house at 78 Clinton Street was temporary home to Goldman more than once. Building on the Langbords' role in promoting the Yiddish drama in Toronto, their daughter, Eva, became an actress and a US stage star (winner of the 1936 New York Critics' Circle award for her lead role in Maxwell Anderson's *Winterset*) before returning to Canada in 1952 as casting director for CBC-TV. Thus even Eva, like Millie Desser, formed part of the loose radical alliance round Goldman, which included many ties between herself, her family members, and her radical friends on the one hand and O'Neill and Anderson and other such leading figures of advanced American theatre on the other. In fact, less than two years before Eva's success in his play, with its radical theme, Anderson had made a trip to Montreal to chair one of Goldman's late 1934 lectures.

The life of Julius Seltzer, too, gives a strong impression of the Toronto Jewish anarchists. Born in 1881 near Bialystok, Russia, Seltzer encountered anarchists and anarchism, but only after emigrating to New York in 1900 did he become an impassioned devotee of the ideal, mainly due to Johann Most, Goldman's own mentor. A seller of newspapers and maker of corn-cob pipes in New York, Seltzer joined a brother in Spokane, Washington, in 1902, and there established a lending library. In 1907, he moved to Schenectady, New York, where he operated a restaurant until 1911, organizing lectures in the city for Goldman and Berkman. In 1912, after an interlude in Ann Arbor, Michigan, he came to Toronto to become the partner of his wife's brother, who had opened a knitting mill; there he lived and prospered, dying in a senior citizens' home in 1973 at ninety-two, the last survivor of the original Toronto Jewish anarchists. Shortly before his death he assessed what he described as Toronto's "mixed Jewish and English-speaking anarchist group, including Italians, a few Bulgarians, and others" for the historian Paul Avrich: "The people in the anarchist movement were the most wonderful in the world. That alone made the movement great. It was one big family. Some of the best were not well-known but were dedicated, simple people. . . . The anarchist ideal is *zaftig* [juicy]. I am in with it all the time, all my life, always getting great pleasure from it, from the ideas, the people, the comradeship. . . . The ideal is still floating all over the world."[7]

Goldman was immediately impressed with the warmth of such people, but just as in Montreal her love affair with Leon Malmed formed a secret story playing out in counterpoint to the growing excitement of her public life. She objected to her accommodations at the Prince George Hotel. An $8-per-day suite, she said, was too extravagant. She moved immediately to a $4 room with a bath and began looking for an apartment. But her objection to the expense masked another motive, the desire for a private place in which to receive Malmed. She soon had a line on one over a Jewish restaurant at 322 Spadina Avenue: "dirt cheap only $15 but I am afraid it is no good and I may not have the privacy I need".[8] She arranged for a telephone, so that they could speak privately.

Malmed kept up a steady stream of flowers, telephone calls, telegrams, and letters. Flowers came on 29 November, the day of her first scheduled lecture in Toronto; "your glorious roses", she wrote to him, "gave so much color and spirit to the evening". He sent her flowers again on the seventeenth and twenty-fifth of December, when seven tea roses arrived from him to commemorate the seven years since her deportation. In advance of his first visit, she was embarrassed about the "shabbiness of the entrance" to the building; her rooms were two flights up. A few lines from a letter to Malmed suggest the meagerness of the lodging: "I became energetic & got my landlord to put in a few pieces of furniture. Now the place looks a little better & once he gives me a stove all will be well."[9]

To this apartment Malmed came on 6 December, Goldman having delayed an offered visit from her nephew Saxe until the following week. When the lovers parted after "two days of ecstasy", a flurry of letters and telegrams followed Malmed to Albany. Goldman was "quivering in every nerve and muscle with agonized yearning". She had a "great secret", she said. "I love you, I love you more than ever."[10] She wrote him the following week, "There must have been some still voice in my soul which compelled me to make the Canadian trip." She declared a plan to extend her time in Canada and presented it as for his sake. "I am going to stay in Canada until May, so we can be near each other and you can come to me." As in her Montreal letters, she mingled sexual and maternal imagery to describe the passion Malmed excited in her: "I want my child to drink the elixir of love from my breast." That she should flare up when, in the week following their tryst, he telephoned her after four days without letters was characteristic of her deep passion. She wrote to apologize on 15 December, saying she needed his support desperately: "Just now I so depend upon it."[11]

Her reference to the affair as a "great secret" is telling, for Goldman continued to be ambivalent about whether the relationship should be made public. She told Malmed that her niece Stella knew about their intrigue, raising the possibility that it would become common knowledge as the family visited Toronto and met her associates there. At other times, she seemed delighted at the prospect of continuing a close-kept game of love under the very noses of her colleagues, whose disapproval she felt sure of. Telegrams must be couched in circumspect language, she told Malmed, and she said of one he sent her, "How much one can read between the inoffensive lines of a night letter."[12]

Goldman met with considerable success as a lecturer in Toronto, addressing large Yiddish and English audiences. During her first month in the city, she spoke on both of her major subject areas, the drama and the leading social/political issues of the day. She discussed not only Ibsen and Strindberg but also Gogol, Ostrovsky, Turgenev and Gorky, among others. Turnouts for the lectures on the latter three authors were disappointing; she surmised that the lecture dates were too close to Christmas and that older Russian writers were "too remote from the English".[13] She spoke to larger crowds on three topics: "The European Situation of Labour", a lecture delivered at the Labour Temple (headquarters and meeting hall of Canadian organized labour at 167 Church Street), in which she made special reference to the recent British general strike and the then still continuing miners' strike that had prompted it; "The Relationship of the Workers to the Intelligentsia in Future Revolutions", a theme that was increasingly important in her later thought; and "Modern Trends in Education", in which she stressed the individual and the imagination over discipline, drawing on the theories Tolstoy and other Russian thinkers.

Her first lecture was on a Monday evening at the Hygeia Hall, 40 Elm Street; the *Star* called it a "Brilliant Disquisition" and "lecturing *in excelsis*". Her topic was "Henrik Ibsen, Social Rebel and Anarchist", and the reporter wrote that she enunciated through the dramatist "her own philosophy of life. This woman who has helped to emancipate women from their Doll's House and had herself gone to prison for her ideals, was living Ibsenism." On 1 December, the conservative *Mail and Empire*, which in the course of Goldman's stay would often either ignore or castigate her, found her first appearance so impressive (doubtless because it must have been Fred Jacobs who wrote this drama-related story) that its reservations were momentarily overcome: "There may have been many in the audience who profoundly disagreed with the earlier revolutionary methods of the speaker, but none could gainsay the courage and earnestness of her appeal as an advocate of social reform." She concentrated on *The Doll's House, Ghosts,* and *An Enemy of Society.* She concluded her remarks on the essential anarchism expressed through Ibsen's characters and their tragic situations by making a direct appeal to conscience, and obliquely delivering her own self-assessment: "All social rebels . . . must expect to pay the price, but it is better to die having seen the vision than to live a life of safety and comfort in the darkness."[14] Behind such comments was her growing concern with the fact that anarchism was now *par excellence* the doctrine that would have power if ever people acted according to reason but would continue to be powerless so long as they chose positions calculated to bring them respectability and participation within the existing system.

Full coverage in the *Star* on 4 and 6 December of her next two lectures carried her image and message far beyond Hygeia Hall. In her 3 December talk, she characterized the education of the day as "designed for the production of automatons"; classes are too large and too standardized, the average teacher "goes by the rule-book and should be considered a child herself",[15] and the imaginative child is looked on as a hindrance. She pointed to Tolstoy in Russia and Francisco Ferrer in Spain as significant educational reformers, and gave vivid impressions of classrooms that were real rooms with real furniture, with involved parents coming in and out and learning along with their children, who advanced partly according to their own abilities and interests rather than a pre-determined system of subjects and grades.

Two days later Goldman compared Russia and Italy, analyzing Mussolini as a "very cheap imitator" of Bolshevik-style terror and force; she concluded with a prophecy of the imminent downfall of both dictatorships. The *Star* reported that "[r]epresentatives of the communist party of Toronto were present to hear her reaffirm her recantation of Bolshevism. At the conclusion of her eloquent address they subjected her to much critical questioning to all of which she replied with conspicuous readiness and effectiveness." Even more than her skill in thrust and parry, her agility with aphorisms and apposite formulations impressed the reporter. His quotation of some of these gives a relatively rare glimpse into her platform style. "The League of Nations is a living corpse." "Government is a political go-cart for adults." "It is criminal to impose any political theory on the mind of a child." "Trotsky and others with great brains work themselves to death for their idea and also work you to death for their idea."[16]

A 15 December *Star* feature story ("Not Bombs, But Flowers, Fill the Apartment of Emma Goldman in Toronto") commented that she was in the city with a letter of introduction from the British Drama League, and reverently cited the titled names on the board of this "very aristocratic as well as literary body". She paid tribute to her acquaintance Sir Barry Jackson ("if ever I believed in knighthood I believed in that one") as the first man to play Hamlet in modern dress and as the originator, through his Birmingham company, of the then-burgeoning little theatre movement in England. Emphasizing that she preached "the supreme force of ideas", the reporter asked facetiously concerning one of her Russian drama lectures, "Is Griboyadev a secret explosive?" Goldman again drew the distinction between herself and the communists, and commented, "I have come to Toronto under . . . the auspices of the Workmen's Circle, an organization which is doing educational work particularly amongst the Jews." She had lectured on Sunday 13 December in Yiddish on Maxim Gorky, she said, to 600 persons at the Labour Lyceum. She spoke of the interest in her trip not only in Canada but in the American press, and of her happiness that Toronto residence allowed visits from her family: "On Christmas . . . I am going to have a family Christmas Party, the first one in the life of Emma Goldman." (Goldman occasionally celebrated Christmas but only as a secular holiday, and she was not an observant Jew.) She answered "I don't think so" to the question whether she would reside permanently in Canada.[17]

Toronto was proving out. She had been highly successful in her initial lectures and contacts with the press. She was encouraged by the enthusiasm of the comrades, and Malmed had visited. If she was not considering permanent residence, she was weighing the pros and cons of extending her visit; she had originally planned to return to England in March 1927, after making a trip to Western Canada. She already had told Malmed that she intended to stay for his sake until May, and now the Toronto faction was urging her to remain at least through the summer and the 1927–28 lecture season. On 18 December she wrote to Ellen A. Kennan about the benefits this had: "Last but not least is the fact that Toronto is near Rochester which gives me a chance to see my dear ones."[18]

Despite her bitter rebellion against her father's authority, Goldman had always stayed close to her siblings, especially her sisters—and later their children—and her brother Morris ("Moe" as he was called). The week before writing to Kennan, she had visits from her sister Lena Cominsky and Lena's son, Saxe Commins, the New York editor and writer, as well as from Moe. Lena and Saxe arrived on the hectic day, 12 December, when Goldman gave an evening lecture before an audience of 700 and then, along with her family members, attended a party at a restaurant. The family returned in force only about a week later to spend the Christmas season with her; this time, the group included her niece Stella and Stella's son Ian, later to become a distinguished book publisher. The holiday mood was heightened by the parties and other gatherings of the Toronto anarchists. She was increasingly impressed with their enthusiasm and personal warmth. "I have not met a group of such genuine, dear, devoted and eager people in an age", she wrote to Berkman in December. "It would do your own heart good to be with them awhile. I am really enjoying my stay." She told Kennan that "the spirit of the group in this city" was the most heartening aspect of her residence, adding: "Such a . . . jovial and sociable lot I have not come in touch with in years. [P]eople in Europe are dead compared to the bunch here. They took ten years off my shoulders." A surprise party to commemorate her 21 December 1919 deportation from the United States included the gift of a wristwatch. She wrote to Berkman of this meeting, "Yesterday they swept me off my feet with a surprise party to celebrate our deportation, or rather the fact that you and I had survived. . . ."[19]

The *Star* reporter at her lecture that evening had got wind of the celebration and asked her about it. She replied that no party was planned, only the lecture. After the lecture, though, she found herself whisked off to the home of I.N. Steinberg, a figure rarely glimpsed in her correspondence but a radical socialist friendly with Rudolf Rocker and close to anarchism, who had been People's Commissar of Justice in the Soviet government 1917–18 before breaking with the Bolsheviks and coming to the West. "Imagine then my surprise", she continued, "when I was taken by car to the house of Comrade Steinberg where I found the whole bunch, a table beautifully set and the dear people presented me with a beautiful wrist watch, the first in my life. . . . No wonder Rudolf liked it in Toronto so much more than anywhere else." She also reported to Berkman that the anarchists were sending him a $15 Christmas gift and were asking him if he would come to Canada if they obtained a visa for him.

Although pleased with the intelligence and interest of her English audiences in Toronto, she would have preferred them larger. On 22 December she wrote to Malmed that her most recent lecture had attracted 125 persons. "The most interesting thing at the meeting was the announcement I made that I would speak on Anarchism on my return from Winnipeg. The audience went wild with enthusiasm."[20]

In late December and early January, Goldman completed her course of drama lectures, featuring Russian authors including Andreyev and Tolstoy. The *Star* reporter at her Andreyev lecture prominently noted her statement, "God and the police willing, when I return in March [from Winnipeg] I will, before I sail back to England, speak on birth control, anarchism and other interesting topics." To a questioner who doubted whether anyone with such a tragic view of life as Andreyev could be called a creative artist, Goldman shot back, "A great many people can afford to be fools . . . but few can afford to be prophets. A creative artist is not obvious. His function is not to betray, but to portray life. He cannot graft on artificial happy endings. . . . He makes people face life, and most run away from it." Signing copies of *My Disillusionment in Russia* after the lecture, she remarked to one book buyer, "The peasants of Russia think a piece of the rope that hangs a man brings good luck. May Emma Goldman's signature bring you the same luck. Who knows but what they will hang me yet."[21]

As she contemplated addressing political issues more directly, she wondered if her meetings might not be shut down; controversy was exhilarating, but it was also dangerous. She was also expecting at this time a late spring Toronto lecture tour by Rocker, which never materialized; though Rocker could not lecture in English, he would split the small Yiddish audience. As well, she doubted the organizational abilities of the Toronto circle in helping her reach English-speaking audiences, feeling also that they spent too freely, especially in relation to the amount of money she could raise at the few meetings. She complained that they "evidently think I can live on what a lecture a week would bring". The schedule they had made left a gap of five days between her first two lectures, on 29 November and 3 December, and then seven days between her first two Yiddish lectures, set for 5 December and 12 December. She was distressed, also, that the first lecture was supposed to cover Ibsen and Strindberg. "Imagine people being so ignorant that they do not know that it is difficult enough to talk of Ibsen in one evening, let alone such a complex character as Strindberg."[22] She changed the topic to Ibsen only. In letters to Berkman and Malmed, she agonized. Her first Ibsen lecture drew 500 people, she estimated, but the number far from filled the Hygeia Hall, which had space for 1,600. She rarely mentioned her Yiddish lectures to her correspondents unless it was to complain that their frequently large audiences made a disappointing contrast to those of the English ones.

Another frustrating element of that December was the difficulty of preparing for her Western trip. Her Winnipeg contacts were agonizingly slow to act, for reasons suggesting that Western Canada, especially Winnipeg, might no longer be the fertile soil for anarchism she had judged it to be nearly two decades earlier. The chief organizer of her Winnipeg visit was her old friend Samuel Prasow, with whom she had stayed in Winnipeg in 1908 and who had been one of the chief agents in Canada for Michael Cohn and herself when arranging the 1926 trip. Julius Seltzer recalled Prasow as the leader, along with his brother, of Winnipeg's anarchists, the two of them remaining active into the 1950s. Prasow had frustrated Cohn with his rare and tardy responses, and recently he had been doing the same to Goldman; moreover, he was relying on Joe Desser to relay plans and news.

On 27 December, Goldman told Berkman about Prasow's latest message to her, which had come via Desser. She was indignant to learn that the Winnipeg anarchists had not wanted her to speak of Russia when in the city. Prasow had told Desser that, in her paraphrase, "we were living peacefully with the Communists, now since they heard Emma is coming they have declared war upon us and we have taken up the challenge. They have captured the Labour Temple built with our money and money of the Socialists and have voted against us having it" for her lectures. "Peacefully indeed", Goldman snorted to Berkman. She would not tolerate any restrictions from "the damned fools in Winnipeg [who] did not want me to touch upon Russia."[23]

The slowness with which the Winnipeg visit came together meant that by the middle of the month she still was not entirely clear what she would be doing in January. On 11 December she wrote to her former lover Ben Reitman, who had taken the occasion of her presence in nearby Canada to ask for a reunion; he wanted to visit her for his birthday on New Year's Day. She replied that she would not be in Toronto due to a planned weeklong trip to Windsor followed by an extended stay in Winnipeg. (As it turned out, the Windsor swing fell through, but she did lecture in southwestern Ontario, in the city of London.)

The year began with a powerful piece of publicity. On New Year's Eve the Toronto *Star* covered the top of page one of its magazine section with "Toronto's Anarchist Guest, Emma Goldman" by Frederick Griffin, a long article which "for psychologic perception and sympathetic understanding is unlike anything written about me",[24] she said in a column she wrote for *Road to Freedom*. Griffin, a native of Ireland often described as the *Star*'s most skilled serious reporter, called her "from an international point of view the world's most notable woman" and gave a laudatory pen portrait of her character and ideas and an account of her doings and circumstances in Toronto. The piece included a full summary of her career which, Griffin wrote, the anarchist campaigner had recounted to him with "intense feeling [and] a delicious undercurrent of humor" but always with "tremendous restraint, as if her experience and philosophy had long since taught her . . . the religion of liberty to which she so passionately adheres [was] much bigger than a mere desolated hearth, imprisonment, or deportation". She told Griffin that "in the light of the war and of Russia . . . I am more convinced than ever that nothing else but liberty as the basis of society and life will ever solve the present problems of the world". Griffin later became the paper's Soviet correspondent and in 1932 published *Soviet Scene: A Newspaperman's Close-ups of New Russia*, a work perhaps somewhat influenced by Goldman's two volumes on the subject.

Griffin quoted Goldman that she hoped to "die on deck, true to my ideals". He told how he had climbed two flights of stairs to be greeted by the sound of her typewriter from the next room and, a moment later, by a man whom Goldman introduced as her brother "Dr. Goldman" (Moe, who was a radiologist). Roses were prominent: many Canadian accounts comment on the constant presence of flowers in her lodgings; they were often gifts from Malmed. In a few moments she finished her writing and invited Griffin into the room where she worked. He wrote: "'I am not accustomed to this primitive method of heating,' she said once as she bustled over to throw coal on the tall little stove in the middle of the floor which gave the room the frontier flavor of a room in the north country. 'Sometimes I forget about it and it goes out on me.' She said this as if she utterly lacked any sense of irritation or complaint—in the same passionless tone exactly which she used later when telling of her harsh treatment at the hands of the American authorities."[25]

But irritated she was. Before leaving for Winnipeg, she spent a few days packing up her things for a move to better lodgings. Writing to Malmed on 7 January she called her rooms above the restaurant "a dump", and complained of rats and smells; she was angry with Seltzer for putting her there. So she moved to "a lovely place"[26] a few blocks north at 683 Spadina Avenue, rented for $35 a month from Joseph Cleman, whose mailing address she had already used in the late stages of arranging her Canadian trip. Moe stayed in this apartment until she returned from Winnipeg.

Early in January 1927, Goldman lectured in Yiddish to 700 persons at the Standard Theatre, 287 Spadina Avenue (the northeast corner of Spadina and Dundas Street—in later times the Victory Burlesk). Her topic was "The Heroic Women of the Russian Revolution". This was her one Toronto lecture at which local communists, whose conduct she described as usually "bourgeois and counterrevolutionary" in its polite reserve, made an attempt to disrupt her with charges from the floor. For example, a man identifying himself as a veteran of the Red Army took exception to her description of "the martyred women of Russia beginning with the heroic wives of the Decembrists to the women now martyred in Soviet prisons. Showing that in the time of the Tsars these women were at least charged with their offense. . . . Now there is no charge, no trial and the prison terms never end." On 5 January she gave an English lecture on Tolstoy, and characterized her listeners as "a beautiful audience, about 250 people, the cream of the intelligentsia, college professors, students, doctors & whatnot".[27]

She then spent a few days in London, Ontario, where she repeated several of her recent lectures, including one at the Ritz Pleasure Gardens comparing Leninism and Mussolini's fascism. To her Toronto remarks she added an important note. This was that many Canadian anarchists, located in Jewish and other ethnic populations, had been persuaded to put aside their revulsion towards Moscow because of the new Russia's public benevolence to Jews. The London *Advertiser* paraphrased her as stating that the highly publicized Russian land grant to Jews had been a ploy to disguise anti-Semitism then prevalent in Russia and its government. The London *Free Press* also reported her lectures prominently. But the meetings and the money raised for the Russian politicals disappointed her.

When Goldman returned to Toronto and her new apartment on 10 January, she still had two weeks to spend in Ontario before departing for Winnipeg. Her public activities in Toronto ended with a successful fund-raising banquet on 16 January, and a few days later she sent Berkman a cheque for $372, $236.50 of it proceeds from the collection that night for Russian politicals. The banquet had also brought many requests that she stay on in Canada. In its afterglow she wrote to a friend, "I am certain if I would put in as much effort as I did in England the results would be far beyond [what] I had there."[28]

Starting on 11 January, she began using her Winnipeg address (Samuel Prasow's home, 435 Mountain Avenue) on correspondence as part of a ruse to be out of town to as many people as possible, thereby getting some privacy for a much-anticipated visit from Malmed, whom she was expecting to arrive for a week-long stay the evening of the banquet. Her letters to him during the London trip are full of her eagerness: "Everything was empty in me when I came to Canada. I had no hope of a private personal character, I expected nothing much from my lectures. But you came into my life or rather you awakened everything to life like the spring." A visit to a farm outside of London prompted her to write that she was desperate for a place away from "all neighbors", with exotic decor, a "turkish divan", and a spacious bathroom so that she could wash and perfume him, and then herself, for a "love feast".[29]

Malmed did arrive on time but announced at once that he could stay only for three days, a fact which seems largely to have spoiled the occasion, for Goldman wrote him on 20 January to apologize for her coldness that weekend. His announcement had made her "guarded" in expressing affection. There had been a few brief moments of pleasure, she wrote, but seeing his train pull away was "horrible".[30] Her passion for Malmed, which only a few days before she had characterized as awakening an unanticipated springtime, never again brought her unmixed joy. She continued both to nurture and dissect their relationship, but she increasingly grew to feel that all she truly possessed now was a memory, condensed in the burning image of their first rendezvous in Napierville. This she continued to celebrate in letters to him, in which passionate tones mingled with bitter complaints and dismissive appraisals of his shortcomings, especially his failure to catch erotic fire from her repeated kindlings.

5

Winnipeg and Edmonton, 1927

Goldman left Toronto on 24 January 1927, seen off by friends at Union Station. She would be in Winnipeg for five weeks, followed by nearly two in Edmonton, then a brief return trip to Winnipeg. Her hopes for a broader tour that would reach the Pacific had foundered, partly, as she said, because of the expense. In addition to Winnipeg anarchist contacts, her friend Carl Berg, a member of the Industrial Workers of the World, was going to join her to promote her lectures. Berg also planned to go with her to Edmonton and assist her there. As Goldman travelled west, she knew what awaited her. Winnipeg communists opposed the idea of an anarchist using the Liberty Temple and also had persuaded Winnipeg members of the One Big Union—a Canadian workers' association founded in 1919 on the "one union" principle championed by the Industrial Workers of the World—to withdraw their support for her lectures. Nevertheless, she was determined to go through with the appearances and to find out what else might be done.

The trip took her into the home ground of Canadian labour activism. Winnipeg's combination of locally grown Anglo-Canadian progressivism and socialism on the one hand, and the influx of foreign-born workers encouraged by the Laurier and Borden governments on the other, made it a place with a radical reputation. In 1916, Manitoba had been the first province to extend the vote to women. In the same year, Emily Murphy of Alberta was appointed the Empire's first female police magistrate. Only three years after Goldman's visit, the famous Persons Case, undertaken by five Alberta women (including Murphy and the novelist Nellie McClung, who from 1921 to 1926 sat in the Alberta's legislative assembly), ended with a ruling by the Privy Council in London that the term *persons* in the *British North America Act* did, in fact, include women. Winnipeg, where in 1907 Goldman had chided organized labour and advised steps towards a general strike, had become in 1919 the site of the only such strike in Canada's history when more than 20,000 civic and government employees walked out in sympathy with an action by the metals and building trades. Leaders of this historic event included J.S. Woodsworth, elected two years later as Canada's first socialist MP, and the founding leader in 1932 of the Co-operative Commonwealth Federation (CCF).

Goldman's 1927 view of the Western Canadian landscape largely seems to have been without these figures. The explanation might be as simple as the fact that she did not support societal reform focused on government institutions, as such activists as Murphy, McClung and Woodsworth did. She may also have seen little common cause between herself and Western reformers—McClung, for instance—who made temperance a key issue; Goldman regarded prohibition as oppression and a failure, as she had proclaimed in a Toronto newspaper interview. Perhaps most importantly, however, she found Winnipeg's labour activists, even the anarchists who had invited her, to be by and large in sympathy with Soviet Russia and the communist movement she despised. Still, Winnipeg had an air of expansive excitement, having more than tripled in population since her visit in 1908.

In a feature story in the *Free Press* of 28 January she took pains, just as she had done in Toronto, to emphasize the difference between Bolshevism and anarchism, to declare her opposition to communists and "soviet ideas", and to give credit for her visit to the sponsorship of the local Workmen's Circle. The great obstacle faced by anarchism, she said, was popular misconception. "We believe in a well ordered society carrying on their business and other affairs in a sane and sensible way", she explained. "Anarchism is not a menace to the strength or solidity of a nation as many people suppose, but rather it unhampers initiative and makes people self-governing and self-reliant." On the day before, the rival *Tribune* published a brief interview in which she is reported to have said: "Human beings should have the chance to grow up to express their own individualities, and to govern themselves. . . . I believe that we should some day do away with all forms of government." While she spoke with the reporter in the living room of her host and fellow anarchist Samuel Prasow, a "huge bouquet of tulips were delivered to her, which, on glancing at the card, she said were from dear friends in Albany, New York. 'I have thousands of good friends in the United States,' she said."[1] This particular good friend, of course, must have been Leon Malmed.

She wrote Malmed frequently during and just after the trip; they were planning a reunion in Toronto in mid-April. Her letters looked forward to the rendezvous eagerly, with expressions of longing couched in her favourite images: "the miracle of Napierville", "a ride with you in 'our' car", "a ride with red roses". But they also contain echoes of her disappointment at their January parting. Already in December she had jibed at him that his love was "only on paper". While she was in Winnipeg and Edmonton, the epistolary romance called forth from her many criticisms: of his style of living (he was wasting himself on the "treadmill of commercialism"); of his passion (it was not "an impelling force"); of his lack of sympathy for her and her needs (he was so consumed by business as to be oblivious to her sufferings).[2]

At her Winnipeg appearances, the communist opposition of which Prasow had warned did not appear openly—"they are too cowardly for that", Goldman wrote later to Joseph Ishill.[3] Although one undercover Mountie reported to Ottawa that the Communist Party of Canada had discussed Emma Goldman at its meetings and had determined to send hecklers to her lectures, the agent said that the lectures themselves showed no sign of "organized heckling" by any group.[4]

A newspaper account of her first lecture in the city, before a capacity audience at the Regent Theatre, on the subject of labour in Europe, records one challenging question from the audience: "How much was she being paid by capital for attacking Soviet Russia?" On 31 January, the *Free Press* (paraphrased a few days later by the Toronto *Daily Star*) carried an account of her fiery reply, under the head "Dramatic Incident Marks Goldman Meet/ Famous Agitator Gives Questioner Tongue Lashing at Regent Theatre": "'Cannot you imagine,' she continued, her voice rising in anger, 'that a person who has gone to prison for participation in strikes, and has been driven from country to country, is not the kind of person who would sell her soul for money?'" She turned on her accuser. "'It shows the evil side in you when you make that charge, because it shows that you can be bought by money.'" If she were there to proselytize for capitalism, she said, would not the "premier receive me with open arms?" Would she really be lecturing in "small halls" and "under any conditions and circumstances"?[5]

Despite the low level of open opposition, she felt that the communists were working against her effectively. She found even Prasow disappointingly sympathetic to the Bolsheviks. On 11 February, she wrote Berkman that "the Communists have poisoned the masses here". Carl Berg, as he travelled the city to promote her lectures, was told by workers on a streetcar that Emma Goldman "gets fifty dollars for every lie she tells about Russia".[6] In view of such unpromising circumstances, she was proud of her

February programme in Winnipeg—thirteen English meetings and five Yiddish, including one arranged by the women of the city's Peretz Schule and another by the mothers' section of the Arbeiter Ring. Yet, as usual, she was disappointed, particularly in the flatness of the audiences and in the amount of money raised. Her most successful lectures, those concerning social topics and held on Sunday evenings in various theaters, attracted 700 to 800 persons each; but the city did not permit admissions to be charged on Sunday, so these were free events, with voluntary donations. The amount she raised in Winnipeg for political prisoners, including $18 contributed at a small banquet in the home of a comrade, was only $143.

But she garnered publicity for herself and her ideas. The *Free Press* story of 28 January gave a summary of her career and beliefs under the head, "Noted Anarchist Tells Why She Follows Trail She Blazed Years Ago". It stated that her "appearance and gentle manner belie her fiery nature, which has made her name a by-word on three Continents. . . . Miss Goldman did not wish to be classed with those who threw bombs and endeavored to usurp government control by violence. Rather she believes in the principle of educating people to be independent and self-reliant—to carry on their affairs independent of a control or governing organization." On 2 February, Winnipeg's third daily, the *Telegram*, published a similar story: "Anarchy, according to Miss Emma Goldman, famous exponent of that cult, who is now in Winnipeg, is that ideal state when human beings govern themselves without law or governments. . . . In reply to the question when that golden time should come, Miss Goldman did not set the day or hour, but said that we should outgrow government."[6] The *Telegram* concluded with the information that on the evening of 2 February she would lecture in Yiddish "to a group of her own race" at the Hebrew Free School, Aberdeen Avenue, and on Sunday at the Regent. Edmonton, where she arrived Wednesday 2 March, made an exciting, satisfying contrast to the difficulties she had experienced in Winnipeg. She praised it to Berkman as "one of the best places in Canada" and felt she could have stayed on for weeks lecturing. "I . . . reached the most diverse people you can imagine. From girls working in the factory to the Faculty of the Alberta College and University; from the Jewish Council of Women and the Hadassah to the women connected with the Arbeiter Ring; from two big mixed meetings arranged under the auspices of the Labor Party, with masses of people turned away form the halls, to out-and-out labor meetings under the auspices of some of the unions."[7]

The city's interest in her was owing to "three people, none of whom was an anarchist", Goldman said. These were Carl Berg, the IWW organizer who had accompanied her from Winnipeg; Frances Friedman, the president of the Council of Jewish Women; and Emil Hanson, a popular Yiddish writer, who was responsible for inviting her to the city as well as for finding her many speaking opportunities. Mrs Friedman was married to an Edmonton lawyer, Harry A. Friedman; they had come to the city in 1913, and Mrs Friedman had been president of the council since its founding in 1920. In her autobiography, Goldman characterized her as "a staunch and sincere adherent of the present political order". The Russian-born Hanson, whom Goldman called a "Socialist-Nationalist",[8] had arrived in Calgary in 1906, homesteaded near Cochrane, and then moved to Edmonton in 1914, where he became prominent in the Jewish community, especially in the labour Zionist movement (Poale Zion). He was a founder of the city's Arbeiter Ring school. He was called the "Yiddish Jack London" for his stories and sketches of the north and of his native Russia, which he wrote for newspapers.

Her invitation to the city, and the welcome she received, were in part the result of a local political struggle between communists and other radical groups, similar to that which Goldman had experienced in Winnipeg. Hanson had left the Edmonton Workers' Circle to join Poale Zion when the local Council of the Canadian Labour Party, with which the Circle was affiliated, fell under communist influence. When Poale Zion then applied for admission to the Council, the communists strongly opposed the move, but were overcome. Hanson promptly suggested that the Council sponsor Goldman as a lecturer. A debate ensued between the communist members, who knew that she would state that the communists had betrayed the ideals of the Russian revolution, and the others, resulting in a compromise: she would be invited if she agreed not to speak on the subject of Russia. Goldman rejected this muzzling, and Poale Zion sponsored her appearance, with the help of the Council of Jewish Women.

She came to Edmonton expecting to give two English and two Yiddish lectures. Owing largely to the efforts of Friedman and Hanson, she found herself speaking fifteen times in a stay of twelve days, and being the guest of honour at a banquet that raised $33 for political prisoners. On 4 March the *Journal* commented in an interview that "Emma Goldman, pronounced and avowed radical though she be, is a charming and amiable person in conversation, cultured and animated, and as she says herself, far more interested in the welfare and elevation of humanity than in any violent effort of a destructive quality". Bowing to the region in which she found herself, she said that the main purpose of her trip was to learn all she could of the Canadian people and that she looked "to the countryside, the rural life of the farmers to give me true insight". On the same date the Edmonton *Bulletin* reported some of her social views under the headline "'Flaming' Youth has Champion in Emma Goldman, Now in City/Girls Should Not Marry Under 25 Years, Says World's Famous Woman Anarchist—Loves Flapper Clothes". She loved the freedom of movement afforded by short skirts, according to the newspaper, which quoted her to the effect that "the modern woman is a much better wife and mother than the woman of years ago" and that women "undertake their housekeeping today with scientific knowledge and efficiency".[9] That evening, Friday, she was to lecture at the Hebrew School on 103 Street, and on Sunday at the Capitol Theatre.

The *Bulletin* took great interest in her. On Saturday 5 March, it reported her Hebrew School address on education, at which Friedman presided. As she had done in Toronto, Goldman declared that the "little red school house"[10] had been a prison and that the child had to be considered the starting point of education. Partly under the influence of Tolstoy she advocated the abolition of textbooks and of the contemporary concepts of school discipline. Her 13 March address on the labour situation in Europe was given, the *Bulletin* reported, to a capacity house at the Capitol Theatre under the auspices of the Labour Church, Dr R.C. Ghostley presiding. In this lecture, one she repeated often, she warned that growing foreign ownership and control in Germany, and suspicions among Germans that the country was going to be "parcelled off"[11] to foreign capital, was creating a dangerous situation there. She gave a gloomy survey of European labour in recent decades, saying it was now denied all privileges in Germany, was little better off in France, found itself the victim of repression and massive unemployment in Italy, and endured still more appalling conditions in Russia.

The *Journal* waited a day to cover this same lecture, reporting on 15 March that while Goldman was dealing with affairs in Russia, particularly in reference to political prisoners, "a voice in the big audience cried 'Liar.' To this the lady replied that nothing could be proved by calling 'liar.' She said that she was there to tell the truth and nothing but the truth about Russia, however distasteful it might be to some persons." The *Journal* may have delayed the story in order to pair it with another article the same day, detailing her speech at the weekly Monday luncheon meeting of the Edmonton Kiwanis Club, where she was introduced by Harry Friedman as a "much misrepresented woman". The writer reported that Goldman had "in her thought provoking address showed how essential it was that the needs of every strata of society be considered of equal importance, and that a kinship of all mankind be formed". She lectured the Kiwanians on the justice and the benefits to society of limiting the working day and eliminating all special privileges for the few; "those with greater opportunities and privileges [ought to] realize their kinship with and their duty toward the less fortunate" by creating "an ideal in life" and making their goal "so to remould society that conditions would be better, more equal and more just". The *Journal* also published an extensive story on Goldman's relaxed and mellow performance at a luncheon organized for her by the Edmonton branch of the Canadian Women's Press Club. "Emma Goldman, self-styled anarchist, sat quietly drinking tea and talking about such important issues as—Persian scarves and European shopping—in the Women's Press Club room, Civic Block, on Tuesday afternoon. . . . 'Surely progress is being made if a press club can invite Emma Goldman to speak. Until recently, they have been the very people who made it impossible to do so,' said the grey-haired, dynamic, keen-eyed woman as she rose to her feet and charged the room with her forceful remarks." Acknowledging that female journalists had been almost uniformly friendly to her, she nevertheless chided women in general that they were "experimenting" with a "superiority complex", that they should not be content with their achievements but "be awake to the stirring of the masses". Her longstanding criticisms of liberal and progressive feminism as materialist, conformist, nonrevolutionary, and actually supportive of the social status quo were delivered with enough force to prompt the *Journal* to head its article "Contented Woman Stumbling Block in Path of Progress is Belief of Emma Goldman".[12]

In Edmonton, Goldman stayed at the home of Harry and Lena Margolis, 10171 94 Street. Harry was manager of the Dominion Bottling Works at 10172 94 Street, a family concern that employed the Margolis sons, Garry and Samuel, who lived at home, and Harry's father, Max, who had a neighbouring house. Lena Margolis was perhaps Goldman's closest connection in Edmonton; she belonged both to the Edmonton Ladies' Progressive Club and the Arbeiter Ring, and helped Goldman make sure, after she had left the city, that these groups continued working to raise money for Russian political prisoners. "It was difficult for me to leave Edmonton and so many dear friends", Goldman wrote later to Lena from Toronto, "but I consoled myself that I may be able to return for a longer stay. I only wish I had not wasted so much time in Winnipeg. I should have preferred ever so much to be with you and the other friends, and to meet the interest which my visit succeeded in arousing."[13]

One topic people in the West frequently raised with her was the view of Russia provided by Scott Nearing, who had visited Edmonton a short time earlier. She told both newspaper reporters and questioners at her lectures that she did not doubt the sincerity of his reports about Soviet Russia but that his evidence was not convincing. His trip had been managed, she said, and did no more than show him "a mere surface of Russian reality".[14] In fact, Nearing, who was promoting his 1926 book *Glimpses of the Soviet Republic*, was dogging Goldman's steps to some extent. When she was in Montreal, the New York communist magazine *New Masses* had proposed him as an opponent in a debate over Russian communism, demanding that she travel to New York for the event (which of course was impossible) and rejecting her request for 50 per cent of the gate, much of which she would have donated publicly to Russian political prisoners. She had countered with an offer to debate in Canada for a fixed fee. "I do not think anything will come of it", she wrote Harry Weinberger from Montreal at the beginning of November. The matter then dropped until a 27 December letter from William Fraser of the People's Forum of Montreal enclosing a letter from Nearing, who was "meeting with your denial of all he keeps saying everywhere". Writing later to another correspondent and basing her remarks on Nearing's letter, she exploded that Nearing had refused to debate her in Montreal because he had "'been informed (misinformed) Miss Emma Goldman had sold herself to the Capitalistic Press.' Imagine a man like Nearing depending upon what he has been informed. But he and the rest of them know perfectly well what they are saying is false. . . ."[15] And now, having avoided confronting her directly, here he was in Canada. His appearance in Toronto had already led to her being challenged there on her portrait of Russia, and she was meeting the same difficulty in Edmonton.

To Goldman, Nearing's conduct resembled that of another pro-communist representative, a Canadian with whom she was involved in an angry correspondence during her Western trip. The controversy grew out of an exchange at her 22 December lecture in Toronto. Henry Lynch, the chairman of the Electrical Communications Workers of Canada and organizer of the Toronto section of the Socialist Labour Party, challenged her to debate one Comrade Silver, whom he identified as a leader of the party, on the subject of the Russian regime. In response to a letter repeating the invitation and offering 15 January as a possible date, Goldman replied that March would be more convenient (the proposed date fell in the period she was keeping free for Malmed's visit) and made two requests: one, that she receive more information about Silver, whose name she did not recognize; and, two, that all proceeds go to Russian political prisoners. Lynch fired back that, as a supporter of the Soviet regime, he had no wish to provide financial aid to "instruments of capitalist interests": "We would as lief contribute to a home for aged and decrepit grand dukes and duchesses."

He also said it was her "own personal doing" if she was not acquainted with the work of her proposed opponent and enclosed a report of a recent debate. It was perhaps not as surprising as Lynch insisted that Goldman, living away from North America, had not learned of Adolph Silver, but Lynch reflected the US Socialist Labor Party's satisfaction with one of its leading personalities. Silver had been put on salary in 1925 to conduct meetings and debates and was known as a "legendary speaker who could tie up traffic". Unimpressed, Goldman replied angrily from Winnipeg that she would not consider the debate; she suspected "people who know so little of the masses of human beings who fill the prisons and places of exile" in Soviet Russia would not "extend fair play or tolerance to a political opponent". Lynch's answer charged that she was "afraid to meet a representative of the Socialist Labor Party" but had "neither the good sense nor the decency to confess" that fear. Lynch repeated the accusation that she was a tool of capitalism in her attacks on the "revolutionary working class government of Russia" and attributed her "sorry and contemptible role"[16] to her anxiety to enter the US.

There is no record of a response. Goldman referred to Lynch in an early March letter as a "venomous creature",[17] a kind of prophecy, since it soon appeared that Lynch had submitted their entire correspondence to the Socialist Labor Party's official newspaper, the New York-based *Weekly People*, which printed it on 9 April, after she was back in Toronto. The letters are accompanied by Lynch's version of her 22 December lecture in Toronto, which varies substantially from the accounts in newspapers (which Lynch accused of pro-Goldman bias) as well as in Goldman's letters. Lynch claimed that he and two other questioners repeatedly reduced her to confusion, that she was "struck blind" at their questions, that she "either ducked them entirely or gave an 'answer' which was no answer at all". He concluded, "It's generally understood she is trying to get herself into the graces of the capitalist forces of the United States so she may go back there."[18]

This was mainly lies and wishful thinking on Lynch's part, but he was correct that her hope of entering the US, stirred by Don Levine's visit with her in Montreal, did remain alive for some months. In letters from November through January, she and Levine half-seriously considered an unannounced trip to the border as a stunt for getting her in; they toyed with the idea that she would try on the way back from Winnipeg. The worst that could happen would be that she would be denied entry or deported once recognized. Such an outcome, she projected, would be valuable publicity for her concluding Canadian lectures, planned for Montreal in late spring 1927. At the same time, various channels for getting back to the States legally were being pursued. Goldman asked her New York lawyer, Harry Weinberger, to look into the possibility and her Montreal friend, Rose Bernstein, organized a "little committee" to help. Levine encouraged Goldman to believe that she might cross the border. He consulted with officials in Washington on her behalf, continuing to stir her hopes over the succeeding months even when he had bad news. On 15 December, he wrote that "for the present your admission through consular channels, by securing a visa beforehand, is not to be considered". The US State Department, headed by Secretary Frank Billings Kellogg, had recently met both international and internal opposition to its handling of two would-be US visitors: Alexandra Kollontai, the new Soviet minister to Mexico, who had wanted to pass through the country on her way to her new assignment, and Countess Catherine Karolyi, the wife of the first leader of the independent Hungarian state formed at the end of the Great War. After only a few months in office, Count Mihail Karolyi had turned over the government to the communists and gone into exile. The countess filed suit against Kellogg when denied permission to enter the US in order to visit her family; she spent part of the fall of 1926 in Montreal while the matter progressed, but eventually withdrew the action and returned to Europe. The resulting criticism, Levine believed, was motivating the State Department's hot-potato treatment of Goldman's claim; officials at State told Levine that she was really a matter for immigration authorities in the Department of Labor. Even had the State Department been willing to grant her a visa, he said, "It would, I am sure, please you little to face America with a passport bearing Mr. Kellogg's approval, after his stupid treatment of Karolyi."[19] She agreed.

On 8 April, however, the day before the Lynch correspondence appeared in the *Weekly People*, a letter from W.S. Van Valkenburg reported that Secretary of Labor James J. Davis had given Don Levine a final, definitive no to the request that Goldman be allowed to enter. "He intimated that the proposition was out of the question 'at the time' and I think we may console ourselves by accepting the situation as the product of developments in Haiti, together with the Chinese problem as being the real reason why the adventure cannot be permitted by the Department. The heads of both Departments with which we have to do are yellow to the core, a circumstance which makes the attempt impossible just now."[20] Marines who had invaded Haiti during Woodrow Wilson's administration had been involved in sporadic violence leading to Haitian deaths during the occupation, which lasted until 1930; Goldman would soon be commenting on unrest in China, where Western troops were called to respond to attacks on missionaries.

Goldman wrote Levine a week later and thanked him for his efforts. Even had she been admitted, she soon would have been deported, she claimed. "Certainly I would not have been silent on some of the glaring evils in America."[21] In later years, entry into the US would loom again as a necessity, as the only possible vindication of her life and work. For the remainder of this first Canadian trip, however, she spoke without regret of being barred, expressing a sort of pride that she was still regarded as too dangerous, and too principled, to be admitted.

On her way from Edmonton back to Toronto, Goldman returned to Winnipeg briefly, 15–17 March, to give three further lectures. One of them represented a significant triumph. As a result of her speeches and activities during her previous five weeks in the city, the "men in the O.B.U. [One Big Union] of independent minds" had decided that they had been deceived regarding her by the communists and that "they should give their members a chance to judge for themselves", she wrote in the *Road to Freedom*.[22] As a result, she was able to deliver her lecture on European labour to several hundred persons in the union's hall. In addition, she soon heard that the anarchists had gained an ultimate triumph in the struggle for the right to use the Liberty Temple. An agreement was finally reached ensuring that members could invite any speaker they wished.

Although many of the lectures she gave in Winnipeg and Edmonton were free, she nevertheless took in enough money from the trip, over and above that which she specifically raised for political prisoners and, as always, strictly set aside, to clear her own debts. She received extensive newspaper coverage, renewed her acquaintance with Winnipeg pals from 1907–08, and made new contacts in Edmonton. So encouraging was her reception on the tour, especially in Edmonton, that she wrote from the West to Berkman, inviting him to consider a move to Canada. There was scope for work there, she said, and they would be able to build a movement; she sought to entice him with the idea of founding and publishing, from Canada, a new anarchist periodical, which he would edit. Berkman declined, saying it would be the same in Canada as everywhere else: the first enthusiasm would die away. Besides, he was more interested in writing than in editing. The project he had in hand, a book entitled *The ABC of Anarchism*, was leading him to think that the Russian Revolution "opened problems which the Anarchist theories have never earnestly considered before and certainly never solved".[23]

6

Spring and Summer 1927

When Goldman arrived back in Toronto on 19 March, she immediately spoke out on a local court case that was attracting international attention. Ernest Victor Sterry had been convicted of blasphemous libel for what he had written on the God of the Old Testament in his periodical, the *Christian Enquirer*. Sterry, fifty-five, who lived at 11 Lee Avenue and had a place of business on Yonge Street in whose window he displayed his offending publication, was not so much a political radical as a religious free-thinker. The Buffalo *Evening News* (28 March) and New York *World* (10 April), in stories on the case that emphasized Goldman's involvement, stated that Sterry—"a stormy petrel in England, his birthplace, and later in New England and New York"—had once sold pamphlets for Goldman in New York City.[1] Relocated to Toronto, he had written in the *Christian Enquirer* in early 1926 that the Bible contains "hundreds of passages relative to the Divine Being, which any moral and honest man would be ashamed to have appended to his character", that the divinity "preferred the savory smell of roast cutlets to the odors [sic] of boiled cabbage . . . and would often have slaughtered the whole bunch if cunning Moses hadn't kept reminding him of 'what will the Egyptians say about it'".[2]

Sterry was accused under an old British law with publishing "unlawfully and wickedly and with intent to asperse and vilify Almighty God [a] scandalous, impious, blasphemous, profane and indecent libel of God, the Holy Bible, the Holy Scriptures and the Christian Religion". The case went to trial on 15 March. Sterry's cause was not helped by the fact that he already had been sentenced, on 1 February, to four months for theft of $200 from Joseph Ying on a charge arising out of a real estate transaction. The Toronto *Daily Star* story on the opening of the trial mentioned his earlier sentence for "theft from a Chinaman" as well as the nature of his support ("the crowd pouring in comprised many Jews" and, "it was said", some of "Sterry's American followers"). The *Daily Star* noted too that Sterry's lead lawyer, E.L. Cross, was "coloured".[3]

As proceedings began, Sterry, "walking lightly" to his place, bowed "smilingly" to spectators and to Judge Emerson Coatsworth, senior judge of the County and Surrogate Court. He conferred with his lawyers in a voice that "echoed through the court like a shout", and stared around the room twiddling his thumbs as Cross spoke. The defence pointed out that many authorities had stated publicly what Sterry was accused of publishing: that the "Old Testament is nothing but mythologies", in Cross's words.[4] Cross also claimed that the indictment had not been proved since the writings in question had not been shown to be indecent. Coatsworth's charge to the jury, a sermon from the bench, was quoted at length in the Toronto *Globe*: "It is always painful to hear any person question any part of the Bible." He allowed for scepticism but said it must be "couched in respectful terms" and told the jurors to consider whether Sterry had "passed the limits of . . . respectful expression" in terms "so indecent . . . as to outrage the feelings of our people and constitute the crime of blasphemy."[5] The guilty verdict was returned after a twenty-five minute deliberation.

Goldman approached the case as a threat to free speech, but she was cautious about any further involvement. She wrote to Berkman two months later, "with the idiotic blasphemy law which is very rigid one does not know just what may fall under it. I certainly have no desire to go to prison for the Lord." In interviews, Goldman scolded a prominent Toronto Baptist minister, Rev W.A. Cameron, who had issued a written protest against the conviction. She "Berate[d] the City for Cowardice" and could not "Understand Why Lovers of Liberty Neglected to Help Sterry": so summarized the headlines of the *Star*'s 21 March three-column story on her remarks. Goldman told reporters that she supported Cameron when he said, "Religious persecution by civil authority is a return to the old days of religious slavery. Courts and judges are not appointed to interpret the doctrine of God or correct views of the Scriptures." But she did not agree with the timing of his statement. "Why didn't he say that before the trial? It might have helped a lot. I doubt if there would have been a conviction if public opinion had been aroused or if a few prominent people had had the courage to say in public what they said privately. There would be less injustice if people resented it before it took place. There is not much use banging on the door of a prison after it has been locked." Not only cowardice but also indifference were to blame, she said, for if "Toronto's lovers of liberty" had feared to act, they easily could have called on British and US champions, whom she named. She also gave the commanding police officer in the Sterry case, Inspector David McKinney of the Morality Department, a long list of famous authors in whose books he could "read innumerable passages which would revolt him."[6]

American newspapers reported Goldman's, as well as Cameron's, statements on behalf of Sterry and the establishment of an appeal fund. "Clarence Darrow may yet get a chance to appear in a Canadian court",[7] the New York *World* speculated, but Sterry never mounted an appeal. Why not? Probably to avoid the one-year maximum sentence. Sterry had to serve sixty days at the Jail Farm, but this was made concurrent with his previous theft sentence, and was to be deported to England. The latter condition was actually suggested to the court by the defendant's assistant counsel, Nathan Waldo. Moreover, Sterry himself agreed to the deportation order, even though five years' Canadian residence was a compulsory bar to deportation and he was a sixteen-year resident. The case not only attracted press and public attention throughout the English-speaking world but also prompted initiatives in the British and Canadian parliaments to remove blasphemous libel from the criminal code. In the House of Commons in Ottawa, the bill was sponsored by the socialist leader J.S. Woodsworth. As for Sterry, by 1931 he was back in Toronto, working as a salesman at the Frank Waddington Company, an auction house on Adelaide Street East, but there is no record of any contact between him and Goldman during her 1933–35 residence in the city.

The New York *World*'s narrative of Sterry's misadventures dramatically stated that as soon as he was convicted, "along comes Emma Goldman, Anarchist, who has been touring Canada lecturing on drama and literature."[8] The newspaper sensed a sea change. As Goldman had promised her Toronto audiences in December 1926, she was now speaking on political issues. Moreover, she was involving herself in specific local causes. This was a striking change from her original approach to Canada. First, in Montreal, and later during her initial weeks in Toronto, she had limited political comment to lectures on Russia and European labour and a few remarks in newspaper interviews on issues equally remote or ones dealing with political theory and principle. But in the West she had spoken on both anarchism and birth control, the latter an especially sensitive topic likely to raise local ire. Encouraged by the response, particularly as she began to consider a longer residence in Canada than previously planned, she began to feel that she should have come prepared to address Canadian questions and relate them to the anarchist cause. Perhaps she also was beginning to gain an understanding of her Canadian environment and a sense of how far she could step safely.

She set up a busy programme of lecturing for the end of March and the whole of April. The demanding schedule, calling for talks on both drama and political subjects, was prompted by her need to support herself through the four lectureless summer months and her desire to build an audience for the autumn, when she intended to organize two series of talks, one on drama, the other on anarchism and current affairs. Over the summer she worked on writing and promoting her lectures. She also expected to raise money and gather materials for her autobiography. In addition, she was looking forward to more visits from family and friends, especially Malmed, who still intended to visit in April.

She began by speaking Thursday 24 March at Hygeia Hall on the birth of modern American drama and the growth of the Little Repertory Theatre. Another drama lecture two days later, on Eugene O'Neill, was quickly followed by one criticizing western and Christian missionary involvement in China: her first major speech in Toronto on a controversial issue of the day. The China lecture caused Goldman considerable trouble, for she was no expert on the subject, and in Toronto she was cut off from the knowledgeable friends with whom she often would discuss such unfamiliar themes. China was in the news just then and was of concern to radicals, because of British and American military responses to violence there against European nationals. The conflict was occasioning widespread debate. About the same time as Goldman's China lecture, the reformer Agnes Macphail also commented in Toronto on the Chinese crisis. Macphail had been in the Commons since 1921, the only woman sent to Ottawa in the first general election in which Canadian women enjoyed the franchise. Like Goldman, she ran afoul of conservative orthodoxy for her low opinion of the missionaries.

Goldman spoke on the evening of Sunday 3 April in the Madison Theatre on Bloor Street. According to the *Star*'s report of her lecture, "China, the Fettered Spirit Unbound", she stated that western nations were using "the most despicable means in order to destroy" China. She was referring to the opium trade, and to what she saw as a provocative use of missionaries to justify a supposedly defensive intervention. She detailed Chinese industrial and child labour conditions, which she pointed out would never be tolerated in the West. Yet she called on Europeans and North Americans not to interfere but rather to leave China "politically, economically, and spiritually free" to evolve in its own way. She stated that the Chinese were motivated by justifiable anti-western sentiment, not merely Bolshevik propaganda as was being claimed. Although she was an enemy of the Russian regime, she said, she was "with Russia" insofar as it opposed imperialism in China.[9]

The *Star* reported in some detail on Goldman's account of the way in which anti-foreign and anti-missionary feeling had developed in China. Goldman stated that Protestant mission work in China had begun when a missionary entered as an "illegal guest of a trading firm". The foreign powers exacted extraterritorial rights long ago. Now, just as on earlier occasions, particularly during the Boxer Rebellion of 1900, British and American soldiers entered the country to "defend" the missionaries. In this way, she said, the church related itself to the gun. (Strangely, the reporter for the conservative *Mail and Empire*, in a circumstantial and grudgingly admiring report on the lecture, wrote that "Miss Goldman, as we recall, did not attack the Christian missionaries, so we are cheated of the congenial duty of defending them.")[10] The *Star* gave separate coverage to indignant response from churchmen. "That any statement made by Emma Goldman regarding missionary enterprise should be materially discounted, was the opinion expressed by missionary leaders to-day. . . ." Dr Frederick Stephenson, secretary of the new United Church of Canada's missionary board, said, "The reference [to the origin of Protestant missions in China] is hardly worth taking any notice of, as the data are all open to study and the source of the conclusions is not one likely to impress thinking people." An anonymous church source went further: "One might as well accept the pronouncement of the heathen world as give value to the avowedly anti-Christian attitude of this woman. Her record of iconoclastic utterance is well known, and her instability is internationally famous. She was all pro-Russia until she went there and is now all anti-Russia. That trip seems to have paid her well. . . ."[11] When pinked on their own soft parts, conservatives did not scruple to lift and use communist formulae.

Goldman herself regarded the China lecture as perhaps her most successful in Canada to date, due to its large, attentive, and impassioned audience. Press accounts make it possible to gain a vivid picture of the event. A violinist and a pianist who had to struggle with a broken piano played warm-up music. "A pale young lady with a flaring, red garment, with a grave face and hair dressed to discourage dalliance", the *Mail and Empire* reported, "introduced *Miss* Goldman in precise terms." The reporter continued:

Like the speaker of the evening and all otherwise assisting, the audience was made up mainly of Jews. . . . Many of those present were young Jews and Jewesses and the prevalence of spectacles on so many youthful faces suggested that it was mainly a crowd of students. There was hardly any laughter and little applause. Miss Goldman, apparently, does not seek either. But she got a close attention that was a greater compliment to a speaker than any vociferations could have been. The only interruption to an address that lasted an hour was caused by the ghostly creaking and crackling of the whole wooden works of the balcony whenever somebody sought to steal out.[12]

Summarizing some of Goldman's arguments, the *Mail and Empire* story gradually turned into a rebuttal, sometimes by means of innuendo, such as its characterization of the audience or the flippant remark, "Only an unavoidable absence prevented Mr. Sterry from bowing his compliments." But at other times it took the form of direct riposte. To Goldman's analysis of the British opium trade, the reporter rejoined, "If it is true that the British forced opium on the Chinese, it was also true that it was the Chinese who smoked it, and that the majority of Chinese wanted it. So if we are to respect the will of the majority in conformity with sound democratic practice, the imperialist British have something to be said for them after all." The newspaper found that Goldman's "square face and short, thick figure" reminded it of both Beethoven and the labour leader Samuel Gompers and that her "not so lovely" pronunciation was that of "the Russian Jew who learns the English language in the United States". Yet even the *Mail and Empire* could not deny taking from Goldman "the impression of courage and essential decency", even though "[m]uch that Miss Goldman said has unfortunately escaped us".[13] She had collected $90 at the lecture and had enjoyed the audience filled with "young artists". She was thankful for her brother Moe's job of organizing and promoting. The *Mail and Empire* had noticed "sidemen making change as a matter of course and without embarrassment" and doubted "if an equal congregation in a Toronto church that night proved as generous." Due to what Goldman called the *Mail and Empire*'s "attack", as she wrote to *Freedom* in London and the *Road to Freedom* in New York, the theatre's "landlord took fright and would not again let us have the hall. Neither could we secure another theatre." On the very day of the lecture she wrote to Malmed that she had called off a lecture in London, Ontario, when the organizers had been able to guarantee her only $30, of which $10 would have gone to pay for her return train fare. She was "dead tired", having "kept a terrible pace since I saw you last".[14] That same day she also wrote to Berkman that she now would stay in Canada, because Rudolf Rocker's lecture tour there had been called off.

On 9 April, as Goldman was looking ahead to the remainder of her spring lectures, she received news from Massachusetts that the convictions and sentencing of the anarchists Bartolomeo Vanzetti and Nicola Sacco had been affirmed by a board of appeals and that the men were to be electrocuted for their supposed roles in a 1920 hold-up and murder. Her sense of helplessness at being unable to lend effective aid often seemed to render her activities in Toronto pointless and insipid. Yet active involvement in the campaign to avert the executions took centre stage in her life only gradually, partly because, as she admitted, she initially underestimated the possibility that the sentences would be carried out. The day after receiving the news, Goldman lectured on the historical development of anarchism. The meeting went well, confirming her determination to give an entire course of lectures on the subject and making her speculate still again on the possibilities of raising an effective movement in Canada. On Sunday 24 April, in "Destruction and Construction", she addressed the subject of revolution, how it should be conducted, and what should follow it. She analyzed whether workers know how to run their industries, and explained her perceived need for the intelligentsia and artists to collaborate with the working classes. She asserted that at first a revolutionary society would retain as much as possible from existing institutions in order to facilitate the people's material and psychological adjustment.

The final trumpet blast of Goldman's spring season was her birth-control lecture at Hygeia Hall on 26 April. The Social Hygiene Council of Toronto, which owned the hall, knew two weeks beforehand that Goldman planned to use the date to speak on birth control, and despite its advanced stands on many issues, tried to wriggle out of the agreement. Goldman had just finished writing her lecture, she told Berkman in an 11 April letter, when the council telephoned and asked to be released from the contract. They "claim the Catholics are after them", she wrote, but attributed their cold feet to the fact that a doctor associated with the council was then on trial for the death of a patient during an abortion. She talked privately with her reporter friend Robert Reade, who told her the council's potential refusal of Hygeia Hall would "make a corking story for the *Star*"[15] and help to promote the lecture. Two days later, the Council backed off when she demanded a $200 reimbursement. In its treatment of Goldman, the council revealed its tendency to be scientifically progressive but socially cautious. In March it had publicly "disapproved" beauty contests and asked Mayor Thomas Foster "to take some means of discontinuing them". On the very day of Goldman's lecture, the council's general secretary, Dr Gordon A. Bates, spoke at the King Edward Hotel to inaugurate a "social hygiene campaign" involving "education for parenthood", "a new war ... against venereal disease", and twice yearly physical examinations because cancer and tuberculosis "caught in their early stages mean a life saved".[16] At the same time, it shied from associating itself with Goldman's political positions, as distinct from her drama talks, which placed it in a zone of vanguardism this side of serious controversy. In such wavering, the council typifies not only Toronto in the 1920s but also the city's Victorian heritage, for England itself had reacted to the French Revolution and the Romantic movement with a similar mixture of conservative political gradualism and social progress within the existing order. Indeed, this balance has dominated the political conformation of Western Europe and North America since the end of the Napoleonic era.

In her lecture, which attracted a paying audience of 800 and made a profit of more than $200, Goldman approached birth control as an essential element of women's rights and strictly avoided discussing contraceptive methods, advising that each person should consult a clinic or physician. Thus she avoided trouble with the law. "Emma Goldman did not, so far as we know, give any instruction or indicate any method or means of instituting birth control, or means of preventing conception, so nothing can be done under section 20 of the criminal code", reported Inspector McKinney of the Morality Department, whose nose Goldman had pulled over the Sterry case. "If she does . . . then I will have something to say about it."[17]

The liberal (and Liberal) *Star* cagily presented its coverage almost entirely as an extended interview on birth control with Dr Charles J. Hastings, LLD, DSc, MD, medical officer of health for the city. "From what I have seen of . . . Emma Goldman's lecture, it appeals to me as having been a very sane address. I like the angle from which she attacks it . . . as constituting a part and parcel of women's rights." Hastings went on to discuss birth control itself in terms of real sympathy and social concern tinged with a sinister Malthusianism at the opposite ideological pole from Goldman's ideas and ideals. Mothers often are solely burdened, he said, with the care of children, whereas "the father has little to do besides providing for the family". It is "little short of criminal to permit unlimited reproduction of the sub-normal type, and also even of the fairly normal type; bringing into the world families that the parents are absolutely incapable and will be incapable of supporting. . . ." Overpopulation, a cause of war, had already arrived in China as well as in Italy and other parts of Europe, he went on, and would arrive in the United States in ten years. Hastings spoke of the gross injustice imposed on the poor by barring them from birth control information, when "those better off in material things have been practicing birth control for years." Dr T.C. Routley, secretary of the Ontario Medical

Association, refused comment, as did all the clergy contacted by the *Star*. Dr Bates tried hard to disengage the Social Hygiene Council from the controversy, saying, "We neither support nor oppose birth control and, of course, assume no responsibility in respect to anything Miss Goldman said."[18]

The birth-control talk concluded the most hectic part of Goldman's late spring lecturing. A coda was a series of four private drama lectures, beginning on 5 May, arranged by the Toronto sculptors Frances Wylie and Florence Loring to help her raise money for the summer. Although she praised the artists in her autobiography, she told a correspondent, "Their intentions were certainly admirable, but the result was poor. The attendance was hardly worth the effort." The *Mail and Empire*'s drama critic, Fred Jacobs, attended the first of these talks, "The Theatre in Russia Before and After the Revolution", and wrote on 7 May in his "Monday Nighter at Large" column, "I went with feelings of doubt as to whether Emma Goldman, the propagandist, would overweigh the views of Emma Goldman the artist, but to my delight I listened to a calm, dispassioned description of what has happened to the theatre in Russia under the Soviet regime, with conclusions that commended themselves at once to the commonsense of the hearers." Jacobs felt that Goldman brought her audience "into intimate touch" with great authors. "It is not often that a woman whose life has been so largely directed to extreme propaganda", he wrote, "realizes that art, in its essence, is something quite removed from the materialistic considerations affected by propaganda and that the arts are not only something different, but something supreme."[19] Goldman must have appreciated the praise, but among both radicals and conservatives, among both those who honoured and those who discounted the arts, she encountered this same failure to comprehend her position: that just because art is "supreme" it is the very opposite of "something quite removed". The weekend following the drama lecture reported by Jacobs, Goldman took a quick swing to London, where on the evening of 8 May she repeated to an audience of 200 her Toronto lecture on China. On her way back to Toronto, she stopped briefly in Hamilton, where she was interviewed by the Hamilton *Spectator*.

At about this same time, Malmed precipitated a crisis in his and Goldman's relationship by cancelling his April visit, pleading illness. Goldman arranged to have her brother Moe go to Albany to examine him. The visit must have been an uncomfortable one for Moe, who arrived to find that Malmed's wife had discovered Goldman's love letters, which Malmed had kept locked in his desk. Goldman wrote Malmed on 10 May to say she was "shocked beyond words" at his "carelessness". She made a request that, she emphasized, she had already made repeatedly, that he return the letters so that she could keep them safe and also use them for an "important purpose", her planned autobiography. "Your obsession to become the richest real estate man is driving you to the brink," she fumed. To Van Valkenburg, who was privy to the affair, she complained that Malmed was not motivated by love in his desire to keep the letters but rather by the same acquisitiveness that drove him in his business dealings. What Goldman required from Malmed was a change in their relationship. After first stating that she would never write again, she relented: she *would* write, but not to his shop; he should rent a post office box. In the midst of threats and demands, the two arranged to meet on the Canadian side of Niagara Falls. On 18 June she wrote to Berkman, "Tomorrow I am to meet Leon Malmed in Niagara, if he does not have another attack and his wife does not tie him to her bed."[20] The rendezvous was unsatisfactory. Goldman wrote to Malmed on 14 July that he had ruined the trip by discussing business—echoing the complaint she had voiced repeatedly since February. She also was troubled, she went on, by his request that they keep the romance secret, forgetting her own longstanding ambivalence on this same subject. Her disappointment with him was linked to contradictions in her thinking about love. She pressed him to be discreet at the beginning of their liaison but later excoriated his own request for secrecy. She ridiculed his materialism but was stung if he did not supply her with flowers or contribute to her autobiography. She rebuked his lack of commitment to her and to their common cause. Yet Malmed was whom she wrote to when, alone in Toronto in the late summer, she had to contemplate the approaching deaths of Sacco and Vanzetti. These shifts are to some degree surface and semantic rather than substantial, but Goldman did not trouble to make clearly expressed distinctions that would disentangle her apparently conflicting positions.

Several writers on Goldman's love affairs have commented that she was drawn to younger men whom she mothered and mentored. She was looking for a partner who would share her concept of living life dangerously and to the fullest, but she also was quick to try molding a likely candidate to fit her expectations. In her love letters, she frequently casts herself as mother, showing little conscious concern that her blending of the mothering role with that of sexual partner might contribute to the dulling of pleasure that was a constant in her reports of failed amours. Another favourite image in her letters to Malmed perhaps most neatly captures the nuances of their relationship and also parallels her connection to North America: she speaks of Leon as her chauffeur, that is, a servant, a dependent, and yet one in a position of control due to his technical competence and capacity for action. To Goldman, North American capitalist society was increasingly inert from the point of view of radicalism, yet its well-to-do liberal and progressive members offered a lot of attention and material aid. Such people now perforce composed her main constituency; she was engaged in trying to evoke their generous passion, and in that sense was in a leadership position, the dominant society's superior and critic. But she also was beholden to them, forced to take the dependent and grateful attitude of a wife or mistress. She had to face the fact that, when she lashed out at it, the system tolerated her not entirely because of her persuasiveness and correctness, nor entirely because progressives found in her an ally, but rather because she was powerless.

Goldman wrote once to a woman going through a divorce that the most difficult achievement was to maintain a friendship with an old lover, as she prided herself on having done with Alexander Berkman. Not surprising, then, that Malmed never entirely disappears from her list of correspondents, that in her next Canadian visit, with its brief swing into the US, he organizes a lecture for her, and when the autobiography appears, feels close enough to her to write her of his shock that he was not even explicitly mentioned. Who was the real Malmed? Was he the cowardly Babbitt of Goldman's bitterness, the shining knight of Napierville, or the heroic anarchist whose support for the Sacco and Vanzetti defence fund during summer 1927 caused his application for US citizenship to be denied? The answer is elusive, because he himself left relatively few traces, compared to the commentary on him found in Goldman's correspondence, where his image is crossed by the ever-shifting reflection of her ideas, needs, and moods.

Until May 1927, Goldman had little time in the rush and anxiety of other public projects and personal dramas to renew herself as a world figure, and gain some financial security, by publishing her memoirs. The search for funds began in earnest when W.S. Van Valkenburg wrote Goldman in early May that a US anarchist, Howard Young, wished to raise money for her use. Young's suggestion did not refer to the autobiography project but rather his hopes of helping "a veteran of the movement [who was] in temporary straits". At first, she declined the offer, warning that people would get nothing for their money. Within a week, however, she agreed that Young could begin approaching potential contributors to an autobiography fund. Goldman was determined to leave the money untouched until she returned to Europe to write.

Within the first two months, almost $700 was collected. She was sufficiently encouraged to write Berkman that she must stay in Canada to help with fundraising. Of the $700, Peggy Guggenheim, the millionaire arts patron, had supplied $500. Another contributor was Sid Jacobs, a Chicagoan she had met in January 1927 on the train to Winnipeg. He had introduced himself, saying that he recognized her from a picture his mother kept on the mantle in their home, and Goldman praised him to Berkman as "good material". Like many others she met, he began their talk as a supporter of the Russian communists but ended up sending $100 for her political prisoners' fund and, later, a similar sum in support of her autobiography. After the original spurt, however, the fundraising slowed and brought many annoyances. Young left Van Valkenburg alone with the work and went off on a cruise. Then Goldman was furious that Margaret Sanger, the birth-control advocate, had been included among recipients of a mailing to request donations. Sanger declined to contribute, but Goldman said that she had no wish "to write [her book] with the help of small souls",[21] explaining that she had had nothing to do with Sanger since Sanger had dropped her some years before when they had both been campaigning on the birth-control issue: the incident had been another example of a progressive, interested in a specialized if important reform, not wishing to associate with a notorious radical who championed complete revision of the social and political systems. Next, Goldman was mortified that a brief editorial soliciting funds on her behalf had appeared in the *Road to Freedom* and even more distressed, after complaining to Van Valkenburg, to learn that he had put it there himself. Don Levine, who had represented her in her efforts to be admitted into the US, then suggested to her that a committee be formed to seek the funds for the project. This motion was accepted: the group included Kathleen Millay, Howard Young, and Bolton Hall, but it seems to have accomplished little. Nevertheless, in letters to Berkman, Goldman began considering what form her autobiography should take, a subject which would be sounded repeatedly, and often acrimoniously, in their correspondence over more than four years, as the process of writing and publishing the book dragged on. At her requests, visitors over the summer brought old letters for use in the task. The prospect of getting access to Ben Reitman's archive of Goldman letters probably spurred her to welcome him for a long visit, from 27 May to 5 June. Reitman brought 500 letters. She was disturbed to find him much changed and in ill health.

When *Living My Life* was finally published, Goldman confessed to having underestimated the threat facing Sacco and Vanzetti and the importance of their case to anarchism. "So overpowering were the proofs of their innocence," she wrote, "it seemed impossible that the State of Massachusetts would repeat . . . the crime Illinois had committed in 1887" in condemning the Haymarket martyrs. "How could I have believed that Sacco and Vanzetti, however innocent, would escape American 'justice'. . . . Only after I had come to Canada did I fully realize my mistake. Talking seemed inconsequential and futile. Yet it was all I could do to call attention to the black deed about to be committed. . . ."[22] The two Italian immigrants had spent seven years in prison while appealing their case. Much of the delay had been forced by the effectiveness of anarchists, later joined by liberals and communists, in publicizing their plight and informing the world about the trial, an egregious distortion of justice and law. Vigorous, sometimes violent demonstrations in many countries awakened American interest and had led to domestic protests that persuaded Massachusetts Governor Alvan T. Fuller to appoint a special board of review. While condemning the trial judge's actions and statements, the board affirmed the court's verdict and sentence. That Sacco and Vanzetti were clearly innocent, as Goldman claimed in her autobiography, was a principle of anarchist propaganda.

At first, Goldman's connection to the case was through letters from Van Valkenburg, who wrote frequently in late April and May about his frustrations in trying to raise funds for their defence. There was little money and energy among their fellow anarchists, Van Valkenburg reported. What money did come in was from communists, who of course projected themselves into the limelight and used the case as a means of generating publicity and good opinion for their party. Goldman replied on 14 May, "The irony is that they [the communists] are making a splurge for two Anarchists, while they drive and persecute the Anarchists at home." Anticipating the failure of campaigns to save them, Goldman feared Sacco and Vanzetti's deaths would accomplish little: "To me the pathos in the Sacco-Vanzetti case is that such fine material should be sacrificed for nothing at all." Still, there is no record of her taking any action on their behalf until 19 July, when she wrote them a letter at Van Valkenburg's request: "Be tender with Sacco", he had written. "He is a crushed & broken man. Vanzetti is a philosopher, this ordeal has made him a halo bearer." Goldman's letter, which she reproduced and circulated widely, contains a likely explanation for her silence. Praising them as "heroic souls whom years of inquisition and agony have not been able to break," she apologizes for not acting sooner, "but the consciousness that my name may be used against you made it impossible for me to write". She assured them that she had been spreading news of them everywhere she visited. On 4 August, Goldman heard that Governor Fuller was allowing the execution to proceed. "I feel my isolation from intellectual friends or those who are kindred spirits to our ideas more to day than I have felt since I am [sic] here", she wrote Malmed. She followed with another letter two days later, commenting bitterly, "As to my work here it never seemed more futile, inadequate and stupid. Drama, sex, other idiotic things when even the savage murder of two innocent men fails to move the masses to real action."[23]

On 11 August, she was urged to lead a protest by a group of forty meeting with her to plan her autumn lectures. The meeting was organized by Esther Laddon, to whose house, at 132 Lytton Boulevard, Goldman had moved on 9 August rather than pay a rent increase at 683 Spadina Avenue. The protest was held 18 August at the Labour Temple. Goldman's lecture was entitled "Sacco & Vanzetti, The Crime of the State of Massachusetts". She gave a comprehensive history of the crimes alleged against the two men and of their trial, emphasizing the strong evidence in their favour and the equally strong indications of irregularities in the court proceedings. The men were convicted because they were foreigners, had opposed the war, spoke imperfect English, and held unpopular social views, she said, and she encouraged everyone present to agitate on their behalf. Her arguments were aimed at demanding a new trial rather than a commutation of sentence. On 19 August the *Mail and Empire* quoted a resolution drawn up at the meeting and sent to President Calvin Coolidge, Governor Fuller, and other US officials, demanding "the right of a new trial" in a case that the resolution characterized as an "outrage upon our common humanity". The only other result of the meeting was a disappointing collection of $51.

A visitor in Toronto who witnessed Goldman's activities on execution day was Freda Diamond, daughter of Morris Goldman's longtime lover, Ida. "She had a phone in her room and it rang all evening long. There were calls from all over the world, but especially from Boston, pleading with her to do something. But there was nothing she could do, and she knew it. For someone as positive as Emma, she was quite modest, not at all like the commander-in-chief many took her to be. 'What can I do, what can I do,' she murmured very quietly, anxiously. Then came the call that they had been electrocuted. We were devastated."[24]

Her work did not stop after the executions, although she was fighting a serious illness at the time. She spent much of the following week in bed with what she reported as a cold in her spine. On 1 September, the very day of the Sacco and Vanzetti memorial meeting, she wrote Malmed that she had lumbago and needed to be treated with "electric rays" (she underwent this procedure for several weeks and later spoke of "violet rays" and "artificial sunlight"). The memorial meeting, held at the Standard Theatre, attracted 1,200 persons, who heard not only Goldman but also Alex Cohen of the Amalgamated Clothing Workers, who spoke in Yiddish, and the Rev Salem Bland, a prominent liberal Protestant whom Goldman introduced as "one of the only Canadian intelligentsia who had the courage to come out publicly to the support of the two men" (as she was paraphrased by Royal Canadian Mounted Police agent number 30 in a report to "O" Division, Western Ontario District). Bland received a "great ovation" after he proclaimed "the men were innocent [and] condemned the present system". Goldman, besides serving as moderator, spoke last, emphasizing that the two men had been anarchists and stating that they were murdered because they had dared to challenge American capitalism. "In this connection she brought in a very nice definition of anarchism", the RCMP observer commented, adding that the "audience was composed of foreigners chiefly, predominantly Jewish, with a sprinkling of English speaking people". Writing in *Freedom*, Goldman called the memorial meeting "one of the most impressive affairs Toronto ever saw". But all her efforts did not remove her feelings of failure and futility, which the two men's plight had deepened. She wrote Evelyn Scott on 3 September that "the Sacco and Vanzetti conspiracy convinced me that all my efforts over the period of a lifetime were in vain, that no headway was made not only with my work but with the work of hundreds and thousands of others who tried desperately to bring some light to the people of the United States. What hope can one still retain if such a crying thing could happen as the butchery of the two wonderful people on the 23rd of August?"[25] Despite her discouragement, she took a number of other initiatives in the Sacco and Vanzetti affair: she wrote to Rosa Sacco to offer help, and she investigated various ways that texts in support of their cause might be published.

During September, her health and spirits gradually improved. Her correspondence shows her reaching out again for new interests. Esther Laddon's daughter, Ora, then a high school student, remembered how Goldman dominated the large Victorian house, staying up all night talking on the telephone, drinking "a good deal of whiskey", waking up late in the mornings, and receiving "droves" of visitors from the United States. Like Eva Langbord, Ora aspired to be an actress, and Goldman, whom the girl found "wonderful . . . full of original ideas . . . liberal in her views about young people",[26] gave her an introduction to Fitzi Fitzgerald at the Provincetown Playhouse. Ora went to New York in 1928 and immediately found herself, partly due to Goldman's influence, acting in an e.e. cummings play.

7

Reliving Her Life

Goldman was planning to be virtually a one-woman free university for Toronto. She and her committee drew up an elaborate programme entitled "Emma Goldman's Lectures on Drama and Social Topics", listing her performances at Hygeia Hall between October and December. One could subscribe to a double course (eighteen lectures) for $4 or either the drama course or the social and literary course (nine lectures each) for $2.25; a single admission was 35 cents. The Emma Goldman Lecture Committee was headquartered in the law offices of Carl M. Herlick at 72 Queen Street West. A progressive with ties to radical causes, Herlick was an Austrian-born graduate of Osgoode Hall who had been called to the bar in 1915. He was a member of the YMCA and the Hebrew Benevolent Society, at the same time as belonging to the Arbeiter Ring and serving as its lawyer. One of Goldman's anarchist comrades, Mollie Kirzner, was his stenographer. The programme's circular featured lengthy appreciations of Goldman's literary style by Rebecca West, Frank Harris, and H.L. Mencken.

The list of the lectures shows what a torrid pace she maintained that fall.

11 Oct.: George Bernard Shaw, His Life and His Works
13 Oct.: The Menace of Military Preparedness
18 Oct.: Shaw continued
20 Oct.: The Child and Its Enemies ("the new approach to the child")
25 Oct.: John Galsworthy, His Life and Plays
27 Oct.: Evolution vs. Religious Bigotry
1 Nov.: Galsworthy continued
3 Nov.: Walt Whitman
8 Nov.: Ibsen's Symbolic Works

10 Nov.: Has Feminism Achieved Its Aim?
15 Nov.: Ibsen continued
17 Nov.: Crime and Punishment [a lecture on the legal and penal systems,
         not Dostoyevsky's novel]
22 Nov.: American Prize Plays
24 Nov.: Sex—A Dominant Element in Life and Art
29 Nov.: Contemporary British Drama
1 Dec.: Why I Am an Anarchist
6 Dec.: Contemporary British Drama continued
8 Dec.: Art and Revolution

Many of these lectures were covered and quoted extensively by the *Star*, gladdening Goldman that she had been able to reach large numbers of people beyond Hygeia Hall. Between 26 October (the day after her first Galsworthy lecture) and 18 November (the day after her "Crime and Punishment" lecture), the newspaper devoted five substantial stories to her ideas, giving provocative accounts of her remarks on Galsworthy, evolution, organized religion, and feminism; its reporting reveals that the originally scheduled 8 November Ibsen lecture was changed to one on contemporary British drama and that the 15 November continuation of Ibsen was replaced by a lecture on contemporary Irish theatre. Of her eight lectures in this span of three and a half weeks, only two were not covered, the 1 November continuation of Galsworthy and the 3 November remarks on Walt Whitman.

John Galsworthy, whom most people today would associate with the British television soap opera made from his novel cycle *The Forsyte Saga*, was in Goldman's view the greatest living dramatic artist, to be compared only to Gerhart Hauptmann. His plays, such as *Strife* (1909), with its examination of the relationship of managers and workers, and *Justice* (1910), which analyzes the brutalizing and criminalizing effects of imprisonment, were often built round concerns important to her. She quoted approvingly Galsworthy's dictum that "the drama should lead the social thought and not direct or dictate it."[1] On 8 November she castigated Canada for indifference to serious British plays: "'Although Toronto is so pro-British, it evidently does not care much about British drama, or wish to know much about it,' said Emma Goldman to her audience of some two hundred and fifty people,"[2] the *Star* reported, capturing what was probably, at least in part, a snide remark reflecting her disappointment at the size of the audience. That evening Goldman had something substantial to say about the

work of Harley Granville-Barker, Elizabeth Baker, Stanley Houghton, Alan
Monkhman, St John Hankin, Clemence Dane, and Githe Sowerby, among
others. She summarized and analyzed such now forgotten plays as
Granville-Barker's *Waste*, Hankin's *The Last of the De Mullins*, and Baker's
Chains, to show how they criticized limits to idealism imposed by convention, family and respectability, and exposed the drudgery endured by suburban clerical workers (we would say "white collar"). Her style in the
literary lecture comes through in the *Star*'s account of what she had to say
about Elizabeth Baker's *Chains* and its hero, Charley Wilson:

> The dull round grinds into Charley's soul, and after struggling in vain, he
> makes the great decision, and arranges to go to Australia, and there with
> his young wife, live the life worth while, and carve out the future that he
> feels will never materialize in the treadmill life he endures. Just as all his
> plans are made, he is thrown back by the shy intimation that a little stranger
> is expected, and his plans for escape . . . are dashed to the ground. This play,
> said the speaker, was centred around the unwanted child.

> Madame Goldman said of Charley in this crisis, "Just as he was about to
> burst his chains, another unbreakable bond is affixed. He sees that he is
> finally fettered and submits dully to a continuance of the old, weary, soul-
> cramping existence which, for one instant, he had hoped to escape."

Many of Goldman's lectures on literature were designed in this manner to
place the prestige of art and of the artist's insight behind her own attack on
the restraints of custom, traditional morality, and received ideas. The play
by Yeats ("Mr. Yates" the *Star* called him) that Goldman chose was *Where
There Is Nothing* (1902), an awkward but personal work that vividly ex-
presses the poet's suppressed desires to lash out at and destroy hidebound,
unjust structures in religion, politics, society, and custom. As the hero, Paul
Ruttledge, says, "I want to pull down . . . the building of the world—to put
a crowbar under the gate and a grappling iron over the towers and uproot
it all." Goldman commented that the play was "of immense social importance, revolutionary importance, as it teaches that law and the church must
be destroyed".[3]

Anarchism, in such presentations, might seem to be reduced to extreme
individualism, which Goldman always abhorred, both in its philosophical and practical varieties. In her political writings and her literary lectures
alike, she balanced insisting on freeing the person from traditional constraints with stressing that to deserve such freedom each person must be-

come committed to valid responsibilities and to social idealism. In her British drama lecture, for instance, she matched the Baker play and its protest against the impositions of family and children with Granville-Barker's *Waste*, which she took as critical of the shallow, dependent wife of the idealistic politician who is the central figure. For Goldman, the politician showed a proper adjustment to both private life and social action whereas the wife represented the person who uses traditions and attachments to prevent others from acting freely and creatively, binding them too closely to the domestic. In addition, she criticized the wife for shirking the responsibilities of motherhood: "Do we, having blundered into a good thing, make the best of our opportunity?" the *Star* quoted her as asking.[4]

The alternating lectures on social issues sometimes treated similar ideas. On 27 October, in "Evolution and Religious Bigotry", she commented acerbically on the Baptist assaults on Darwinism (only two years earlier, in 1925, the famous Scopes monkey trial in Tennessee had resulted in the conviction of John Thomas Scopes for teaching evolution). Goldman gave a history of both Catholic and Protestant "persecutions" of scientists, but crafted her remarks primarily to underline a general point: the defence of intellectual freedom and its strenuous pleasures. "Her own conclusion to the lecture was a clarion call to the youth and people of to-day to fight 'the reactionary forces which would keep you from achievement and would bring you back to darkness, ignorance and superstition.'"[5]

She changed the title of her 10 November lecture "Has Feminism Achieved Its Aim?" to "Is Woman the Equal of Man?" and reviewed women's social status and achievements from the beginning of history to the present. Women, she believed, had three-quarters emancipated themselves, intellectually, politically, and economically, but now needed to emancipate themselves "sentimentally"; there had not yet been a female Shakespeare, Beethoven, or Wagner because women were not yet free "in the sense and to the extent" that such artists had been. To complete the task, women needed (in the reporter's paraphrase) "clear sheer downright common ordinary nerve. Woman persisted in cloaking herself with formalities and superstitions and prejudices . . . and until she threw these off she could not succeed to her complete emancipation." Goldman also sounded her consistent criticism of orthodox feminism: it fell in with the false emancipation offered by the system's tendency to break down all other social forms from which a person might derive value in order to integrate everyone, women included, into the economy. The *Star* wrote, "And the lecturer's significant contention was that the mere exchange of the dull drab monotony of the home for the dull drab monotony of the factory or office or salesroom did not lead to independence, to emancipation, but was merely an exchange of [one] form of slavery for another, and was the real reason why so many girls and women still seek freedom in matrimony."[6] "Crime and Punishment" was reported the next day under the provocative headline "One Law for the Rich Another for the Poor/Emma Goldman Claims Wealth Plays Its Part in the Court Deliberations". She commented that "when the same thing is committed by two different men, belonging to two different groups of society, they are treated differently by the public press and the courts." With this idea she connected another, the use of official and popular viewpoints as a sort of alternative law, such as when anyone who "goes against" established principles is regarded as a criminal. She used both objective information and her own prison experiences to illustrate these points and to attack the penal system. She called prisons "chambers of horror" and "universities of crime"[7] and rebuked the third degree and the lash. Another high point of the autumn lecture season was "Why I Am an Anarchist", which proved to be the most successful of all, attracting the greatest audience and the liveliest interest.

In the audience for one of Goldman's first lectures that season were J.F.B. Livesay, who had moved to Toronto to manage the Canadian Press, and his daughter, Dorothy, then an undergraduate student at Trinity College, University of Toronto. Dorothy Livesay considered the encounter with Goldman important in her personal, literary, and political development, and she recounted it prominently in two of her memoirs, *Right Hand, Left Hand: A True Life of the Thirties* (1977) and *Journey with My Selves* (1993). She emphasized that her father's suggestion was a bold one, which expanded her education far beyond the traditional university curriculum. After the first lecture together with her father, she attended many others with one of her more adventurous classmates, Jean Watts Lawson, who later became a member of the MacKenzie-Papineau Battalion that fought on the Republican side in the Spanish Civil War. Livesay preserves a vivid image of Goldman: "The first time I saw Emma I saw the very warm human person—like a Viking to me—though she was a *teensy woman*, five feet, five inches, like Queen Victoria! Long blond hair turning grey, deep blue eyes [hidden under] very thick lenses . . . a sunshiny person with wonderful humour and a wonderful smile . . . and yet tremendous strength. . . ."[8] The two young students attended both the literary and the political lectures. "Emma Goldman not only gave literary lectures, but she spoke as an anarchist and as an ardent feminist, advocating birth control." Goldman influenced Livesay's reading. "Our thirst for more led us to read Shaw's *The Intelligent Woman's Guide to Socialism and Capitalism* and the works of Marie

Stopes, as well as *The Dance of Life* by Havelock Ellis."[9] Although Livesay's political beliefs eventually took a communist and then a socialist direction, she permanently prized Goldman as a model of commitment to the politically engaged life. "Emma Goldman's stand had the solidity of a piece of sculpture; there was no fear in this woman. She took a stand. Everything about her was taking a stand. . . . We were started on a direction completely the opposite from that of our fellow classmates."[10]

Although the drama lectures were better attended than those on social topics, Goldman complained constantly of the small audiences: 350 for the first Shaw meeting, 200 for the lecture on sex. After the first eight events, she had raised only $67 over expenses, although she was pleased at the end of the series to be able to send Berkman $300 she had collected for political prisoners. She no longer believed, however, that she could make a living for herself through lecturing in Canada. So she decided to turn down the continuing requests of Toronto friends that she stay in the country. During the fall, she wrote to Berkman that she was replacing the "lost illusion" of finding a home in Canada with another goal: to write her memoirs. Her disappointment with Canada, however, was part of her gloom over the larger world situation. Now that she had explored Canada, she told Berkman, she knew that there was "not a field for me" in any country. She complained of colleagues "who promise much and keep nothing, people to whom Anarchism is really a vice one indulges in occasionally when it costs little".[11] Her friends, especially Berkman and Joseph Ishill, recognized this malaise. "Since the year 1917," Ishill wrote to her in November, "I find that you not only have lost spirit but a great part of that vivacity which thrilled the many that heard you. But since the World War, that condition seems epidemic among our anarchists. . . . It is tragic for a rebellious spirit like yours to feel itself skimming the earth with maimed wings but you are not a lone example." About a month later, Berkman wrote, also in response to one of her Canadian complaints, that, in his opinion, there would be no place for Goldman in the US either. "In your letters to me as well as to other people, I find much more emphasis on the tragic aspect of the case, so far as you personally are concerned, than about the tragedy of the thing so far as An. and the An. idea and propaganda are concerned. . . . It seems to me there is no field in the world for the propaganda of An. ideas, at least not just now."[12] "There is a field in Canada," she retorted, "but one person cannot plow it." In a November letter to Van Valkenburg she confessed that her Canadian venture had not been a failure considering how much lecturing she had done and how the word anarchism had at least been uttered in the country. Nevertheless, as she told Berkman, the nation remained "virgin soil" for the movement. Perhaps her dissatisfaction was due to fatigue. On 1 December she wrote to Sadie Robins, Van Valkenburg's companion, "It will all be over very soon—only two weeks more. I have already announced to some of the friends that after December 9th I will get me an honest-to-God jag and then go to bed and sleep for as many days as I can. It is ridiculous for an old war horse like myself to get into such a state of depression over the preparation of lectures. . . ."[13]

Her last weeks in Canada were spent resting, receiving visits from friends and family, and conducting correspondence and fundraising related to her autobiography and her return to Europe. On 25 December the Laddons gave her a Christmas party at which flowers from Leon Malmed arrived, and on 5 February the Reades hosted a farewell party. She made a few public appearances in the days before leaving the city, including one at a banquet on 29 January, two lectures before the Toronto Theosophical Society on 2 and 5 February, and a lecture on 7 February about two books by Judge Ben Lindsey, *The Revolt of Youth* and *Companionate Marriage*. The farewell banquet, attended by 100, was a success. Congratulatory telegrams arrived from Michael Cohn, Ben Lindsey, Theodore Debs, Arthur Leonard Ross, and many others. Ben Reitman had asked to come, but she discouraged him from making the trip. The chair, her physician and friend Dr Maurice A. Pollock, made an appeal on behalf of her autobiography fund that, she said, "met with an immediate response of $500 of which the good Doctor alone subscribed $100."[14] One sour note was the presence of Malmed, whom she had not seen since their disastrous meeting at Niagara Falls in July. In the interim, they had continued to correspond sporadically, and Malmed had sent her flowers for Christmas, her birthday and other occasions, and, more important, had finally returned the letters she needed for the autobiography. At the banquet, he did not speak to her and made no contribution to the evening's fundraising. Despite her bitterness, she was soon asking him for one more romantic meeting, to come to her at Montreal or Halifax on her way out of Canada. But she was also concerned about a final reckoning: she wanted him to return a watch, a token which she had given him when they were first together in Montreal in November 1926, but which now she needed because the wrist watch she had received in Toronto in December 1926, as a part of the memorial event marking the anniversary of her deportation from the US, had broken.

Her mood on leaving was by no means entirely negative. At her last Toronto appearance, the lecture on Lindsey's books, she was "again made to realize that I had not wasted my time and energy [by the] many people [who] came forward to make all sorts of offers if only I will continue my work and not leave [and who] made me promise that I would return." As she departed, she congratulated herself that she had come on borrowed money and was now debt free, that she had succeeded despite Cohn's prophecies of failure, that she had evoked genuine interest and affection from the Canadian comrades, and above all that she had made "Anarchism heard in its true sense and meaning where it had formerly been misrepresented and reviled." She went to Montreal, arriving on 9 February and staying only nine days. There too she found herself warmly received, and felt that the atmosphere in the city had changed decisively, that the "poison spread" by communists during her 1926 visit was gone. Her meetings were well attended, so much so that she regretted that they all were in Yiddish except one, on Walt Whitman, held at the home of the Caisermans. These lectures and her Montreal farewell social were organized by the group she had set up in 1926, the Women's Relief Society for Political Prisoners in Russia, which she considered "the most positive achievement of my visit to Canada" because of the hundreds of dollars it had raised in its fifteen months' existence for "the victims in Soviet prisons".[15] In the afterglow of warm goodbyes, she was touched by deep affection for Canada. "When I have finished my autobiography," she wrote to Ishill from Montreal on 14 February 1928, "I may again come to Canada. I seem to have made friends who want to work for my return."[16] She was leaving with her debts paid (except for $300 she borrowed from Malmed sometime during the trip) and enough to cover her fare. In addition, she had about $1,100 towards the autobiography: far short of the $5,000 she had told Theodore Dreiser she needed, but sufficient for getting started. Moreover, she was going to her own home, since friends in the US had arranged to buy for her the cottage in St Tropez called Bon Esprit, where she had spent the summer before coming to Canada in 1926.

On 18 February, Goldman travelled to Halifax, where she embarked for France on 20 February. She had been in Canada almost exactly seventeen months, and she tried to sum up her trip. Drafting a report for the *Road to Freedom*, she came to the conclusion that Canada was virgin but fertile territory for anarchism, for there as elsewhere people were disillusioned by the postwar state, by growing economic difficulties, and by "the Russian delusion". To exploit this opportunity, however, would require "systematic work, going up and down the vast stretches of the country lecturing on Anarchism and various kindred subjects." Still more important, her travels and lectures had revealed that classic anarchist texts no longer appealed to current "realities of life",[17] regardless of how well they might present the movement's political theory and ideals. So she appealed for the creation of a new educational literature. Perhaps this was in part a public pre-apologia for the time she was going to spend and the book she was going write on a modern life in anarchism: her own.

But her plan for the autobiography fell apart within a few days of her return to St Tropez, where Berkman and his lover, Emmy Eckstein, were waiting for her. As Berkman had feared, Emmy and Goldman began to quarrel, and Goldman was left alone in St Tropez while the lovers settled in St Cloud near Paris. Berkman's letters to Goldman and others invariably blame Goldman's intolerant treatment of the younger Emmy. Berkman already had written to Goldman in Canada that they would have to talk about Emmy, whose feelings were easily hurt and whose jealousy was easily ignited. The three of them living together seemed impossible and maintaining two households meant a considerable drain on their finances. Berkman returned to St Tropez frequently for brief visits, and Goldman saw him whenever she visited Paris, but they remained essentially apart while the autobiography was written.

Goldman did not start the autobiography alone. Emily ("Demi") Coleman, a longtime correspondent and friend of Saxe Commins and a frequenter of Peggy Guggenheim's social set, was living in Paris and offered to move in with Goldman at Bon Esprit and provide secretarial help. On the eve of her fifty-ninth birthday, Goldman wrote to Evelyn Scott that she was determined to finish the book in one year, by June 1929. With Demi's help, she established a routine of writing longhand for three weeks, followed by a week of dictation, which Coleman typed. In five months, they had accumulated almost 200,000 words, but the material covered only the time up to 1900. Still, Berkman wrote encouragingly that she was "more than half"[18] done, and Dreiser said he would certainly be able to find her a publisher.

Demi, too, quarrelled with Goldman, but remained on the job for a year. Letters to friends, which Goldman dictated to Demi, often commented that their battles were a pleasure for them both. Still, the year ended without an acceptable draft, and nearly two more years passed before the book was completed. Goldman had never before attempted anything on such a monumental scale. The life she set out to reconstruct from the letters and papers begged from friends—a poor replacement for the archives seized by the US government in 1917—had been tumultuous, multifarious, and always layered with argument, as much with her closest associates as with her numerous enemies. Now she was supposed to craft one story for everyone: the masses she wished to awaken to anarchism's ideals; the officials of the governments that she had worked all her life to subvert but which still had power to frustrate her hopes; and her supporters, both those in the anar-

chist movement and others devoted to her through family loyalty, friendship, or common cause for social change. Those closest to her offered advice and warnings. Arthur Leonard Ross, a lawyer and friend, asked her
before she started to make no admissions regarding her role in the Frick
assassination, saying, "Should you entertain any illusions concerning your
reentry into the Promised Land, what vestige of hope there is will be dissi-
pated by the publication of the story." She replied warmly that "it will be
out of the question to consider your suggestion of eliminating the story . . .
my connection with Berkman's act and our relationship is the leitmotif of
my forty years of life. . . ."[19]

If the life she was telling was politically controversial, it was also personally bitter. The events she was reviewing, no matter what self-satisfying
message of personal determination and brilliant strategy they might contain for her to savour, reminded her that her ideals repeatedly had failed to
change the world. She would not soften the horrors she had seen—after all,
each one was part of her indictment of the evil society she opposed. At the
same time, she had to prove herself vindicated by her devotion and to
demonstrate that, despite the movement's failures, she had valid reasons to
maintain her convictions.

Perhaps the most difficult of these convictions to celebrate was one that
always had put her at odds with her anarchist associates: her ideal of love
and her relationships with men, all of them rich in early satisfaction but
ending with her rueful forgiving of a man she had loved but found unwor-
thy. How she might rehash these relationships concerned her friends. Mollie
Steimer and Senya Fleshine, from *Mother Earth* days, wished her to omit
any mention of Ben Reitman, and Berkman cautioned her against mentioning *any* of her lovers. In constant letters exchanged from their separate
homes in France, Berkman and Goldman argued about their old love affairs. Tensions over people from the past, such as Ben Reitman, spilled over
into acrimonious exchanges about Emmy. Which of them had hurt the
movement more by the lovers he or she had taken? Which had suffered
more from getting involved with younger partners? Was the world more
unkind to women with younger lovers than to men? And so on. Whatever
could have possessed her, Berkman wondered, to have been so taken in by
Reitman, a glib but obviously empty figure without a gift to recommend
him. Goldman replied that she was perfectly aware of Reitman's weaknesses: "I knew Ben inside and out two weeks after we went on tour; I not
only knew but loathed his sensational ways, his bombast, his braggadocio,
and his promiscuity which lacked the least sense of selection." Then she
turned on Berkman. What chance had he and the others given Ben to prove

himself? Hadn't they forced him to be the thing they accused him of being? "Had you and the other friends concerned in my salvation recognized this, had you shown Ben some faith ... [he] would not have become a renegade." By contrast she forgave Berkman, grandly, for his weaknesses, his "naivete" about the women with whom he himself became involved. She felt herself superior, because "it requires deeper love and more exalted experiences to love those in our life in spite of their faults. That's why I will continue to love you to my last breath, Sash, old scout."[20]

During this period, Goldman was in frequent communication with Reitman. She wanted more of her letters back; in January she wrote him asking for those covering 1915–17. She warned him not to let anyone else read or copy her letters, fearing that others might see what they revealed in ways that contradicted the story she was about to tell. Although for a time she would break off contact with Reitman, apparently because of bitterness over reliving Reitman's desertion of her when she was arrested during the Great War, it was Reitman rather than Malmed who dominated her thoughts about love as she worked on the story of her life. Moreover, she had to contend with Reitman's eager suggestion that they resume their relationship—an idea in which she found some solace against the pain of Malmed's coldness. As a result, the love that had been so prominent a part of her decision to come to Canada was downplayed in the autobiography, in which Malmed is treated as a friend only, and even then disguised by a fictional name—Bass.

She fought with Berkman about many other subjects as well. In July 1928, just as she began writing, they were arguing about the methods of revolution. She insisted that "if we can undergo changes in every other method of dealing with social issues we will also have to learn to change in the methods of revolution." In November 1928, even as he was encouraging her to hope that she was more than half done, she was in agony over how Berkman had betrayed her by his criticism of Leon Czolgosz, the assassin of William McKinley. She wrote on November 23, "As to your stand on Czolgosz, I find it just as absurd now as I did then." Berkman's response was bemused: why did she still feel such anger over an event from so long ago? He added that he had been right in Russia when he had taken longer than she did to reject the Bolsheviks. "Your opposition to the bolsheviks seemed to me too sentimental and womanish. I needed more convincing proofs, and until I had them I could not honestly change my attitude. After all, I think that is the difference of the male and female mentality." Berkman sounded this same theme in a diary entry shortly after: "She thinks I don't understand her struggle in writing and living through the past. It's no use arguing about it though. Our outlook is different. Her attitude to things is very feminine."[21]

When Goldman submitted a first draft to Berkman early in 1929, he told her that months of reworking were needed; in his diary he commented that "she was laid [up] in bed the day following our talk about her book." He felt consternation that she had portrayed him as "too harsh, too much the fanatic." In February, she wrote to complain that their living apart was holding up the autobiography's completion. She would not send the manuscript to him at St Cloud and indeed could not let it out of her hands on any account. There was no solution except for him to come to her for as long as she needed him. Addressing his attachment to Emmy, she said that she, Goldman, would have sacrificed staying with a lover even "if the separation would mean for the rest of my life."[22]

The Rockers visited her for summer 1929, and Rudolf Rocker mentions in his memoirs how hard and painfully she was working. Negotiations with Alfred Knopf in New York were going on throughout this period, with Saxe Commins and Arthur Leonard Ross handling the direct contacts, but with Goldman taking so active a part that Ross reported to her she had gained a reputation at Knopf as an exceptional businesswoman. She mocked the compliment: why were people always surprised to meet a woman who understood business? But she also explained the project's vital importance to her. "My book is my first and last chance in life to get enough material results to secure myself for whatever few years there are left me to live." In September she signed a contract which provided a $7,000 advance, half on signing and half on completion, which was to be March 1930. She was to receive a standard 10 per cent royalty on the first 5,000 copies sold and 15 per cent on all copies thereafter. She spent the winter in Paris, thus closing the distance considerably between herself and Berkman, who remained at St Cloud with Emmy. Berkman reported that the project was taking its toll on Goldman's health. She suffered from fallen arches, damaged eyesight, swollen veins, and emotional fatigue. Goldman had experienced no suffering in her life equal to the agony of reliving her bold career: "The writing of my book has proven the hardest and most painful task I have ever undertaken or gone through. Not even when I thought I would have to go the way of Czolgosz did I feel such agony as I have since last June. It is not only the writing, it is living through what now lies in ashes and being—made aware that I have nothing left of the personal relations—from all who have been in my life and have torn my heart."[23]

On 1 March, as the Knopf deadline neared, the French government ordered Goldman expelled. In an account written some weeks later, she described the brutal suddenness of the arrest—"you must leave France at once"—and her skillful pleading, which bought ten days' grace, during which time she was able to secure the services of a renowned lawyer, Henri Torres, who succeeded in having the deportation cancelled. The attempt to remove her from France had been based on a directive that dated from her 1900 trip, when she had visited Paris for a birth control conference on her way home from medical studies in Vienna. A few days after the 1 March order was served, she wrote to Milly Rocker, "The whole world is a prison and most people have turned into jailers." In any case, now Berkman was deported, and Emmy became Goldman's house guest at St Tropez for three weeks. "I could live in our house with her for years, I am sure of that", she wrote. "But how it will be to have Sasha and her I don't know."[24] Getting Berkman back into France was a year-and-a-half legal and public relations effort which resulted in the government's granting him special severely restricted temporary residency. When he reentered France, however, he and Emmy did not move to St Tropez but rather to Nice.

On 29 April 1930, Goldman wrote to Arthur Leonard Ross that she had sent "the fifth and last instalment minus two chapters."[25] This description undoubtedly reflects her growing weariness. She suggested the book end with her 1919 deportation from the US. Her suggestion that she should omit the story of Russia came in a letter dated just two days after Berkman's deportation. How Berkman would be able to support himself became a matter of growing concern for her; she spent summer 1930 in Germany, where one of her activities was searching for writers whose works Berkman might translate. Knopf formally rejected the text of the autobiography as she had delivered it, lacking the story of Russia and the rest of her life to the present. So Goldman reluctantly went back to work. Finally, in February 1931 the book was done in its final form, but wrangling with the publisher continued. She wanted a one-volume edition priced for the poor, retailing at a maximum of $5. Knopf stuck to its own concept and released *Living My Life* in two volumes at $7.50 for the set. She forever afterward regarded this as a crucial error and the cause of the book's commercial failure.

Finishing her memoirs left her without a purpose. She must find one, she wrote to Berkman, as "it would still be insane to go on merely eating, drinking, and having a roof over my head." While they were waiting during the summer for the book to come out, they worried that Berkman faced deportation again, on charges from the United States that he had killed someone in Canada (where in fact he had never set foot); they were still fighting to get his status regularized in France, where he was required to report regularly to have his papers renewed. Otherwise, the summer passed in argument as the old wrangles over Emmy revived. Berkman incited Goldman by announcing that he was considering marriage to Emmy and then expanded on his familiar ideas about women. "In almost all works of women (autobiographies, novels, etc.) you will find the frank confession of . . . their unsatisfied urges. You'll never find it in any man's work. You may find in it a strong sex urge, as say in Frank Harris' works, but never an unsatisfied urge."[26] Tough words for a woman to hear from her old lover, a man who has a younger mistress whom he complacently praises to her.

Living My Life is an unwieldy thing, almost 400,000 words in its two volumes, which are of roughly equal length but disproportionate in many ways. Eighteen of fifty-six chapters are devoted to the Reitman period. The era following her 1919 deportation occupies only five chapters, one of which presents the story of the months in Soviet Russia in 200 pages, whereas most chapters are fewer than twenty. This material on Russia, added at the urgent demand of the publisher, is actually somewhat redundant in view of *My Disillusionment in Russia*. She might have crafted this section of the autobiography as a contribution to the ongoing discussion of the merits of Soviet communism versus anarchism, a dialogue so important to her prospects for gaining an audience in America and Europe, but instead she merely gave a breathless recitation of events. The centrepiece of the action is really her relationship with Reitman and the glory years of touring on behalf of *Mother Earth*. Up to that period, she moves rapidly through her early anarchist education and organizing, the fugitive years after Berkman's attempt on Frick, her various lovers, and the story of her own independent career, which focuses on her emergence from anonymity. Even more unsatisfactory is the surprising sameness of the way she describes events and incidents, always shaping them to deliver some vindication of her position, her powers, her ideas and insights. She seems to have had difficulty creating sufficient objectivity with which to form judgments and develop a coherent concept of her life's overall shape. She was re-experiencing the life she reread in her letters, not reflecting on it, and was unable to get beyond settling old scores as if they were ongoing controversies. The clarity with which she always had seen her own position seemed to block her from doing more than simply narrating a series of vignettes, drawn from memory refreshed by her sources. The breathless immediacy of her stories reflects how closely she was working from the letters. Reitman's large letter supply may help to explain his prominence in the book.

Reaction to *Living My Life* from those who knew her was generally disapproving. Berkman, of course, disputed the manner in which he was rendered, and Reitman expressed agonies of confusion over what she had written about him. Malmed was disappointed too. Why had she not said more about their affair? She answered, "Well to a large extent because it ended so disastrously. . . . Our old friendship should have remained free from anything erotic. The main reason, however, was I did not wish to add to the conflict in your home."[27] Another factor was her fatigue. Her affair with Malmed had been coextensive with her 1926–28 Canadian residence, the whole of which occupied part of her sketchy nine-page final chapter, one of those Knopf forced her to add.

Reviews were mixed, and bore on the life portrayed as well as the portrayal. "Over thirty years of violent, almost frantic activity—to what end?" Thus Lawrence Stallings in the New York *Sun*, adding in a by-then hackneyed reference to her marriage that she was now "resting in the bosom of her legal husband". In the *New Republic*, Waldo Frank criticized her "failure to understand Russia", which he attributed to the "anarchist failure to understand and hence to work upon the world". Others called the book "interesting . . . as sheer reading" and "frank, direct, and brisk". The most positive review, and the one that Goldman liked best, came from Freda Kirchwey in the *Nation*, who alone laid positive emphasis on the great amount of personal material included. Goldman regarded this as an example of specifically feminine insight, and indeed the autobiography can be seen—in contrast to the assessment of such commentators as George Woodcock, who find it unforgivably egocentric—as an expression, admittedly not so coherent as might be wished, of her understanding that the political and the personal are interdependent. Perhaps the most annoying theme of the reviewers was the idea that her life was over. *Time* wrote, "Now that Emma Goldman's career is finished, you may even find it possible to add a kind of warmth in your disapproving admiration of her."[28]

Goldman disagreed with most of the reviews she commented on, even those which she considered the most appreciative. Sales were disappointingly slow, and ultimately she never earned back her $7,000 advance, and hence never derived any further income from the project that she had hoped would "set her up in life". Also, she felt that anarchists had not defended her sufficiently. In one letter she called the book a "material flop", but then hurried to add, "Of course, it is not the fault of the work, rather it is the prohibitive price and the unfortunate moment for the appearance of the book," with the Depression underway. She had "never felt so beaten". She wrote to Berkman: "I know there is no place where I can or will gain a footing and once more throw in my lot with our people who continue the struggle for liberation."[29] In the months that followed, she began to hope she might be wrong, to think once again that Canada might, for all its limitations, be such a place.

8

Clinging to the Chance of Canada

The financial failure of *Living My Life* was the death of Goldman's dream of a new career as an author and of her hope of financial stability and employment for Berkman as well, for they could have continued collaborating as they had done during the *Mother Earth* period and in the days of *My Disillusionment in Russia*. Instead, as 1932 began, they faced the grim prospect of having to scramble again for every dollar, with Goldman returning to the lecture circuit she had hoped she might put behind her or at least make more comfortable and profitable by the prestige that was supposed to come from the autobiography. In February, she toured several major German cities and also the Scandinavian countries. Her target was the rise of dictatorship in Europe: she warned that Hitler might soon follow Stalin and Mussolini into power. While on the road, she teasingly wrote Berkman that she was considering an article about Germany that would include an interview with Hitler; to get it she would have to conceal her identity by using her married name, but she envisioned an excellent piece, highlighting the terrible poverty and despair she saw throughout the country. In the end, of course, she abandoned the plan, as she had no cover that she could use to get close to Hitler. On the contrary, she was threatened with violence by Nazi party members. Such harassment soon became a constant worry for her and not only in Germany. Her lectures throughout Europe were targets now from both extremes of the political spectrum, and she was frustrated that when she attempted to speak from an anarchist perspective, her statements went largely unnoticed except when one side or the other, fascist/reactionary or communist, co-opted them as weapons to use against its opposition.

Berkman meanwhile was struggling to find some way to earn money and chafing that life would have been simpler for him and Emmy if they had been able to live with Goldman in Bon Esprit at St Tropez. The barrier to this, according to Berkman, was Goldman. In November 1932, he wrote to his one-time lover and co-worker Fitzi Fitzgerald, "E.G. is dictatorial and interfering, and she has a way of making life miserable for you without saying anything to which you can give a rough and suitable answer. The more is the pity. And the worse of it is that E.G. herself has not the least idea of it. She is a great woman in some ways, no doubt of that; but living close with her is just impossible."[1] For more than four years they had heated epistolary exchanges on what was troubling them, whether phrased in terms of abstract concepts or of personalities. Which sex was criticized more for taking a younger lover? Was Emmy the spoiler in the menage, or was it Emma? Despite this, Berkman could still claim that Goldman was unaware that in his view she was responsible for making it impossible for the two of them to be together.

A year after publication of *Living My Life*, Goldman was suddenly stilled. The whirlwind who had stormed out of the US towards Russia, only to storm out of Russia towards the West in order to correct its mistaken notions about the Russian Revolution, and then stormed out of England to Canada and out of Canada towards the promised resurrection of her autobiography, felt "completely torn out from my moorings". She expanded on this in a letter to Berkman: "I am in the worst state of turmoil I have been in in years. In addition to being neither able nor willing to be caught in that muddy mob stream, I also feel an alien everywhere."[2] At the very heart of the winter lecture season, she worried that the few dates she had, including one in Germany, were at risk because of the increasing power of the Nazis. She wrote Berkman that even if Hitler were elected, as she expected he would be in the upcoming vote, she would honour her commitment if the group that had invited her still wished her to try. Berkman was against a trip to Germany, feeling it was too dangerous. Goldman's resolve was not tested, as after Hitler's election in March 1933 the invitation was withdrawn. At this time she was in England for the release of the British edition of *Living My Life*. At the 2 March luncheon, organized by Rebecca West, with entertainment by Paul Robeson, and with many of her literary friends in attendance, Goldman created a stir that reached Canada by refusing to allow a toast to the king. The Windsor *Star*, along with many US newspapers, reported the event as, in the words of one, "a deliberate snub to King George".[3]

To be feted in London and make an anti-monarchical stir was cold comfort for Goldman. The loss of Germany as a site for lecturing and work, and the prospect of being denied the Scandinavian countries as well, reduced her European territory to Britain and the Netherlands. She rarely spoke publicly in France, in part, she said, because of the cliquishness of the anarchists there; but she also must have felt that doing so would threaten her own residency and Berkman's. She did make one of her public appearances in France about this time, speaking in Paris in Yiddish. The city was already beginning to show the effects of Hitler's rise: many radicals, including Rudolf Rocker, were arriving, having fled Germany just ahead of arrest. Along with Max Nettlau, Rocker kept encouraging Goldman to think of Spain as a prime field for anarchist activities. She had long been familiar with the anarchist movement there, and one of its heroes was also one of hers. This was Francisco Ferrer, whose focus of reform was education and whose models of modern training of children Goldman embraced. She had celebrated Ferrer's courage and his pedagogic theories in her autobiography as well as in *Anarchism and Other Essays* (1914). Ferrer's ideas, combined with those of Tolstoy, provided the educational methods she had championed in many lectures on the subject, including those given in Canada in 1927.

Anarchism had been a part of Spanish life, particularly in northern Spain, since the nineteenth century. The militant Federación Anarquista Ibérica (FAI), founded in 1927, built on Ferrer's work and that of other early reformers and revolutionaries in its opposition to the dictatorship of Primo Rivera. The FAI allied itself with the Confederación Nacional del Trabajo (National Confederation of Labour, or CNT), founded in 1910 as an anarcho-syndicalist association of trade unions operating particularly among textile workers in Barcelona and miners in the northern provinces of Asturias and Oviedo. Both organizations operated underground while Rivera was in power. Soon after returning to Europe from Canada in 1928, but before settling down in earnest on the autobiography project, Goldman had visited Spain with Henry Alsberg. She returned unconvinced that anarchism could take root in Spanish society, a perception that failed to recognize the extent to which it had already done so, and was probably based in part on her assessment that liberation had not improved certain important aspects of Spanish society. She told correspondents that for the Spanish male, a woman was nothing but a breeding machine. The paternalism of the culture discouraged her from thinking of the country as a focus for her work, as did her lack of the language. Still she followed the unfolding story in Spain during the writing of *Living My Life*. The Rivera dictatorship ended in 1930, and King Alfonso XIII went into exile early the following year. She took time to send Nettlau a letter expressing her happiness at the overthrow of the Spanish monarchy and her hopes that in Spain anarchism might have a real proving ground at last. She was disappointed and challenged by the decision of some anarchists to vote in the April 1931 elections and to accept government posts. Even if the purpose of entering government was to participate in dismantling central structure, as these anarchists maintained, was there not a dangerous abandonment of principle involved?

In autumn and winter 1932 she began thinking of Spain again. The times were heady there. The anarchists who had supported the 1931 elected government had done so partly in the expectation that plans to grant autonomy to local communities would proceed quickly. This was a point of particular concern in Catalonia, the northeastern province with a tradition of separate culture, language, and institutions dating to before the formation of modern Spain in 1492. Catalonia was granted essential autonomy by the central government in 1932, a part of sweeping reforms undertaken in land distribution, education, and other spheres. But conservative opposition to the Madrid government solidified round bitter rejection of these reforms, and Goldman's fear that this opposition would be particularly dangerous for anarchists made her decide again that Spain was not for her. Indeed, many Spanish anarchists, far from seeking compromise, were objecting that the pace of legislated change was much too slow. Violence grew on both sides, and Madrid, fearful of conservative complaints that it was incapable of keeping order, took such harsh measures against opponents, including the pro-reform rebellion led in January 1933 by Casas Viejas, that many anarchists came to agree with Goldman that there was no place in government for their ideals. As a result, in the November 1933 election, wholesale abstention by anarchists and others, protesting what they took to be the government's betrayal, led to the formation of the new government by conservative politicians.

During summer 1933, Goldman met Mabel Carver Crouch, a prominent American liberal who encouraged her to consider a return to the US. Crouch promised that she would do everything she could to support this initiative and involved Goldman's friend and disciple Roger Baldwin and the American Civil Liberties Union, which he led. She also organized a committee of prominent writers, educators, and publishers to champion Goldman's entry. Among the members were Alfred Knopf, Sinclair Lewis, Fannie Hurst, Sherwood Anderson, and John Dewey. Goldman was so encouraged by the possibility that she began making plans for a North American visit, which would also include Canada. She began contacting Canadian friends, including Esther Laddon in Toronto and Rose Bernstein in Montreal, for help in getting her fare and arranging places to stay and to lecture.

The main focus of her hopes was now the United States, which led her into a heated argument with Berkman. Goldman talked to Crouch and others about the possibility that she and Berkman could return together, although she said that Berkman would only consider such a move on his own terms. This phrasing, with which Goldman clearly wished to underscore Berkman's courageous independence, drew a bitter complaint. Berkman said that since he knew with certainty no such terms would ever be offered, it was false to say he would consider a return. He would never go back, and she had compromised him by suggesting anything else. She already was compromising her own position, he wrote, by her willingness to have people approach government officials on her behalf. He regretted that on this, as on so many other matters, they did not agree, but he was adamant. Goldman replied that only a return to the US would validate her life, and she would not stop working for vindication, as she has stressed repeatedly in her autobiography.

The autumn 1933 lecture season began with her committed to the North American trip, yet increasingly anxious. What would happen if North America fell through? As October began, many details were still not in place. The plan was that she would go to Canada and from there enter the US; no direct entry into the US would be attempted. Arrangements in Canada were going slowly. "I am not deceived about my chances in Canada. Times there are as frightful as in the states. But anything will be better than inactivity, or isolation here." She wrote Rocker that the Canadians were "slack" and "lazy", lacking the necessary skills as organizers or fundraisers to make the trip worthwhile. Later in the month, she wrote again that she had heard nothing from Montreal: the Canadian anarchists, she complained, had "shown no interest whatever in my offer to come."[4]

In the meantime she was writing repeatedly to Esther Laddon about arranging the money for her ticket. By the end of the month, from Montreal, Rose Bernstein was in touch with promises of welcome and a gift of $50. Laddon told her that $200 would be coming soon for her fare. This raised Goldman's spirits. She responded to Crouch that such enthusiasm had given her "a sense of new life".[5]

With these hurdles overcome, Goldman addressed other worries. She feared leaving Berkman alone, especially under the pressure of his ill health and financial worries, for what she termed on one occasion a "wild goose chase" in Canada. Then, too, she wondered whether she would meet an uncomfortable challenge at Canadian Immigration, a financial means test which she saw no way of meeting unless she were to lie about prospects of income from a supposed book project. She told Milly Rocker that she would bluff her way into Canada if she had to, because she was determined to go, and yet she felt bitter about her chances. "I haven't got your faith in the Jewish comrades and there are n[o] others. I know how I had to drudge seven years ago, what misery, what disappointments. And I am sure it will not be better now. But I have no choice really. A thousand times rather the bitterest struggle for our ideas than the useless and meaningless existence of St Tropez."[6]

In late November she went to the Netherlands, only to have her planned lecture on dictatorship cancelled in Rotterdam; she was escorted to the border. Although Berkman congratulated her on still having the power to impress and frighten, Goldman saw the event as a warning that she must take even more care in her attempts to reenter the US. Attention called to her planned visit would perhaps cause American government officials to co-operate with Canadian authorities to deny her entry to Canada. Therefore the publicity necessary for successful lectures must be avoided if she was to enter Canada and the United States at all. Roger Baldwin assured her that she should make the trip, that negotiating for the visa from Canada would be better for her, even if it meant she had to risk money for the voyage and still not be allowed to enter the US.

Aboard ship, Goldman sent Ben Capes a disturbing picture of her prospects. "Do not imagine I look to much success in Canada. There is no one to help with meetings. Our comrades were never too efficient to arrange English lectures. Now they are fewer, poorer, and even less of account." Still, she wrote, she felt compelled to "cling to the chance in Canada".[7] When she arrived in Halifax on 10 December, she did in fact have to lie about her finances in order to get into the country. On the way to Montreal, trying to rebuild old bridges, she wrote Malmed about the great hope that she might be able to enter the US at last, the hope which had inspired her so much on the 1926–28 trip, and asked how the Depression had affected him. By 12 December she was in Montreal telling Stella to send letters to Rose Bernstein's house at 798 Champagneur, Outrement. She was uncertain how long she would be there but, encouraged by the reception, wired Berkman that she would stay for at least a few days. He misunderstood the message and at once sent word to Stella that Goldman had been detained by the police.

On 13 December she sent Roger Baldwin a list of possible lectures in the United States, because Baldwin had written her before she sailed that chances were still good for admission but there would have to be government approval of her lecture subjects. Her list included: "Germany's Tragedy, the Collapse of German Culture"; "Hitler, a World Menace"; "Dictatorship, Right and Left: A Modern Religious Hysteria"; and, "Fascism, The Theory of Despair, Not of Hope"—approximately the same course that she delivered in Toronto in January. As she wrote to Berkman a little later, she was much encouraged by her Montreal reception, so much warmer than the one seven years earlier. Her four days in the city "had been like a mad-house. I had to see about two hundred people." She hoped that she had prepared the ground for her return and "successful meetings"[8] there.

She left Montreal on 15 December and the next day was writing friends that in Toronto she had filled out her application for a US visa without any difficulty and expected an answer in two weeks. As she waited, she stayed with her friends, Esther and Max Laddon, at 132 Lytton Boulevard. Esther Laddon held a small reception for her, and she was told that the Jewish community would help to organize lectures in the city. The offer was encouraging but the political atmosphere in Toronto seemed to her tainted and constrained, and she feared that she might have troubles with the police. Referring to Chief Constable Denis C. Draper and his success at preventing Communist Party meetings in Toronto, she wrote to Berkman, "I understand they have a chief of police here who suppresses every meeting. What he will do with mine I can't tell. One thing is certain. I'll not be able to talk on Anarchism for instance. I'll have to stick to Germany, Fascism and Dictatorship. Literary subjects will be alright. Well, I'll see." To Harry Weinberger she exclaimed, "Imagine declaring the Communist Party illegal,"[9] alluding to the 1931 incarceration of Tim Buck, its general secretary, and seven others, for sedition under Section 98 of the Criminal Code, which prohibited advocacy of the violent overthrow of government.

The landscape had indeed darkened since Goldman had last been in Toronto and Canada. Perhaps the reactionary mood she now found in the city was partly an echo of her own previous presence. The police crackdown on what were deemed radical groups dated from late 1928, a few months after her departure for St Tropez. Draper's actions against communists and others were enabled by a 1929 Toronto Police Commission ban on all public addresses not in English; licenses could be stripped from anyone who rented meeting space to groups or events considered subversive. This ruling was actually used to break up a 1929 gathering at the Standard Theatre in commemoration of Lenin's death and to detain speakers. On 4 December 1933, little more than a week before Goldman's arrival, the Standard featured the first and only performance of *Eight Men Speak*, a dramatization of the plight of Buck and the others, part of the campaign leading to their release in 1934. Seeing a sold-out house, the Toronto Police Commission prevented a second night by threatening to revoke the theatre's license. Goldman likely would have heard talk of this development from the moment she stepped off the train.

On 20 December the Toronto *Daily Star* welcomed Goldman back to the city with a long interview by her old friend Robert C. Reade. "Emma Goldman is back in Canada and Toronto after almost six years of absence," Reade wrote, announcing her plans to speak after the New Year on "the Nazi menace". She told the *Star* how an atmosphere of gloom, like that in early 1914, was pervading Europe, and said that in the three-year "period of aloofness" required to write her memoirs "the trend to Fascism became painfully apparent to me". She spoke of the "ghastly irony" that Mussolini had recently welcomed a high-ranking Soviet official "when the prisons and islands of Italy are crowded with Communists. But Bolshevism and Fascism everywhere are able to fraternize with the common bond that they both hate and extirpate the individual." With regard to Hitler and his party, Goldman quoted H.G. Wells's jibe that "they are clumsy louts hating all ability" and went on to detail atrocities against intellectuals and common citizens, individuals, and groups. At least one instance deserves to be quoted.

> Perhaps the worst case brought to my personal attention was that of Erik Mühsam, a poet. His house and all his belongings, including a library of 5,000 volumes, were seized. He was beaten mercilessly. His beard and his hair were pulled out. The swastika was cut in his forehead with a pen-knife.

> He was forced to dig a grave and, standing beside it, in danger of being thrown into it, was compelled to sing the Horst Wessel song. That's the song, you know, which speaks of the joy of Jewish blood spurting from the knife.[10]

She again paid tribute to this poet and anarchist in an article on political refugees in the *Nation* in 1934; by then he had been murdered. Drawing on her anarchist network, she was able to report that following "his death in July [1934], announced by the Nazis as 'suicide,' his widow was shown his tortured body, with the back of the skull crushed as if it had been dragged on the ground, and with unmistakable signs of strangulation." To the Toronto *Star* Goldman recalled that, in 1932, when German friends said their was no danger of Hitler's leading a government, "I saw his Brown Shirt troops parading in the streets and beating up their opponents. It was only too obvious that he was getting into power. . . . He could have been destroyed years ago but his opponents were both too stupid and too cowardly to do it." In the interview, Goldman knocked over the comforting self-assurances of the day one by one. Hitler's government is weak because it is nearly broke? "German industrialists so far have been behind him. He has been adequately financed by the heavy industries. . . . But the real danger from Hitler is in what he will do when his followers clamor for something concrete economically. When they ask him for bread, he will have to give them blood." Surely he cannot make war given the antiquated and dilapidated state of the German military? "The feeling in France is that Germany is well able to-day to carry on war. There is fear in France and there is fear in every country in Europe which I have recently visited. In fact, there is almost panic in Belgium." But isn't Naziism an isolated and despised phenomenon? "[T]he Nazis are not so much without support abroad as you may imagine. In every city in Europe they have agitation centres. Their propaganda covers the world. Wherever there are Fascists, there you can find friends of Hitler."[11]

In describing Germany, Goldman painted a clear, vivid picture of one of the basic cases of a modern nation controlled by rigid authoritarianism, massive propaganda, suppression of free speech, and socialization for conformity, all backed by terror and threat. "There is indeed an opposition," she said, "secret, sullen and silent. . . . But how is that opposition going to do any effective protesting? They are disarmed. Hitler's party is armed. He also has the police and the army. There is no free press. No, I see little chance of destroying Herr Hitler from within. The Germans are not like the turbulent and riotous Spaniards. They are docile and submissive."[12]

As Goldman planned her Toronto lectures for January, she simultaneously continued her plan to enter the US. First, she had to get a letter substantiating her claim to permanent residence in France. Then, she had to send her passport to Ottawa to have the US added to the countries for which it had validity, and this met with the objection that she should have applied from France, and would first have to obtain France's permission for travel. The US consul in Toronto told her that it was highly unlikely that she would be allowed to enter the US. "After all Miss Goldman, the law is there. I don't see how Washington can get by it,"[13] he said. She was relieved to discover that the man had no real control over her destiny, she wrote to Roger Baldwin. Still, she was so nervous that she was having trouble sleeping. She also told Baldwin that Toronto colleagues were urging her to start lecturing and that if the visa did not arrive within a week she would try to organize meetings. These people had helped to pay her expenses, she said, and they were entitled to meetings. Although the *Star* article of 20 December shows she had intended from the start to give Toronto lectures in January, she doubtless regarded these as postponable, because she intended to leave for the States on the first date permitted by her visa.

While she waited, Goldman came to feel that staying in Toronto required getting out of the Laddon house. Although Esther was a close friend and valuable helper, Goldman regarded her husband as a "Babbitt" and reported that he had been "nagging" his wife because "my presence and telephone calls had disturbed his comforts." Also, the house was a forty-five minute streetcar ride from the city centre. Relations were strained even further when, in the last week of December, Goldman was injured in an automobile accident when the Laddons' car skidded on icy streetcar tracks. The Laddons' son, Ben, had been driving her back to the house in what she described as "beastly weather, bitter frost and rain freezing to ice by each drop". When he tried to move around a car standing still at a corner, his car would not move off the slick tracks but kept sliding forward until it collided with the other vehicle. Ben Laddon was uninjured but his brother-in-law, also sitting in the front, was badly cut on the face and wrist by the broken windshield. Goldman, in the rear, felt "a sensation that my legs are being cut off"[14] as the front seat slid backward, pinning her in position. She was in considerable pain and unable to walk, but went home to the Laddons' in a taxi. Although her legs were badly bruised, the major ill she suffered from the accident was probably the serious cold contracted while waiting in the sleet for the taxi. Responding on 30 December to Arthur Leonard Ross's news that the current hold-up in approval of her visa was due to the opening of Congress (scheduled to convene on 3 January), she commented that she would not in any case have been able to go immediately, as a high temperature, shooting pains in her chest, and a "vicious"[15] cough sent her to hospital that day. She acted to better her situation by moving into Apt. 12 at 601 Spadina Avenue in the second week of January.

Meanwhile, the Toronto committee for her lectures met on 3 January, and shortly afterwards a programme was set up at her favourite venue, Hygeia Hall. She was to speak first on conditions in Germany, then on "Hitler and His Cohorts", "The Collapse of German Culture", and finally "Dictatorship Right and Left: A Modern Religious Hysteria". She wrote Berkman and Emmy Eckstein, "I have stepped into a hornet's nest since I reached our comrades in Canada. I have already seen more people in the last six weeks than I have in all the years living in France. . . . And last but most important my lecture notes I had done nothing about until a week ago have just kept me swamped with work."[16]

Ross had been correct to fear the mood of Congress. The Department of Labor was planning to place a liberalization of immigration laws, and a proposal to admit German refugees, before the House, and feared that news of Goldman's readmission, even for a brief visit, "would determine the reactionary elements in Congress to oppose the projects", as Goldman put it in a letter. Not only did this delay approval of her visa, it prompted officials, who already had pre-approved her lecture topics, to demand restrictions on her speech. Roger Baldwin wrote to her that the "chief objection to your speaking on political subjects is that as an anarchist you would doubtless arouse attacks from some quarters that you were advocating the ideas forbidden by the immigration law". Could she abide by this restriction? The very constraints that Berkman had predicted were now appearing. She wrote Stella with some self-doubt and criticism in her tone, "Well, my dear, I have accepted the gagging condition of the Dept. of Labor." She continued to rail about the department's foolishness in imagining that literary topics "can be treated without analysis of the soil from which they sprung". But she was realistic, dismissing as "childish" Baldwin's and Ross's idea that after arriving she would gain more liberal treatment. "Once I am in the country," she wrote to Stella, "Wash. will keep me to the letter of the law and not the spirit."[17]

In early January, rumours about Goldman's negotiations began to surface in the American press. The New York *Sun* reported that efforts were being made to "gag" her. The story was brought to her attention by reporters from the Canadian Press wire service and the Toronto *Mail and Empire*. But her fears over the controversy's possible effects were quelled when her visa was granted on the same day she moved to her own apartment, 9 January; she would be admitted for three months, beginning 1 February. She wrote to Berkman that, with the exciting trip in prospect, it "will be hell to live here three weeks in the gloom of my place". The new apartment was pitch dark even in the day, having a wall directly in front of its one window. "One has been spoiled by the light in St Tropez."[18]

News of Washington's decision resulted in her being "fairly mobbed",[19] she reported, by the Toronto press, and becoming the object of a heady bout of attention in American newspapers as well. The US consul in Toronto seemed determined to spoil her hopes, however, again telling her that despite the visa she was still unlikely to get permission to enter and further frightening her by deciding to check whether Canada would readmit her once her visa expired. Her complaints about this treatment caused Arthur Leonard Ross to get the Department of Labor to send the consul strict instructions to issue the visa.

Now her plans for lectures and public appearances in the US began to grow firm. She already had received and ridiculed an offer to lecture on the vaudeville circuit ($200 a week for three six-minute talks a day). She was quite anxious, though, that someone effective be found to put the meetings together, because she hoped the tour would turn a profit for her as well as vindicate her ideas. The last three weeks of January found her busily sifting offers and proposals from a variety of booking agencies. Also, she was dealing with Alfred Knopf, who planned to issue an inexpensive one-volume version of *Living My Life* to coincide with her visit. It was priced at only $3 and was to appear on 10 February in an edition of 2,000 copies.

On 17 January she wrote to Berkman and Emmy about her first Toronto lecture, which was in many ways a gratifying success: eight hundred persons in attendance, six hundred of them paid admissions. She was disappointed in press coverage from the *Star* and disheartened by the amount of work involved in getting out the big audience, with almost no one, only one energetic friend, a visitor and old cohort from the *Mother Earth* era, assisting her materially. In addition, as she informed Arthur Leonard Ross, she was having difficulty concentrating on her Canadian work. "I have to sit hours at the machine typing letters. I have to supervise all the details of the arrangements here. And to cap the climax I had to dash out early this morning to address a strike meeting." Nevertheless, she felt her work in Toronto was both rewarding and valuable, even necessary, given the restrictions she had accepted on what she could say in the United States. The flurry of publicity surrounding her carried to the United States the frank and controversial political content of her Toronto lectures, in which she chided and warned the leaders and opinion makers of all democracies, presenting balanced—and devastating—assessments of their own behaviour and that of Hitler and Stalin. Commenting on her lecture on dictatorship, which she characterized as a form of religious hysteria, she wrote to Thomas Bell, "I am so glad that I am able to discuss this and similar vital themes in Canada, since it shall not be possible to do so in America."[20] She was disappointed by the fact that her usual journalistic ally, Robert Reade, no longer worked on the weekday *Star* but rather on its Saturday magazine, the *Star Weekly*. The *Mail and Empire*, however, covered the first talk extensively and fairly, and on 18 January the *Star* carried a lengthy and commendatory opinion piece on her and her lectures. She was delighted. By the end of the month, she was able to write Milly Rocker that her "work here [was] nearly finished".[21] The four events had an average attendance of 450 and had shown a small profit (admission was 25 cents a head, rental nearly $100). The *Star* article she so enjoyed gives a glimpse of the content, and of Goldman herself as she seemed at this time to friendly Toronto commentators. The piece was bylined "The Observer", the journalistic *nom de guerre* of the liberal

Protestant minister Salem Bland. He wrote: "In her appearance in Hygeia Hall last Monday she seemed to me to have mellowed and broadened, though her energy seems as ebullient as ever and her intellect as nimble and clear." In that first lecture, "Germany's Tragedy and the Forces That Brought It About", Goldman enumerated four main culprits: the German Social Democrats, the Prussian Junkers, the principal leaders of the country's heavy industry, and the communists. The Social Democrats received the heaviest criticism, first for having submitted to the Kaiser in 1914 and then for having become, after the war, "poverty-stricken in revolutionary ideas or impulses", in Rev Bland's paraphrase. The Social Democrats had been content to accept Hindenberg, who had immediately betrayed them to Hitler. Her analysis of the communists in Germany, while balanced, was withering. They were responsible for the lack of a united front against Hitler, for they wished to dominate the left and spent more energy in fighting socialists than in fighting Hitlerites. Goldman argued that they had subverted every organization that tried to work with them; in a few years she was to experience personally, in Spain, a similar disaster caused partly by similar tactics. "Until the Communists will learn to co-operate and be tolerant and give a share to others", she commented, "there will never be a united front against such devastation as has come on Germany and now threatens the world." Bland applied to Goldman Heinrich Heine's famous words, "lay on my coffin a sword, for I was a brave soldier in the liberation war of humanity", and wrote of her, "I doubt if our shrewd and practical age has produced another woman or man who has more steadfastly and heroically fought for liberty." He did not scruple to associate her with Christ, on "Grand Inquisitor" grounds: "it is difficult to think of Him looking around at things as they are in Canada to-day and not saying things which would create distaste in some influential people." A revenant Jesus would probably be denied the right to speak, Bland continued, but "I am glad that Canada has never excluded this outspoken, but fair-minded critic of modern civilization, and that under the genial tolerant spirit of President Roosevelt the United States has laid aside its hysterical fear of this gallant soul." Readers were then commended to the remaining lectures as "an informative and fair-minded though condemnatory treatment of a momentous revolution".[22] This and similar contemporaneous reactions to Goldman's treatment of European events prove that not everyone in the 1920s and 1930s missed what has become so obvious in retrospect, that her facts, derived from the international radical network, were better than those possessed (or at any rate used) by democratic governments, and that her analyses were much more intelligent and accurate than theirs, perhaps because she was unbiased by groundless hopes for an easy continuance of profit and comfort.

One person deeply impressed by her lectures was an Italian workman and anti-fascist organizer named Attilio Bortolotti, who became a friend for the remainder of her life and assumed great importance at its end. A native of Friulia, he had been an instinctive radical since his teenage experiences in the Great War and had adopted anarchism in 1922 as a result of the writings of Enrico Malatesta and other classic anarchists, which he had discovered in the course of his work in Detroit and Windsor in the effort to save Sacco and Vanzetti. For a decade he had been struggling to find or build an adequate anarchist group in Canada. Moving from Windsor to Toronto in late 1929, Bortolotti at first was isolated from both the radical and the Italian communities, but in August 1931 (or perhaps 1932 or 1933: his recollections varied) he printed and distributed five hundred leaflets for the anniversary of Sacco and Vanzetti's executions and as a result met Italian socialists and communists. Soon he had located and befriended a fellow Italian anarchist, Ruggero Benvenuti, and began participating in the Matteotti Club, a mainly socialist organization named for an Italian radical political leader upon whose assassination in 1924 the impulsive Bortolotti had burned his Italian passport (a fact that contributed to later difficulties involving Goldman). Gradually, Bortolotti and Benvenuti attracted a number of likeminded Friulians and Italians and founded Il Gruppo Libertario, which published an anarchist newspaper, *Il Libertario*, and organized a "filodrammatica", coordinated by Bortolotti, to stage dramatic works with a libertarian message at the Labour Lyceum and at an old church converted to a meeting place by a Russian, Bulgarian, and Ukrainian anarchist group, headed by one Vasiliev. "We left the [Toronto] socialists and Communists far behind," he proudly remembered, "when it came to plays and recitals—followed, naturally, by dancing—for twenty-five cents a person."[23]

At this period Bortolotti attended Goldman's lectures, and after one of them he was introduced to her at a reception at the home of Maurice and Becky Langbord. His entry into her circle came through Morris Simkin, whose printing shop had prepared the Sacco and Vanzetti commemorative leaflet. In 1986 Bortolotti gave an interview to the Toronto anarchist magazine *Kick It Over*, in which he recalled Goldman's lectures, and his first encounters with her, just before her US trip. He remembered that "she delivered three lectures which were a masterpiece at the Hygeia Hall. . . . The title of the first lecture was 'Hitler and His Cohorts'. There were about 2,000 people there. Of course, the Jews felt that they wanted to hear what Hitler was doing, although he had just begun to persecute the Jews then." Elsewhere Bortolotti commented that he was "flabbergasted by the way she spoke, with her energy, with the beauty of her sentences. She was nothing to look at—short, fat, unattractive—but when she spoke, with that fire in her, you forgot everything. In front of you was something that transcended looks." His most vivid memory was his advice to her against accepting the US-imposed ban on mentioning politics. "Then Emma got a permit to go to the States. She asked for six months and they gave her three months, warning her not to speak on anarchism. She accepted it, and discussed it with me one evening, and I said, 'You're prostituting yourself Emma.' She looked at me—you should have seen it—this fiery, deadly look. She resented it very much."[24] Bortolotti's objections echoed the admonitions Goldman received from Berkman, of whom the young Italian, with his fiery commitment, reminded her.

But Goldman's course was set, and besides, she was too busy to consider monitory voices. On the twenty-eighth, she gave a Jewish meeting, "a very big affair and a very nice audience" for which "the comrades worked very hard . . . especially Joe Desser and Maurice Langbord." The following night saw her concluding English lecture, that on "Dictatorship Right and Left". No wonder that a week earlier she had warned Arthur Leonard Ross "not [to] be surprised if you meet a very tired lady Feb. 2nd." She left herself a day to arrange last-minute details before setting out 1 February for what she often had characterized in recent letters as "going into a Vesuvius".[25]

9

To Vesuvius and Back

Goldman crossed into the United States at Niagara Falls on 1 February and arrived quietly at Pennsylvania Station in New York the next day. The small welcoming party consisted almost entirely of family members. According to an interview in the New York *Sun*, she purposely avoided Grand Central Station because she had heard that a demonstration in her honour was being planned there. "Not many people know this", she told a *Sun* reporter, "but, though I have addressed thousands, even hundreds of thousands, of meetings in my life, I am always very uncomfortable when I am in the crowd, especially if I am the center of its attention." The reporter recorded that another member of the party, the professional booking agent James Pond whom she had hired to arrange her tour, was irate at the poor size of the welcome: a minor detail but a telling one, because differences of opinion about the proper conduct of Goldman's public appearances developed quickly. Goldman told the *Sun* that she would leave New York on 17 February for lectures in Boston, Philadelphia, and probably Washington. She was glad to be back, she said, and hoped to live the rest of her life in the US, but she was determined to speak freely and would leave the country at once if any attempt were made to censor her. The article makes no specific reference to the Department of Labor restrictions over which Goldman had agonized, but what she said suggests that she was already testing her bonds. "I don't think they are losing very much sleep in Washington over anything I may say", she ventured. "The only thing, perhaps, is that they don't want too much said about Hitler. There is trade, you know, with Germany, and too much criticism—but I shall not stay if to stay I have to be what they call 'good'."[1]

At her first public speaking appearance, Goldman called Germany a "nation led by degenerates". Through Roger Baldwin, she heard soon after that the German ambassador had protested and that the Department of Labor wanted her to know that she should avoid saying things that would lead to any further formal complaints from foreign representatives or from members of Congress. Goldman persisted. She wrote Berkman that in a lecture on "The Drama in Europe" she had "led blows straight from the shoulder on the menace of Fascism and dictatorship".[2]

Despite this brinksmanship, and the FBI agents J. Edgar Hoover had trailing her, Goldman stayed the entire ninety days, and the first few weeks held golden promise. On 11 February a crowd estimated at 2,000 stood outside New York's Town Hall to catch a glimpse of her when she went in to speak at a Community Church memorial service in honour of Peter Kropotkin. She was invited by several magazines, including *Harper's*, the *Nation*, *Redbook* and the *American Mercury*, to write articles. She had the services of an enthusiastic, well-connected publicity agent in Ann Lord, who was being paid by the Pond Bureau to travel in advance of Goldman and make arrangements for her visits. At an appearance in her American home town, a packed house of 700 crowded Rochester's City Club until 3 a.m. listening to her answer questions about her career. But the hopes excited by this early fervour faded. During late February and much of March, Goldman was travelling frantically in New England and in the Midwest to engagements with disappointingly small audiences and receipts. She blamed Pond, writing Arthur Leonard Ross that "Pond has completely ruined the magnificent opportunity my re-entry into America has offered". The halls were too large, the admissions too high, the publicity ill-directed. Pond, in turn, blamed her. There was "a national anti-Emma Goldman sentiment",[3] he reported to Goldman's niece, Stella Ballantine. Pond claimed that Goldman and her friends had misled him about her drawing power. He felt cheated.

Other explanations were offered too. Evelyn Scott told Goldman that the communist boycott of her meetings was probably to blame, since liberals in the US were by and large communist supporters now. Her nephew Saxe and others suggested to her that young people were no longer interested in anarchism; they were looking instead for the sort of relief that communists promised. The prominent New York newspaperman Heywood Broun, who chaired Goldman's 28 February lecture at the Broadwood Hotel auditorium in Philadelphia, devoted one of his "It Seems to Me" columns to a smug if vivid account of Goldman as a "gallant figure but also a futile one [who] just couldn't compromise" and who belonged to a vanished era when American radicalism "in addition to being far more fierce . . . had, perhaps, a greater measure of dignity" than in 1934. Cursed with the "fatal" temperamental defect of being unable to compromise, she was now "an old woman without a country, a party or a following. . . . There is no regime to which Emma Goldman can give approval. But she has her dream and her integrity."[4]

Broun espoused a middle-brow social Darwinism in averring that nature "will not permit such inflexibility" in a world in which "[e]very man in his inmost heart wants not liberty but license" and that the "life force", in society as in nature, hedges this frightful instinct with circumstance in order to bring about growth through "selection, adaptation and the happy miracle of accident". Failing to adapt to this truth, "Anarchists have gone the way of antediluvian mammals" into extinction. "In principle and emotion", Broun continued, "I'm all for Emma and against Charles Robert Darwin. The only trouble is that he happens to hold all the aces. No political and economic ideal has ever been as pure as that which Emma Goldman advocated." The self-congratulatory, practical, and disabused tone, and the philosophical complacency of this rejection of her ideal—and of any ideal not embodied in a powerful party able to deliver influence and position to its adherents—well represented what Goldman knew she was up against in the dominant society. She began to fear that she "had been forgotten and no longer represented a drawing force".[5] But she also took Broun's ideas apart—tacitly, for she never referred to him but only to the prevailing temper of American culture—in the writings later prompted by her US visit.

During the last few weeks of the tour, Goldman's own theory of the reason for low attendance received some vindication, as lower prices and more intelligent publicity produced large audiences at meetings organized by old friends and colleagues. Starting on 21 March she made sold-out appearances in several Chicago venues (a crowd of 2,000 heard her at the New Masonic Temple) and then began a triumphant progress through some of the same cities, including Pittsburgh and Detroit, where she had met with disappointment only a few weeks earlier. These late successes, and the thought of what she might have done if she had controlled the whole tour, made her frantic to return to the United States again.

Chicago was the turning point in still another respect. At a lecture in Lincoln Center there, she met an osteopath, Dr Frank G. Heiner, thirty-six, an admirer of her work since his first reading of *Anarchism and Other Essays* ten years earlier, who was at this time doing graduate work in sociology at the University of Chicago. She wrote Berkman on 9 April that she had met just the man they needed to begin an anarchist renewal in the US, a man who understood American psychology. Before she left Chicago, she made plans with Heiner for publishing a pamphlet series. Heiner promised that he, too, in emulation of his hero, Goldman, would begin speaking publicly about his commitment to anarchism. The fact that Heiner was blind and that she was about to be forced out of the country did not slow them down. She was exhilarated, although also puzzled and doubtful, when the married Heiner's letters to her during her last few weeks in the US revealed that he admired her not only as a campaigner for anarchism but also as a goddess of love.

This new offer of romance came at a time when Goldman was meeting one old flame after another. In Chicago, she encountered Ben Reitman, who had written her repeatedly during February and March and had taken a hand in publicizing her Chicago lectures. His only regret, he wrote after their meeting, was that she had offered no word of encouragement that they might be lovers again. Leon Malmed helped to organize a meeting in Albany on 15 April; he and Emma, too, met briefly, although his expressions of interest in her seem primarily to have taken the form of concern for her material welfare, a sympathy which she found too little, too late. Even Arthur Swenson, her young Swedish lover from the early days of her flight from revolutionary Russia, surfaced to write to her sentimentally about their past together. Swenson was the one to whom Goldman most frequently compared Heiner when she wrote to her new friend about love.

Heiner's letters pursued Goldman back into Canada, which she entered with only minutes to spare before her visa expired on 1 May. She went directly to Montreal, where one newspaper said, "Radio signals were already warning police officers to look out for her." She told reporters that she had not expected an extension of her visa. "I knew that there were plenty of people who would think the United States government would be safer if I got out before May 1!" She had found the US "more liberal" than she remembered. "The liberality of the present administration in the states was responsible both for my being permitted to return, and for the lifting of the sense of repression, enabling the people freely to come and hear me, and to listen in far more receptive mood." Roosevelt's New Deal, she added, was "a very sincere attempt"[6] to deal with society's ills, but one she was sure was doomed to fail, only serving to prop up an old system and encouraging people to look to Washington for miracles.

She told reporters that she would be in Montreal for two weeks and would deliver two lectures in English before going to Toronto. In the event she stayed three weeks, lodging first at the Ford Hotel, where she gave her initial interviews, and then moving to Meyer and Rose Bernstein's home in Outrement. Ann Lord was still with her, and did much of the work of booking space at the Windsor for 14–15 May and publicizing the two talks, which were to be "The Hitler Regime, and the Forces that Brought It About" and "The Collapse of German Culture". As always in Montreal, Goldman was impressed by the religious, ethnic, and linguistic divisions that separated the city's residents into communities that seemed to her "a million miles" from one another. "Here it is doubly hard because the French are under the thumb of the Catholic Church and the English and Canadians are difficult to reach." She wrote Rudolf Rocker, who had recently delivered five lectures to Jewish audiences in the city, that she would be giving two as well, although she doubted that she would be able to add much to what he had recently told Montreal's Jewish community about Germany. She wished that Montreal Jews would take more interest in reaching other segments of the city, an initiative which, never strong, actually seemed to have decayed since 1926–28: "I think it terrible that the Jewish comrades concentrate all their efforts on Jewish propaganda",[7] Goldman stated.

She was delighted and surprised when crowds of 350 turned out for each English lecture. She wrote Berkman: "When I tell you that the Jews live nearly a million miles removed from the life of the natives of the city, you will appreciate how glad I am that my meeting succeeded in bringing out a serious and distinguished audience." According to the Montreal *Gazette*'s account of the second lecture, after her indictment of Hitler's destructive effect on German culture "Miss Goldman was bombarded with questions, and it was here that she burst out with all her old fearlessness and power, tossing back answers as fast as the questions came. Some of the replies were in the true 'Red Emma' style—caustic and biting. Her remarks on Hitler and his aides were even more highly colored than on Monday night when she called them 'beautiful pathological specimens and ripe material for a lunatic asylum'."[8] Spurred by the turnout, Goldman agreed to add a third English lecture on *Living My Life* on the twenty-first, and a social was held for her on the twentieth. Since her final Jewish lecture had been on 18 May (its attendance of 400 provided a profit of $60), her hectic schedule had included events on three of the four nights before her departure for Toronto on the twenty-second.

To Berkman, Rocker, and others, she wrote more warmly than she had during the tour of what she had accomplished in the US. Even if the crowds often had disappointed, she had succeeded in getting the anarchist message to the people through the press, and now she was heartened in the same way by the Montreal newspapers' coverage of her English lectures. Even the French-language press reached out to interview her and report her remarks on Germany. The English journals had sought her views on fascism in Great Britain ("the English people as a whole believe so much in the British Parliamentary institutions that they cannot see [fascism's] danger"). In *La Presse*, she was described as one who, despite loving France "passionnement", feared that a species of fascism was already establishing itself there due to a national "respect pour l'autorité militaire, trop regardée comme unique embléme de l'ordre". Speaking in French with the reporter, she repeated that she was "not Red. Not capitalist but not communist. Very simply, I preach liberty for the individual."[9]

The crowds were larger at her Jewish lectures, and yet she was disheartened, she wrote Heiner, that she saw in none of the various "foreign language groups" an understanding of anarchism as anything but "an economic theory of the future. Not a spiritual force for immediate regeneration. Not a liberating, beautifying ideal of their lives. . . ." During the few weeks in Montreal, Heiner was added to the small core of correspondents, such as Rocker and Berkman, to whom Goldman confided a freshened hope for anarchism. She was beginning to be drawn into a love dialogue with him as well. On 6 May, she wrote, "I thought my days of awakening a grand love were over. . . . Every pore in my body cried out against the injustice of a world that grants man the right to love until his highest age though he may never have been young, never consumed by the forces of passion that scorch one's body and one's spirit. The right denied my sex. . . ."[10] She believed that he loved her but she still feared to pursue an affair. She did not want to hurt his relationship with his wife and daughter. She also suspected that he would reject her eventually because of the difference in their ages. Nonetheless, before leaving Montreal she was broaching the possibility that Heiner visit her in Toronto, even if only to work on anarchist projects. On 22 May, her travel day between the two cities, she wrote, "I really don't know whether the fires in my soul you have lighted are love. Or whether it is my emotional hunger for love, for intimacy. . . ." But at the same time that she expressed herself so doubtful, she was preparing for a love affair. Instead of staying in Toronto with friends, she rented an apartment for the summer at the Westminster, 152 Bloor Street West, to which she moved on 29 May, the day after delivering her only lecture of the spring in Toronto, "My Impressions of America and the New Deal". Both from the platform and in interviews immediately after her arrival, Goldman congratulated the US for its new freedoms but predicted failure for the New Deal. "An attempt to better conditions from on top by decrees and codes made by those in power is bound to fail", she told her audience at Hygeia Hall on 28 May. Five days earlier, in an interview with the *Daily Star*, she had criticized the pledges of a "new deal" for Ontario then flying in provincial politics. "It's a sort of autocracy you have here and at Ottawa, I always thought", she said. What was needed everywhere was for social change "to grow from within". Turning to international affairs, she warned that western governments' obsessive pursuit of communists was leaving them vulnerable to fascism, which was dangerously gaining ground in France and England. On 30 May one successful aspect of her US tour was concluded when Albert de Jong wrote from the Netherlands to acknowledge receipt of $1,002.87 that she had raised and sent to Europe for "our comrades".[11]

For a short time, Ann Lord, who had accompanied Goldman from Montreal, stayed on in Toronto and helped her with the first article she was writing in response to her American tour; like her Toronto lecture, it was entitled "My Impressions of America". The piece was an initiative of her own; she was uncertain whether she would be able to find a publisher for it, and she had to move on quickly to the articles she had agreed to write for specific US magazines. About this same time, Goldman was interviewed by a prominent Toronto journalist and columnist, Hye Bossin, who published an admiring account of the meeting in the *Jewish Standard* on 29 June. Bossin described Goldman as one who "will not compromise in any way, even at the price of a peaceful old age. . . . When in England, she criticises the monarchy; on German soil the former republic [which had been in power when she spoke there]. In Russia she lashed the government while at the same time throughout the land resounded the executioners' guns. In the United States, the scene of her most recent pilgrimage, though restricted by Washington in her criticisms of Germany, she nevertheless succeeded in discussing the forces that helped bring Hitler into power and the menace he and Fascism represent to the world." Bossin shed a kindly light on the question of Goldman's changing audience. "Peculiarly enough, her lectures bring out a less proletarian type than the average radical lecturer. Her audiences are largely made up of the 'Home-and-School-Club' type." In addition, Bossin provides a rare public record of one of Goldman's almost constant private themes, the sometimes difficult relationship she had with Jewish communities in Canada, and especially with their radicals of various stripes. When he asked her about the Zionist movement, Goldman said that she saw a home in Palestine as "at best but a place of temporary refuge for those from places where the Jew cannot breathe". Jews should seek full rights wherever they were living: this was the sort of drive for equality she saw among American Blacks. Moreover, she characterized attempts to ground a renewed sense of Jewish identity in a religious revival as "the result of suffering and despair". Without giving any names, she described some Montrealers as falling into this error. "In Montreal recently I was surprised to see a revival of Yiddishism in a certain circle always considered radical. For a while I thought I was back in a Russian village of years ago. The works of a young Jewish poet were being praised, works that were chiefly with a religious background. I consider that a form of retrogression."[12] It seems quite likely that one of the people she had in mind was her longtime friend H.M. Caiserman, who by the late 1920s had been influenced by the growing intellectual influence of the Poale Zion movement, which proposed to reconcile Zionism and socialism and to promote the creation of a Jewish socialist workers' state in Palestine. Goldman continued to regard such a dream as a version of bureaucratic statism.

Writing, especially without Berkman near at hand, was always difficult for Goldman. Her progress on her many and varied magazine projects was further complicated by Ann Lord's departure on 16 June, when Goldman was still at work on a promised *Harper's* article on the individual's role in society, for which she was working from an essay on the same subject that Berkman had sent her. She completed an article on communism promised to the *American Mercury* on 18 June and the *Harper's* article four days later. Soon after, while she was contemplating her next piece, an essay on political exiles for the *Nation*, her article on impressions of America was rejected by *Redbook*. Early in July she was still reworking it when she heard from the *American Mercury* that her essay on communism would appear in September and October with a "few discreet cuts" to satisfy length requirements. Then, George R. Leighton, the editor of *Harper's*, rejected the essay she had sent him. "As it now stands the article is . . . a philosophical treatise. What we need is an article that shows how you put these principles and beliefs into practice." She responded to his criticism not by revising but rather by drafting an entirely new work, the important essay "Was My Life Worth Living?". This left her with the original essay on the individual still unsold. Dealing with editors was a torture for her, because of her dread of rewriting, but even more troublesome was her growing financial desperation. The magazine essays and articles were the only source of income she had for the summer aside from a monthly allowance from her brother Moe, and when the stipend did not arrive she wrote Stella on 14 July for $15. She was "dead broke", she reported, and "just down right sick over the *Harper's* business".[13] Although a cheque from the *American Mercury* for $192 ($200 minus $8 US income tax, a deduction Goldman challenged) arrived two days later, and Moe's allowance soon after, Goldman was not entirely relieved. She did not want to depend on money from Moe and his wife, and her living expenses until meetings began in October would take up all the funds she had in hand. Where was she going to get the $200 to mount a tour, either in the US or in Canada? She tried the American impressions article with *Harper's* while struggling through a reworking of the essay on individualism. On 30 July, the *Nation* accepted her article on political exiles but complained it was too long, necessitating still further labour to prune and modify it.

All her writing and rewriting kept her close to the Toronto apartment, where she was often occupied with visits from family, including her brother Herman, now seemingly recovered from a troublesome illness of the spring and early summer, and others, such as her new Chicago friends, Jeanne Levey and her husband. She went occasionally for a weekend in Muskoka, a region of lakes and hills north of the city. On one occasion she took some family members to visit the Arbeiter Ring youth camp run partly by the Langbords. But she was still overwhelmed with paperwork, which now began to include preparations for October lectures in Toronto. Millie Desser, daughter of Joe Desser, one of the chief organizers of her 1926 trip to Canada, was now her secretary. Goldman was able to pay her only a few dollars a week pocket money.

Despite such frenzied activity, Goldman spent much of the summer feeling alone. There was no anarchist community in the city, she informed her friend Albert de Jong. "The Italians are active in their own language group and so are the Jews, but their work never reaches the public. I will try hard this autumn to gather up whatever little material I may find here." Her sense of isolation was aggravated by growing worries over Berkman, who had been complaining for some time about the burdens of translating Rudolf Rocker's massive *Nationalism and Its Relation to Culture* into English. Goldman began to suspect that part of the problem, at least, was due to illness. At the end of July she told Berkman to rest while the weather was hot and urged Emmy Eckstein to tell her what medicine had been prescribed for Berkman recently. To Stella she relayed that Emmy was doing almost all the typing now, that Berkman was "weaker and weaker". She cautioned Heiner against mentioning Berkman's poor health when writing to France. What Berkman needed, she told Emmy, was "a passport to come to Canada".[14] For the time being, she encouraged them to stay on at Bon Esprit, where they had been living, sometimes Berkman alone, sometimes the two of them, for the summer. She hoped that they again would consider trying to make their home there permanently with her.

In the meantime in Toronto, Goldman found two remedies for her loneliness. One was a new youth-oriented anarchist group not unlike that she had encouraged Heiner to form in Chicago. She reported to de Jong that she had "called a gathering of young people, students and workers for this coming Thursday. It will give me an opportunity to see whether it is worthwhile [to make] any future effort". The meeting went well. Thirty-five people came, she told Frank Heiner, maybe even some communists, and the discussion was lively. "Last night convinced me more than ever that there is keen interest in our idea."[15] The group started regular meetings, although she informed Heiner that she was worried because there was no sign of the sort of talent that would be needed to keep it alive once she left Toronto. The other remedy for loneliness was Heiner himself.

Throughout most of the summer, Goldman's passionate letters to Heiner mingled desire with doubt. She treated his projected visit to Toronto as a certainty and discussed plans, but at the same time she kept expressing reluctance about a love affair. Early in June, she wrote him that she would certainly meet his bus when he came to visit. "You moved me to tears with the announcement that [your mother] reads to you. May I do it for you when you will be here? I mean if there will be time left to read?" But a few days later she was telling Berkman that her love for Heiner was doomed, that she would never be allowed into the US for any extended time, and that even if he visited Canada, she would soon be returning to Europe. The next day, while suggesting in a letter to Heiner that he come to Toronto in July or August, Goldman wrote him that she feared she would disappoint him. On her birthday, she expanded on what was worrying her. "I cannot get away from the fact that I am ages older than you. I am sure you will tell me that not the years but spirit counts. And that your imagination sees me young. I understand all that. But understanding everything does not mean feeling at ease over certain facts that stare one in the face."[16]

Goldman protested that she would not hurt Heiner's wife, Mary. Yet what seemed to trouble her most about the correspondence over the summer was her knowledge that Mary read incoming letters aloud to Heiner. She complimented Mary on her liberalism in a letter written 23 June: "What overwhelms me is your wonderful capacity to share all the intimacies of Frank with women who come into his life. It's almost like being present at the intimacies that should remain the most sacred private affair between the two concerned." Goldman seemed to be probing, testing Heiner's claim that Mary would tolerate any lover he sought as long as it was a woman Mary could respect. At the same time, she seemed to be asking for sympathy. "As to feeling free to write Frank as I should like that is of course impossible. Yes, I know you are marvellous. But it is my own feeling about you my dearest. I should never want to see Frank again or to write another letter were I to feel I am causing you pain."[17] Frank answered within a few days of this letter, setting 16 August for his visit and offering the reassurance that Mary never saw his letters to Goldman. Goldman began offering details of their time together. She would take him to the Toronto Islands, and there was a lovely drive along Lake Ontario, and a beautiful park (she meant the Scarborough Bluffs) they could visit.

But she was also waiting to hear back from Mary, a letter which did not arrive until shortly before the visit. In this remarkable communication, Mary began by apologizing for the delay, since she wanted to reassure Goldman that she accepted the affair, even welcomed it. Goldman was the sort of woman who might direct her husband into a more independent way of life. Many of his lovers, including the one he had been involved with when he met Goldman, Mary said, had aggravated the problem of his dependence by acting towards him in the same smothering, all-protecting way that his family had from his earliest childhood. Assuring Goldman that she was interested only in helping her, Mary nevertheless painted a bleak picture of the life into which her own involvement with Heiner had led her. What she hoped for and envisioned had been to free him of dependency; instead, he seemed drawn to women who would reproduce his mother's style. He had been on the point of ending their marriage to take up with such a woman, Mary wrote, on the very evening when he heard Goldman lecture in Chicago. Goldman, Mary felt, was the person who could "encourage him toward . . . the only real approach he has ever had toward . . . independence—his work in sociology."[18]

Goldman took Mary Heiner at her word. She would welcome Frank as her lover when he arrived in Toronto. Letters all but stopped for the next two weeks. One day she wrote a quick note to Berkman, to apologize for her silence. Heiner was in the bathroom, she said, or she would not have written. His blindness made her reluctant to leave him alone for even a moment, but beyond the pathos he inspired was the ecstasy of pleasure. "Heiner is the greatest event of the last seventeen years. He embodies all that Ben was lacking plus Ben's primitiveness. . . . The more painful will be his departure."[19]

During Heiner's visit, she gave little time to other activities, including her new group, but she worked with it in arranging a public memorial for Sacco and Vanzetti on 27 August. At this event, she wrote Berkman, Heiner spoke "beautifully", as did one of the group members, an Italian comrade she does not name, possibly Attilio Bortolotti. Goldman, who chaired and also delivered remarks, reported that the memorial was poorly attended but that at least her group could "reach the masses" with its message in a way that others, including socialists who had held their own memorial the previous night, were unable to do, for they had failed to attract press coverage. Just before Heiner's departure, Goldman invited the group to her apartment to get to know him. She wanted him to talk about sociology, psychology, and anarchism. "He held them spellbound for two hours", she wrote to Berkman on 30 August. "Bear in mind most of them were students in these very branches. Yet they told me that Heiner had brought home to them the relation of Anarchism to these subjects."[20]

10

We Cling to an Ideal No One Wants

Goldman clung to the memory of Heiner's visit. She wrote Stella at the beginning of September, "It has increased my faith in humanity to find in Frank such an indomitable will to overcome all the terrible difficulties his handicap has put in his way. And it has strengthened my belief in freedom as the highest expression of man. You see dearest I found in Frank complete harmony of ideas, in the world we aim to build, in our need for art and beauty and in complete fulfilment of my woman soul. Is this not a great wonder, at my age? And in this cold and ugly world." The cold and ugly world, however, touched even the love in which she gloried: the sorrow of separation made returning to her writing very difficult. "I have tried to buckle down to the work I must do on the article and lectures", Goldman wrote Heiner on 5 September. "But so far I have not succeeded. Your spirit hovers over me and is in every corner of the apartment."[1] On 20 September she left the quarters they had briefly shared to take two rooms in a house at 471 Brunswick Avenue, the new home of her friends the Langbords.

Her letters from Toronto in September and October, both to Heiner and to other friends, are filled with hopes and frustrations. Heiner could be the new US leader that the anarchist movement needed desperately, she believed, and she urged Berkman and other friends, such as Max Olay, to support and encourage him. Goldman and Heiner plotted strategy for Heiner's anarchist agitation in Chicago, and she was able to follow every step of her lover's work with a new student group, similar to the one she had organized in Toronto. At the same time, she worried about the obstacles between them. She was still barred from entering the US. Even if she could return to Chicago, she told Emmy, a frequent recipient of her romantic confidences at this time, she would not enjoy the visit because of the possible harm such a trip would do Mary. Only slightly less unlikely was that Heiner would travel again to see her, in Canada or in France. She was haunted by the possibility that their separation might be permanent. She wrote him that each day was fraught "with fear and hopelessness that there will be no return of the two magic weeks your visit had created for me."[2] Moreover, although she delighted in Heiner's passionate letters, the pleasure was diluted by awareness that anything she wrote to Heiner was read aloud to him by his wife.

Still, Goldman accomplished a great deal in September. The *Harper's* essay was sent to Saxe Commins for editing, and by month's end Goldman's revised manuscript was on its way to the magazine. Many long days went into preparations for a busy schedule of lectures set for October. Goldman also began pressing Roger Baldwin for news on a renewal of her visa, this time possibly for six months; Baldwin replied with a request that they meet in Niagara Falls early in October to discuss strategy. Goldman also pursued Berkman for some reassurance about his condition, and he replied early in the month that she must give up the idea that he and Emmy were conspiring to keep anything from her. He was "more mentally than physically tired",[3] he protested, and well able to go on, although just how the Rocker project was to be completed he could not imagine, given a book far too long and a translation fee ridiculously small.

The Toronto lectures, which began on 1 October with a talk on *Living My Life*, covered a wide variety of subjects and audiences. Topics included the plays of George Bernard Shaw, Russian literature, German literature, the munitions industry, and new approaches to early childhood education. As usual, Goldman's reports on the lectures almost invariably emphasized her disappointments. She had returned to the gloomier pole of her ever-alternating attitude towards Canada: now it was sterile ground for her work. With very few exceptions, she reported, naming Millie Desser and her father Joe, and Maurice Langbord, the old guard had lost all its spirit.

Her hopes for an immediate return to the US were disappointed in October. Shortly after she and Baldwin rendezvoused at Niagara Falls, he met with an American government representative who, citing such reasons as fear of the new Congress and the growing national intolerance for aliens, informed him that Secretary of Labor Frances Perkins was being advised to refuse a new visa until at least a year had passed since Goldman's visit. Baldwin suggested Goldman send Stella on a "private" appeal to Perkins, which he thought would be more successful. On 26 October Baldwin reported that he had spoken personally to Perkins, who confirmed her decision not to grant a visa. He apologized for having misjudged the situation. Being barred from the US was made even more difficult by family worries.

Her brother Moe suffered two heart attacks during October, and Goldman feared that he would never recover sufficiently to return to work. Moe's financial troubles made her own worse by causing her to question the allowance Moe had been providing, her sole steady source of money at this time. She wrote to Stella on 25 October: "I am absolutely determined not to take another penny from Moe and Babsie."[4] Still, in this same letter, she told Stella that her financial worries meant that she had to stay in Canada. She reported the same decision to Berkman, who at this time was beginning to ask when she would return to France. She hated Canada, she said, but at least, unlike France, it afforded her some opportunity to work, even if she earned barely enough to support herself. She was now considering the same sort of extensive lecture series that she had given in Toronto during the fall of 1927, a course of political meetings alternating with a course on literary and artistic subjects. It might run ten weeks, both in Montreal and in Toronto, and at the same time allow her to book additional individual lectures.

She had finally decided that she would make one more try for a visa; and she also was hoping, as she told Emmy, that she might see Frank again. A rising mood was fed by these dreams and also the pleasure she took in her Toronto anarchist group, which during this time was meeting regularly and encouraging her work. The group was "purely proletarian", she wrote to Frank. With little speaking or writing skill among the members, it nevertheless was active in publishing and distributing an anti-war resolution that Heiner had composed and setting up fundraising activities for refugee relief. The group had considerable devotion to anarchism and enthusiasm for her personally, and she was quite interested in its education, holding regular reading and discussion sessions, which she began with Berkman's *The ABC of Anarchism*. She mentioned a number of members of the group by name, including Attilio Bortolotti, and also "a Canadian woman", Dorothy Rogers, and a "lovely young Dutch couple",[5] Dien and Tom Meelis, all of whom would become close to her.

In his reminiscences given to *Kick It Over*, Bortolotti recalled that Rogers, originally a member of the socialist Cooperative Commonwealth Federation, was prompted to switch from socialism to anarchism after hearing Goldman lecture, until "one day she said to Emma, 'I'm glad to call you a comrade.' At that time we had organized the international group who were Jews, Italians, Swedes, Bulgarians. There were about fifteen to eighteen in the group and Dorothy became a member."[6] This recollection tends to imply that Goldman's circle, composed partly of persons she had discovered, also included ones previously gathered together by Bortolotti and his friends.

In another reminiscence, Bortolotti reported that the group met often at Joe Desser's home, and occasionally at "Vasiliev's place", possibly the old church that the Russian group had converted to a meeting spot; he recalled as members Seltzer, Judkin, Steinberg, Benvenuti, Gava, and Thorne. Goldman, about to leave for Montreal, hoped that this body would continue to meet and study in her absence and would still be together if she did return to Toronto in the spring.

Goldman's arrival in Montreal on 6 November excited little public notice. There was no press coverage of the sort that had greeted her in May when she returned from the US, and she soon found that she would have to make her own preparations for lectures. When no audience seemed likely for a drama lecture series, she considered returning to Toronto almost at once; but while she was trying to decide, she arranged to have Millie Desser join her as secretary. Berkman urged her not to mount a series without assurances that it would, indeed, be profitable. She said she would not go ahead without 100 subscribers, but the number with which she would content herself kept dropping. Eventually only fifty persons subscribed. Despite her worries, she conducted her drama lecture schedule while simultaneously reporting to Berkman that she might have to cancel it and return people's money. The course, ten Wednesday evenings, concluded on 13 March, and besides the subscribers usually drew an additional twenty or so individual admissions. She arranged many other lectures, including three at the YMCA on popular social topics, one on *Living My Life* for December, and at least two English and two Yiddish lectures in January and February on birth control, sex, women, and children. Public English lectures she had managed to obtain dealt not only with literary but also social and political themes, some based upon essays and articles she had recently written. Subjects included George Bernard Shaw, Kropotkin, "Art and Revolution", "The Place of the Individual in Society", "The Challenge of the Child", "Youth in Revolt", and "Constructive Revolution".

On 12 November, she made her first public appearance in Montreal, a lecture on Shaw at the Windsor Hotel to 162 paying listeners, with the American playwright Maxwell Anderson in the chair. Both the Montreal *Gazette* and the Montreal *Star* covered the talk, in which she rehearsed her longstanding dispute with Shaw the social commentator. His reports on the Soviet Union, based on "ten days as the favored guest of the government", were unforgivably wrong, and she enlarged on Russian conditions as she knew them, both by experience and research, to illustrate her argument. For instance, while Shaw had praised Stalin as the saviour of the Russian people, four million of them, by anarchist estimates, had died in the 1932–33 famine. "It would not matter if this man [Shaw] were a nobody. But he has tremendous influence among certain people. Incompetent and lacking in courage, he is considered some sort of an idol by those who follow him", the *Gazette* reported her as saying. It was only a matter of time, she continued, before Shaw spoke up for Hitler. "But wait—wait until Hitler is a success. Shaw loves success". Excepting *Candida* and *Heartbreak House* from her indictment, she analyzed Shaw's dramatic works to show that he characteristically "makes just and brilliant criticism of society, but in the end he falls down and is unable to carry through to a conclusion" consistent with the "fine ideals of democracy and liberty"[7] that powered his early thought.

Lectures within the Jewish community remained the profitable part of the trip. Rabbi Harry J. Stern of Temple Emanu-El, for example, arranged an original group of lectures and asked her back several times for additional talks. Among her few helpful supporters were the old guard, Meyer and Rose Bernstein, Sara Caiserman, and Gertrude Zahler (her husband Max was now entirely absorbed, in Goldman's opinion, by his chain grocery store), and two new friends: Gordon Whitehead (an Englishman but, Goldman reported, the most animated one she had ever encountered), and Mrs Anna Aron. But for Goldman the dominant consideration continued to be the lack of effective contact between this community and the English-speaking population of the city. For Goldman, Montreal's two solitudes of Montreal were Anglo and Jewish; for her, the French Canadian majority did not exist, or existed only as some shadowy miasma, the element that made Montreal "Catholic-ridden" and forbidding. The crowds of young people at her lectures on sex and birth control were encouraging, but for these talks she found it difficult to book space, a circumstance she blamed on the Catholics. On 4 December, after four English lectures and a number of well-attended Yiddish ones, she reported to Berkman that she had earned a surplus of only $3.95 from the former and $90 from the latter. Five days later she wrote to Emmy that "my heart is no longer in the efforts in Canada. The damned country has taken it out of me. I am only thinking how to pull along until April when my fate is to be decided between America for six months and France for good."[8]

To make life easier, she kept considering an earlier-than-planned return to Toronto, where friends were numerous and where, she believed, living was cheaper by half. In Montreal "the poorest furnished apartment costs [between] $45 and fifty a month".[9] The one she found on Tupper Avenue (after staying initially at the Ford Hotel) was noisy, especially in the mornings, when workers set out through the streets just when she was trying to sleep after long hours of lecture preparation and letter-writing. When Emmy reproached her for not returning to France for Christmas, Goldman replied in torment that there was no work and no money for her there. At this same time, on 13 December, her brother Herman died, and Goldman's distress was augmented by her cruel exclusion from the United States, when it seemed to her that the new temporary visa she was seeking could have, and by now should have, been granted.

Throughout the month she carried on epistolary discussions over the state of affairs in Spain, various then-current books on history and sociology, the sway Russian communism continued to hold over radicals and youthful idealists in North America, the activities of Heiner and other anarchists in Chicago, and the progress of her anarchist group in Toronto. As well, she mediated a serious dispute at long range. Although Berkman had returned to translating Rocker's book, Rocker, discovering that Berkman was trimming the text, objected angrily that it must be rendered in full. Goldman tried to smooth things over by letter, excusing Berkman's slow progress on the ground of illness. At the same time, she wrote to Berkman, excoriating Rocker's stubborn refusal to condense. She confided to them both how much she wanted to be in France again so that the project could be completed.

Almost immediately on arriving in Montreal, Goldman began pressing Roger Baldwin again for action on her US visa. Conditions were so terrible for her in Canada, and her income from lectures and writing so small, she said, that unless she could get into the States to work she would have to return to Europe. Baldwin soon replied that the Department of Labor seemed unlikely to consider a return even in April; anti-alien and anti-radical feeling in the country was mounting, making a government gesture towards Goldman politically out of the question. Goldman continued for a time trying to find someone of influence to intercede for her. Despite the hopeless prospect, her determination was briefly redoubled when on 14 February 1935 her beloved brother Moe, who had been seriously ill throughout the winter, suffered a blood clot in a kidney and lingered for about three weeks in critical condition, apparently near death. She did not want to leave North American while Moe was ill nor to accept that her being barred from the US prevented her going to him. Then, in the second week of March, she heard from Stella that Moe had experienced a "miraculous"[10] recovery. By 14 March, Goldman was able to report to Milly Rocker that he was out of hospital.

Another reason for clinging to the visa application was the difficulty of giving up hope of renewed contact with Frank Heiner, even as this motive now began to weaken in face of her realistic assessment of the overwhelming barriers to their relationship. From Montreal, she at first wrote him that she finally had mastered the terrible agonies she suffered immediately after he left her in Toronto. She feared to entertain any feelings for him again, since they could not be together. In her unhappiness she returned again and again to the comfort she felt in sharing herself with him and her letters called out for some brief renewal. But when Mary Heiner left Chicago to look for work in Oregon, and Heiner's letters became even more passionate in their expressions of praise and love, Goldman drew back. Heiner's hopes that somehow they could meet again were now unwelcome. Goldman explained to Emmy that Heiner was too dependent on his wife for the separation of the two to be anything but temporary. Heiner himself confessed that if Mary found something worthwhile in Oregon, he would follow her there. Goldman determined to cut herself free from one more North American entanglement.

Another obstacle, however, effectively blocked her return to France: she had earned so little money that she could not afford the fare. Anxious inquiries from friends, including Leon Malmed and Ben Reitman, suggest that she was having difficulties keeping up her usual determination. When Reitman reproached her for not writing, she replied, "Canada is suitable for being buried in and nothing more, someday it may show some feeling but not yet."[11] Her misery and hopelessness made her see her current Canadian situation as a sort of never-to-be-resolved paradox: intolerable and inescapable. As was often the case in the circuitous, repetitive, and slowly evolving course of Goldman's deliberations on personal matters, the way ahead that she eventually chose was an element already present but almost unnoticed for weeks. Already in December, when the Berkman-Rocker tiff erupted, Jeanne Levey of Chicago, who was concerned in the project to get Rocker's book translated, had written her that she, Levey, would provide the fare to Europe, and had reported later in the same month that she had already raised $250 for the purpose.

Levey wanted Goldman in France soon to help Berkman with his translation. At the same time, she asked Goldman to consider a new writing project of her own, suggesting that a book on the great men and women Goldman had known would command a wide audience. Goldman soon received letters from Heiner, Berkman and others encouraging her to undertake the project. The course Levey offered was the one Goldman finally seized on as her rescue. With Levey's assurances of money, she decided in February that she would go to Europe, and booked passage for early May, making arrangements for a brief return from Montreal to Toronto before

sailing. She found that US friends, perhaps touched by the impossibility of
having her return, had now become active in support of her new book
project. A letter campaign on its behalf was started in early March, when
she was winding up her Montreal drama lectures and preparing her brief
farewell trip to Toronto, and perhaps she and others envisioned a sort of
reprise of the *Living My Life* episode, in which she would live in France as
a distinguished author, recoup her prestige, and relieve friends' worries
over her future.

Goldman had one more shock to endure before departing. In February,
Berkman suggested that she sell Bon Esprit. He had a buyer for it, he said,
and she could probably live much more cheaply in Nice than she did there.
She dismissed the suggestion at once. The St Tropez cottage represented
security for her, and for them too. Despite the practical troubles they had
had in the past living together, she felt the future would be different, due to
the new understanding the three of them were now enjoying, the love that
filled their letters, including those that had gone back and forth between
Goldman and Emmy in recent months. But Berkman insisted on pushing
the sale; Goldman steadfastly refused. Shortly after, Berkman wrote to reveal the motive for his unexpected idea: he and Emmy were in financial
crisis. The utilities in their Nice apartment about to be cut off, they had sold
everything they could, and they were going without food, which was ag-
gravating Emmy's stomach problems. They could find nowhere else to live
in Nice. As for the cottage in St Tropez, it was out of reach due to French
restrictions on Berkman's movements (his initial reticence on which fact
had created much of the startling, enigmatic quality of his sudden suggestion to sell).

In early March, Berkman telegraphed Michael Cohn: "Broke and in debt.
Giving up apartment. Urgently need seventy-five dollars. Please cable."[12]
Cohn sent the money. When Goldman reproached Berkman and told Emmy
that she must stop selling her clothes, Berkman replied that asking for
money was hard and that he had waited as long as he could before doing
so. Goldman set about canvassing friends to donate consistently to Berkman
at least enough to pay for rent and adequate food. She was soon successful
at least in having occasional amounts provided to him. Nonetheless he
kept pressing her to sell the cottage and she kept refusing, preferring that he
petition French authorities for permission to reside outside the Nice area.
On 30 March she told a correspondent, with premature optimism, that the
police had allowed this, but on 8 April Berkman wrote that in fact he had
been refused the right to enter St Tropez and now was virtually a prisoner
in Nice.

In the midst of this new crisis, Goldman travelled to Toronto; by 18 March she was reestablished in Maurice and Becky Langbord's home at 471 Brunswick Avenue, writing letters and organizing lectures. During her brief stay (she was to return to Montreal on 22 April), she set up four English lectures on consecutive Tuesdays, beginning 20 March with "The Element of Sex in Life"; it attracted 183 persons. She also arranged Yiddish lectures for 25 March and 14 April (and on 11 April she spoke on birth control in Hamilton). On 27 March, after the first two lectures, she wrote to Frank Heiner that the "meetings here are as disheartening as those in Montreal. . . . My disappointment in Canada is so painful because I put so much effort and work into each lecture." And the following day she informed W.S. Van Valkenburg, "The only question is how long one can go on working for landlords, newspaper advertising and printing. That is all I have done in Canada."[13]

Throughout her 1933–35 North American sojourn, the success of communism, both in nearly monopolizing the attention of radicals and progressives and in neutralizing her own personal impact, had been a frequent theme of her reflections. Now it was repeated in explanation of the meager response she had felt in Canada during the past seven months. "We couldn't reach the workers largely because of the Communist boycott against me" was the opinion she sent to Anna Olay. In fact, communists had abandoned direct disruption and now simply exploited their advantages of wealth, publicity, and organization. "It is insidious because it is done under cover and after all they have papers and facilities because of ever ready funds at their disposal. Time on end they have arranged meetings for the particular evening on which my lectures were announced. They did that last Sunday [25 March] in this city when I had a Jewish meeting. They had a free meeting in the largest hall in town against War and Fascism. As their speaker they had Norman Thomas and a lot of other big guns. Naturally, everybody went there."[14]

Her frustrations surfaced in dissatisfactions with her old Toronto Jewish friends, perhaps augmented by the busy social dance they led her before her return to Montreal. She had hoped to have at least a week in Toronto to rest and prepare for the trip to France but she was taken to "these private dinners which take up time and mean very little." Even the most faithful of Torontonians annoyed her. Maurice Langbord, with whom she was lodging, was "eaten up with egocentrism"; although he was "kindness personified", his motivation was "self aggrandizement" and "to shine somehow as if he were really doing anything".[15]

Such exaggerations seem to have been prompted by the fact that the undeniable energy and commitment of Langbord and others were not dedicated exclusively to anarchism but in fact were oriented more towards organized labour groups. "In fact there is no [Toronto anarchist] group", Goldman complained bitterly to Berkman. "Our comrades belong to one of the Arbeiter Ring branches. True they got that branch to back some of their [anarchist] undertakings. But nothing compared to the work they give the Arb Ring. Especially Langbord who works himself sick for that organization. He it was who built their camp and who slaves for it all summer." In early 1927, Goldman had written glowingly in *Freedom* about the establishment of this camp and its programme of radical education for the young. Her frustration even boiled over into friction with the ever-faithful Joe Desser, to whom she later apologized from Montreal: "I do hope that you will get over your hurt. That you will realize that our work is more important than personal grievance. It is so important that you do, now that we have gathered a few people to our ranks."[16] The "few" were the members of her new anarchist group, which included Dorothy Rogers, Bortolotti and his Italian comrades, the Meelises, and other recent recruits.

On 22 April, she returned to Montreal to prepare for her departure. She was to board the *Ascania* on 3 May and reach Le Havre on the eleventh. The two weeks before sailing were given to social events and her dealing with three committees, of which she had become the focus during the last several weeks: one to organize her Montreal farewell banquet, another formed at Jeanne Levey's instigation to raise $3,000 for her to write her book on famous persons, the third formed at her own prompting to secure donations for Berkman. Gifts were slow in coming for her book project in response to the letter sent to many liberals and progressives over the signature of a distinguished body including John Dewey, Gilbert Seldes, Dorothy Canfield Fisher, and Roger Baldwin. Money, however, did begin to flow to Berkman. The only entirely successful committee was the one arranging her banquet at the Tudor Hall, highlighted by a programme of musicians and singers, "an artistic treat of the highest order", replete with scores of telegrams, letters, and gifts from across the continent. With hopes that the quasi-anarchist drama league that she had formed in Montreal and the anarchist group in Toronto would survive in her absence, Goldman boarded ship the day after this "wonderful farewell evening".[17]

One result of Goldman's US tour had been that the major writings of her late career, apart from *Living My Life*, were produced in Canada, largely in Toronto during summer 1934, in the rooms on Bloor Street which she had rented partly for work, partly for meeting with Frank Heiner. There she produced, often in close epistolary consultation with Berkman, three long essays and a shorter but important statement on the world's political refugees in the period after the First World War, "The Tragedy of the Political Exiles", first published in the *Nation* in October 1934. "Was My Life Worth Living?" followed in *Harper's* in December. Between these two dates, Goldman heard that "The Forgotten Individual" and "My Impressions of American and the New Deal" had been rejected by *Scribners*, the *Atlantic Monthly*, *Forum*, and the *American Mercury*. "My Impressions" was never published but formed the basis of lectures. "The Forgotten Individual", the essay originally rejected by *Harper's* as "a philosophical treatise", was published in December as a pamphlet, *The Place of the Individual in Society*, by the Free Society Forum, a group including Frank Heiner. Finally, an essay she called "our Communist article" in her correspondence to Berkman was published by the *American Mercury* but in a mutilated form that involved her in controversy.

These essays, especially the first three, form a group that continues the self-assessment and self-justification begun in *Living My Life*. The writing of her autobiography was largely a positive attempt, undertaken in hope, to reclaim centre stage and renew her power to animate an effective mass movement. Since then, the scene had darkened. Economic depression enveloped the world, weakening the status and the resolve of workers and further directing all attention to the simplistic capitalism v communism contention. To this had been added the sounds of extreme reaction, especially fascism and Naziism. Transatlantic politics had come to be dominated by tyrannies of the left and right: the dictatorships in Russia and Italy had further established themselves and the terrible one in Germany had arisen. As time passed, anarchism was pushed to the margins everywhere but in Spain. In the seven years since she had set out to retell her story, Goldman had grown old. She was not the only one to notice. When the mass press occasionally turned its eye towards her, she was usually regarded as an interesting example of indomitable futility and irrelevance or else lumped with the Reds and cited as an example of apostasy from their ranks that proved the argument against Stalinist Russia and communism, as though no other radicalism existed. Her late writings scanned this devastated landscape for hope and attempted to refute the notion that her time had passed. On the contrary, her day was coming, it was the future, although she had to acknowledge the present darkness. "The Tragedy of Political Exiles" looked back to a golden age of agitation for freedom, the late nineteenth and early twentieth centuries, when many countries gave haven and allowed free movement to radicals who, "[n]o matter how great their sufferings . . . could arouse public opinion in their place of refuge against the tyranny and oppression practiced in their country, . . . help their comrades in prison with large funds contributed by the workers and liberal elements . . . even ship guns and ammunition into Czarist Russia, despotic Italy, and Spain." For the present, however, the world had been "turned into a huge penitentiary" under worldwide "political conditions . . . more despotic and inhuman than during the worst period of the Czars. The war for democracy [i.e., the First World War] and the advent of left and right dictatorships destroyed whatever freedom of movement political refugees had previously enjoyed." In the 1930s, "every country is afraid of the bolshevik or the fascist germ and keeps the frontier hermetically sealed, even against those who hate every form of dictatorship." She acknowledged that the recent flow of radical refugees from Austria, Germany, Russia, Italy, Poland, Hungary, Rumania, Yugoslavia and "other lesser countries" indicated that "these lands have become the graveyard of revolutionary and libertarian ideals". The essay pointed to the longer ones in linking Bolshevik communism, German and Italian fascism, and supporters of Moscow. The left and right dictatorships proceeded not only by authoritarianism, coercion and terror, but also by all the tools of publicity and propaganda; "character assassination" was added to butchery, and all political opponents, including in Russia the greatest freedom-fighters surviving from the czarist period, were "maligned, misrepresented, dubbed with vile names, and hounded without mercy". In the West, many who condemned fascism "remained indifferent to the Golgotha of the Russian politicals" or even justified it. "All these good people are under the spell of the soviet myth" and would protest "brutalities in capitalist countries when they are condoning the same brutalities in the Soviet Republic".[18] Thus the left and right dictatorships had polarized world politics, and the great tyranny on the left, the Soviet Union, had largely destroyed the world libertarian and revolutionary movement by making Bolshevism dominant and thus making all radicalism seem a tool of Soviet goals.

"Was My Life Worth Living?" and "The Place of the Individual in Society" in large part presented her view of the main mechanisms of control that had evolved in the capitalist and bourgeois democracies. These countries had developed and imposed on their populations a mass personality-type that was modeled on the machines and machine-like techniques that had delivered unprecedented comfort and power. "In fact, the pattern of life has become standardized, routinized and mechanized like canned food and Sunday sermons", she wrote in "Was My Life Worth Living?". The "hundred-percent American" of the then-current catch phrase "easily swallows syndicated information and factory-made ideas and beliefs. He thrives on the wisdom given him over the radio and cheap magazines by corporations whose philanthropic aim is selling America out. He accepts the standards of conduct and art in the same breath with the advertising of chewing gum, toothpaste, and shoe polish." This phenomenon was what constantly strengthened "the whole complex of authority and institutional domination which strangles life" and made Americans "so easily hoodwinked by the sanctity of law and authority".[19]

What was the positive of all this negative? Goldman placed herself with the American heroes, inherently or explicitly anarchist, such as Thoreau and Whitman, who "in the face of persecution and obloquy have lived and fought for their right and the right of mankind to free and unstinted expression". She too had been "deprived of most of the comforts society offers to ability and talent, but denies when they will not be subservient". Yet she had managed to express herself. Such persons bore witness to the fact that anarchism was the most "practical philosophy that has yet been thought of in its application to individual expression and the relation it establishes between the individual and society", making it "too vital and too close to human nature ever to die". But what of the objection that unchanging human nature itself contained the worship of authority she had just criticized? Human nature, she asserted, could change and shake off this slavishness, for its one unchanging, essential, and dominant element was love of freedom, a "craving for liberty and self-expression". Because anarchism "alone stresses the importance of the individual, his possibilities and needs in a free society", it alone "propagates uncompromising rebellion"[20] against right and left, capitalism and communism, democracy and state socialism, with their fundamental agreement on the necessity of government, authority, hierarchy, and privilege, supported by coercion and thought-control.

"The Place of the Individual in Society" further develops many of these points, and makes perhaps the strongest statement of her doctrine that the individual is the basis of society, an idea that had grown in importance with her as she had been forced to accept the waning of organized anarchism. Every form of dictatorship, she wrote, is an "attack on civilization", which in its true sense has always been "a continuous struggle of the individual or of groups of individuals against the State and even against 'society,' that is, against the majority subdued and hypnotized by the State and State worship". Individuality is "the consciousness of the individual as to what he is and how he lives." It is a living and growing thing. Its essence is expression, and it is completely opposed to all concepts of "individualism", which are masks for "social and economic laissez faire: the exploitation of the masses by the classes by means of legal trickery, spiritual debasement and systematic indoctrination of the servile spirit". Individualism converts life into "a degrading race for externals, for possessions". Goldman linked doctrines of individualism to the social Darwinism promulgated by "self-seeking 'supermen'"[21] and to it she opposed Kropotkin's doctrine of mutual aid, founded on the scientific demonstration that cooperation, not competition alone, is a basis of nature.

To her, constitutionalism and democracy seemed modern forms of the alleged consent of human beings to domination by governmental and social systems; but all such systems are inherently conservative, stagnant, and repressive, and have never changed except as "the result of pressure exerted [by] the individual, the man of strong mind and will to liberty"— that is, by revolution whether intellectual or armed. But today the creative individual or group faces the new and terrible task of fighting the tyrannous majority or mass. "[E]ven more than constituted authority, it is social uniformity and sameness that harass the individual most" in a society in which "the wholesale mechanization of modern life" has been deployed to increase that uniformity which is the "strongest bulwark of authority". In this context, Goldman chided the "intellectual proletarian" (the professional person and the white-collar worker) who "foolishly thinks himself a free agent" but is guided by "[m]aterial considerations and desire for greater social prestige" to accept and support a political and social fabric with "no place in its texture for free choice of independent thought and activity" but only for "voting and tax-paying". Anarchism, conversely, stood for the creative individual's distinctive "[d]isobedience to every form of coercion", including the "power of privilege, of money, of the priest, of the politician or of so-called democracy". Still more importantly it stood for "[r]eal freedom ... true liberty", which is "positive: it is freedom to do something: it is the liberty to be, to do: in short, the liberty of actual and active opportunity". Alone among social theories, anarchism "steadfastly proclaims that society exists for man, not man for society".[22]

In terms reminiscent of Heywood Broun's dismissal of Goldman at the beginning of her tour, *Harper's* prefaced "Was My Life Worth Living?" with an editorial note characterizing her essay as "her last will and testament", as an "exhibit" of "*really* rugged individualism unaltered by opposition or advancing age" and as "anomalously" belonging "in the same part of the political spectrum as the gentlemen of the Liberty League"[23] (extreme conservative, pro-laissez faire, anti-government libertarians). In their brief comment, the magazine's editors offered no argument supporting these arch distortions of what the essay itself demonstrated cogently: that Goldman was still vital and opposed individualism on strong grounds, that the basic element of her doctrine was not political liberty for unrestrained economic assertiveness but rather political liberty inseparable from mutual aid and the full creative development of each person.

If *Harper's* represented the tendency to dismiss her, the *American Mercury* represented the tendency to use her. In March (after a long delay occasioned by a change of owners and editors) it printed, under the title "Communism in Russia", part of her excoriation of the Soviet Union as noncommunist both in practice and theory. But the concluding "chapter" on anarchist communism was omitted from an essay that she and Berkman had hoped would be headed "Two Communisms—Bolshevist and Anarchist" and would help reawaken the sense of an alternative revolutionary ideal. The magazine refused Goldman's request to publish an explanation in a later issue. Then, the newspapers of William Randolph Hearst, main promulgators of the anti-alien feeling that continued to make the US government refuse to readmit her, picked up the *American Mercury* piece and made it the basis of a widely republished anti-Soviet article, with a "rotten"[24] picture of her at the top. The only response she could make to this was to complain to Berkman and others, and to publish in the *Nation* a denunciation of Hearst's use of her words.

Publicly, she had put up a valiant if futile defence against the accusation of irrelevance. Privately, she was tired and often discouraged, though never to the point of pausing in her work. "Fact is dearest", she wrote to Berkman as the new year 1935 began, "we are fools. We cling to an ideal no one wants or cares about. And I am the greater fool of the two of us. I go eating out my heart and poisoning every moment of my life in the attempt to rouse people's sensibilities. At least if I could do it with closed eyes. The irony is I see the futility of my efforts and yet I can't let go." Despite her protests to Berkman that "I am as strong as a bull and I have inexhaustible energy",[25] she was tired and full of doubt as she boarded the *Ascania* to leave Canada on 3 May.

Just as in 1928, she returned to France in the expectation that she would live with Berkman and Emmy at St Tropez (Berkman finally having received permission to travel there). The couple met her at the house, which Emmy had cleaned and readied for her. But almost at once the threesome parted, Berkman and Emmy withdrawing to Nice in the face of Emma's bitter refusal, according to Berkman, to be swayed from a dark depression. Blame-laden arguments over how to better their relationship followed. In July, Goldman wrote to Berkman of her distress that they had not been pleasant with each other once in the three months since her return. Berkman, visiting her at St Tropez in August, wrote Stella that Goldman had "arrived from Canada pretty much exhausted, more mentally perhaps than physically . . . more oppressed in sprit than at any former return home. Most probably Chicago was the cause of it."[26]

But Frank Heiner was only one cause, and not the major one. Goldman wrote Roger Baldwin in June, just before her sixty-sixth birthday, "It is indeed disgraceful to be rooted to the soil of one country. Perhaps one cannot adjust oneself easily in later life as one does in one's youth. Whatever the reason I have to admit defeat. The ninety days of my return dispelled whatever doubts I had on that score. I know now I will remain an alien abroad for the rest of my life. Not a happy feeling." Goldman also revealed she was no longer considering writing the book on famous personalities from her past. Not only was the world uninterested, but she was pessimistic about her chances to work again with Berkman. "While he looks much better than I had expected from the reports I got all last year, he is far from strong."[27] The translation of Rocker's work was all that they could expect from him.

Goldman at last simply withdrew from the troubling conflict with Berkman and Emmy. In September, she began planning to return to England to lecture; she wrote C.V. Cook that she remained committed to revolution and in her English tour would oppose war as she had in the past. Repeating an analysis, inherent in her Canadian lectures, of the German Social Democrats after the so-called revolution in 1918, she stated that war against a nation was an ineffective way to prompt social change; only a native movement could address a country's problems.

In October, she left St Tropez for Paris and there received word that Berkman was seriously ill. She decided to go ahead with her trip, but asked Berkman for an account of his health, and angrily questioned his secretiveness when he admitted that he probably had some kind of prostate problem. From London on 19 November, his sixty-fifth birthday, she wrote him that

the one treasure I have rescued from my long and bitter struggle is my friendship with you. . . . I know of no other value, whether in people or achievements, than your presence in my life and the love and affection you have roused. True, I loved other men. I love Frank with a silly, but nonetheless intense emotion. . . . Such an abiding feeling could be better explained if you had always been all tenderness or understanding. But you were not that. On the contrary, you were and are still often harsh and lacking in comprehension of the interior motivations of my acts. But all that is as nothing compared with the force you have been from the moment I first heard your voice and met you in Sach's cafe and all through the forty-five years of our comradeship. I seem to have been born then as woman, mother, comrade and friend. Yes, I believe my strongest and most compelling feeling for you is that of the mother. . . . Men have come and gone in my long life. But you my dearest will remain forever.[28]

Shortly after, she announced to Heiner that their correspondence was interfering with her work; she had no hope anymore of their reunion and would finally have to make a complete break with him for the sake of concentration.

In January 1936, she was disgusted by England's display of grief over the death of King George V, with even the "radical Jews" following the crowd; only "our few [anarchist] comrades" escaped the stain of the "fake" public emotion. Events such as lectures were being cancelled; one of her own, which she held despite the general trend in order to stand out against "such cringing chauvinism", was quite poorly attended. Berkman wrote admiringly that their struggle in the United States together had never been so difficult as Goldman's in England: "It is clear that you have not a very easy field to hoe in England. But it will be the same in England or in the US."[29] An additional annoyance for Goldman was that, as during her 1924–26 English sojourn, she was again being criticized for writing in capitalist publications, an easy charge for pro-Moscow opponents to make in light of her recent essay in *Harper's* and the use of her *American Mercury* article by the Hearst newspapers.

In letters throughout the winter of 1935–36, Berkman and Goldman argued about whether the Spanish anarchists should participate in the elections of 16 February, to help oust the reactionary government that had been elected due to their non-participation in the vote of November 1933. In the event, most radical elements, including anarchist organizations, joined in voting against the conservatives, resulting in the formation of a Popular Front government. Berkman wrote Goldman on 21 March, "Just briefly, for I know you are busy [with work in England]—obviously I am opposed to cooperating with the Communists. But in Spain it seems that the present victory of the radical elements is due to our people having helped them with their votes." Goldman replied a few days later from London, "I cannot agree with the suggestion that anarchists should in grave times cooperate with communists in elections" and denied that the core of the anarchist movement in Spain, the CNT, actually had done so. "We would be spitting ourselves in the face if we approved participation in elections. Fighting

ALL POWER AND ALL GOVERNMENT AS WE DO, how can we help [by] putting anyone into positions of power?" In directly considering the Spanish anarchists (Berkman was relaying his and Goldman's opinions on this point to Spanish colleagues and arguing the question with them), she was willing to take a liberal view: "Every country imposes different methods in certain emergencies. We can only state our own position toward the fundamentals of anarchism. And that has always been opposition to the slick political machine that has ever corrupted the best of people or has paralyzed their efforts to serve the masses."[30]

On 11 February, Berkman had his first prostate operation; Goldman remained in England. His health worsened, as did Emmy's, and on 5 March Berkman asked Goldman to return and help, in view of a stomach operation performed on Emmy. After delaying briefly, Goldman replied she was coming but stayed in England a little longer to complete scheduled engagements. Her 15 March lecture in Coventry drew 1,000 persons; the group was "more responsive than any audience I ever had" in England. Before she arrived in southern France, Berkman had undergone, on 23 March, a second prostate operation. In a letter written that day, he stated, "I have lived my life and I am really of the opinion that when one has neither health nor means and cannot work for his ideas, it is time to clear out."[31] At his request Goldman went to Nice to care for Emmy and for him while he was in hospital. As soon as he returned to his apartment in early June, she withdrew to Bon Esprit.

Seemingly, it was only when apart that they could glory in their mutual love and respect, and Goldman carried the burden that the other two blamed her for this failure. Her return to Bon Esprit alone was a grim period for her; she was isolated personally and politically, lacking all prospects for constructive work or a way to earn her keep. After having insisted in 1934 and 1935 on hanging on to the cottage, she now arranged for its sale. The only place in the world she possessed in which to live inexpensively had proved a failure as a place to work. If she had achieved success with *Living My Life*, if she had been able to return from North America with the celebrity to continue publishing articles, or if the book about famous persons from her past had interested anyone, then she might have been able to remain. But without such work there was no way to live. She was planning to leave, but for where? Palestine? Nice? Paris? In June, her concern over whether she could resurrect herself one more time showed in her letters. She dismissed as only a cultural prejudice the belief that love is impossible for middle-aged women. "I could give you some examples of men of thirty-five having fallen in love with women of sixty. Why not, if the women are attractive, have a young spirit, have a fine and alert mind, and are emotionally strong."[32]

For her sixty-seventh birthday, 27 June, Berkman had planned to come to St Tropez to surprise her but at the last minute decided that he could not make the trip. Celebrating the day with the visiting Dr Michael Cohn and his family, she received a telephone call from Berkman, who assured her that he was feeling better and looked forward to their next meeting. At 2 a.m. on Sunday the twenty-eighth, she received a telephone message from Nice that Berkman had been shot the previous night and was dying. Goldman and Cohn struggled through the complex bus schedules to get to Nice, where they found Berkman in hospital, paralyzed and scarcely able to speak. Emmy, in "a collapse",[33] had been taken to a police station by officers who suspected her of the shooting. Goldman wrote, at Berkman's dictation, an account of what, he said, had in fact happened. He had suffered a terribly painful episode, and Emmy had left the apartment fearfully to find a doctor. While she was out, Berkman had shot himself in the chest. Having signed this document, Berkman lived only a few more hours. Goldman passed the morning and afternoon with him; he died at 10 p.m. Sunday.

The distrust in which Berkman and Emmy were held, which he had often resented as a burden on their quiet, withdrawn lives, was evident in official treatment of his case. Despite his statement, and the evidence of neighbours who saw Emmy seeking a doctor at the time of the shot, the death was treated as suspicious and the request to have his body cremated was denied. He was buried instead. Partly as a result of Goldman's insistent demonstration of the facts, Emmy was freed. Goldman never would forgive her. Why had Emmy left Berkman alone? But even more than she blamed Emmy, she blamed herself. Berkman left a bitter legacy for Goldman: the memory that he had killed himself on her birthday, his expectation that she would provide for Emmy, and his withdrawal from her life. His suicide gave a new dimension to her accusation of injustice against the world. Why had life not allowed her to accomplish what she might have done? In this case, she could have and should have saved him. Guilt had been a cornerstone of their lives ever since the days of the attempt on Henry Clay Frick, when Berkman had gone to jail and Goldman had not been charged. Now she had to assume the guilt of his poignant death. The man against whom every other was measured and found wanting was gone. One of the great friendships, partnerships, and love affairs of the twentieth century was over. Its pitiable end seemed an indictment of all their hopes that freedom to think, to speak, and to love would inevitably bring about a better world.

11

The Spanish Civil War

On 17 July 1936, less than a month after Berkman's suicide, the Spanish Civil War began with a military uprising against the Popular Front coalition elected only four months earlier. Attempts by army units to seize control in many parts of the country, beginning with soldiers stationed in Spanish Morocco, were opposed by workers and local militia groups. After the initial uprising, the Republic retained about half the country, with Madrid still operating as the capital but with Catalonia in the northeast, and Barcelona its capital, the core of resistance. Francisco Franco, stationed in the Canary Islands at the time of the initial uprising, soon joined the army in Morocco and led a successful invasion of the mainland. He was accepted as the leader of the fascist-supported forces by 1 October.

On 18 August, Augustine Souchy, secretary of the Comite Anarcho-Syndicalist, invited Goldman to support the Spanish anarchists by operating a press service and propaganda bureau in London on behalf of the CNT-FAI (National Confederation of Labour—Anarchist Federation of Iberia). He encouraged her to visit Barcelona to gather firsthand information about the community there, which was operating on anarchist principles. She wrote Stella at once, "Believe me my heart jumped and the crushing weight that was pressing down on my heart since Sasha's death left me as by magic."[1] She would remain devoted to the cause of the Spanish anarchists to the end of her life.

Goldman went to Barcelona in September 1936. This, the first of her three visits to Spain during the Civil War, was full of bright hope. The Barcelona anarchists were in control of the city; on every side she saw proof that anarchism could create a healthy society without a costly period of violence. She was delighted by all she encountered. She addressed a meeting of 10,000 people, saying that they were a "shining example to the rest of the world", adding: "I have come to you as to my own . . . for your ideal has been my ideal for forty-five years and it will remain [so] to my last breath."[2] She visited collective farms and factories, travelled to the front lines in the neighbouring province of Aragon, and climbed to mountaintop village schools where the kind of creative educational practices she had been preaching for years were being implemented.

When she returned to England to open the office of information, however, she found life in London as a propagandist disturbingly slow. Great Britain already had declared itself neutral in the Spanish conflict; France and the US soon followed. The commonplace characterization of the Spanish Civil War as a "dress rehearsal" for the Second World War fails to take into account that, while Franco's army was fortified by men and machinery from Hitler and Mussolini, the duly elected government of the Spanish Republic received help from only one of the future Allied powers, Stalin's Soviet Union. For Goldman, the presence of communists in Spain's Popular Front, and the growing influence they held due to Stalin's aid, brought forebodings of betrayals such as those the anarchists had met during the Russian Revolution. Her perspective on the war, which was neither fascist nor communist but rather anarchist, and Catalonian anarchist in particular, made every rapprochement with the Popular Front doubtful on principle. Yet, with anarchists already engaged in battle, she was unwilling to second-guess their decisions publicly, although many of her most intimate associates, including Rudolf Rocker, attacked her for her silence. In private, she argued strongly to the Spanish anarchists that they must not make league with the communists. In public, however, she deferred to their decision, and did not enunciate her principle, which was based on knowledge of communist duplicity and destructiveness to the radical cause dating back to her time in Russia. Only after the collapse of the Spanish Republic did she fully denounce the role of Stalin and international communism. She made the experience of Spain a chief theme of her prophetic warnings against communism, while always remaining careful to make the distinction that "many of the Communists in the International Brigade were sincere idealists who fought heroically [and] were wounded, some mortally"[3] alongside the anarchists.

In May 1937, the communist campaign for control of the Popular Front, which so many anarchists had predicted, and which Goldman now admitted publicly she had feared, led to street fighting in Barcelona. Goldman was in England at the time of the attack on the anarchist-operated telephone exchange and other facilities. She said afterwards that she prized the narrative of the fighting, the only accurate account of what was really happening in Spain, in George Orwell's *Homage to Catalonia* (1938). Orwell's name appears as a member of Goldman-organized relief committees in the months that followed.

She visited Barcelona two more times, in autumn 1937 and in late summer 1938; during the second visit, she received messages of good will from H.M. Caiserman through Samuel Abramson, a young Montrealer in the International Brigades. Abramson had been on the lookout for Goldman for some months at the request of Caiserman, who had heard from her that spring, a postcard from St Tropez wishing him well and inviting him to stay if he came to France. Abramson, who had joined the Canadian Jewish Congress with Caiserman's encouragement before going to Spain, reported that Goldman was "looking younger than ever".[4] He praised the work she was doing for the Spanish in London and sent her good wishes back to Caiserman and to Rabbi Harry J. Stern.

In the letter, Abramson also mentioned that the International Brigades would soon be disbanded and that he planned to return to Canada to work for the Spanish cause. By December, Franco's troops were in Catalonia, driving the Republican army towards the French border. On 5 March 1939, the Republican government left Spain for exile in France, where an estimated 500,000 soldiers and civilians were already in refugee camps. Despite repeated assertions that the revolution was not over, Goldman was now largely confined to attempting to help anarchist refugees to safety in France and elsewhere.

In the early months of 1939, Goldman again decided to abandon England for Canada. In Paris, she attended a meeting of the Republican government in exile, and also visited Amsterdam to put her own and Berkman's papers in order at the archives of the International Institute for Social History. Such diplomatic and housekeeping chores attended to, she turned her thoughts to Canada. She saw it as the best way to find substantial help for the Spanish refugees. But she was under no illusions. "I confess", she wrote, "I am not very sanguine about my chances there, but it will be change which I need very much indeed, and perhaps I can succeed for my heroic Spaniards."[5] She was also drawn once again to the country partly by the hope that she would be able to see family and friends from the US if not actually enter the States; the matter was of special importance to her, because her niece Stella was hospitalized for depression.

Goldman secured passage to Canada for 8 April aboard the Cunard liner *Alaunia* and travelled to Paris to make final arrangements with the Spanish organizations there for continuing her work from North America. On her return to London, she met 160 refugees booked on the same boattrain and ship and spent her final week in England trying to lodge them and organizing a committee to operate on their behalf in her absence. She considered delaying her departure, but could not find a place on a later vessel and would not consider remaining in what seemed to her a dead country. Her feelings for the total body of refugees were intensified by this new encounter with a few of them: "the appalling misery and inner demoralisation among our Spanish comrades here have affected me to such an extent, it brought back my heart trouble in a more acute form",[6] she wrote to Rudolf and Milly Rocker in New York, referring to a troubling health problem, sketchily defined in existing documents. In an August 1939 letter from Toronto to her US friend Hutchins Hapgood, the Chicago novelist who was also one of the first members of the Provincetown Players, she wrote:

> I can tell you now that Spain made the profoundest impression on me of anything that ever happened in my life—much more so than the Russian Revolution. Perhaps it was because in Spain the anarcho-syndicalists and anarchists as represented in the National Confederation of Labor and the Anarchist Federation of Iberia had made the first experiment in constructive work. I do not mean to say that their collectivization was complete Anarchy. Far from it. But it was the nearest beginning that ever happened in the history of the social struggle. You can readily see therefore why I was carried away and why I pinned my faith to my comrades in Spain. Alas it was expecting the superhuman for a group of people even if they had a membership of nearly three million to stand out against the conspiracy of the democracies, the treachery of the Soviet Government, lastly but not least the indifference of the international proletariat. And yet while the Spanish people have been defeated they are not conquered. Unlike the German and Italian people the Spanish militants love liberty beyond life itself. They continue their struggle even in a guerilla way and they will never be content until they have conquered Fascism. It is my abiding faith in my Spanish comrades which helps me to go on regardless of all disappointments and difficulties.[7]

"I shall want to speak on the betrayal of Spain as my first lecture", Goldman wrote from London to Dorothy Rogers in Toronto on 12 March. Desperate for useful work, she arrived in Montreal on 17 April to little public notice and little activity. No fundraising event was held on behalf of the Spanish. She described the Montreal of 1939 as "fascist ridden" and, as ever, "Catholic ridden". The province's controversial 1937 padlock law, named for the padlock with which police sealed a building that had been raided, was still in force, and Goldman described to Rogers the power that Maurice Duplessis' government had given police "to fight Communism": they could "break into your house, collect what they consider Communist literature and disperse a gathering which they interpret as a secret section, though it may be a christening, birthday party, or a wedding". She hesitated about getting together with Montreal friends, even privately, for fear she might bring down such raids, but she did stay a few days with her old friend Rose Bernstein. She began sending letters to people in the United States, including Harry Weinberger, Leon Malmed, Rose Pesotta, and Fitzi Fitzgerald, but by 21 April had moved on to Toronto to a far different, livelier welcome. Anarchists "in full force"[8] met her at Union Station, and the press covered her arrival enthusiastically and announced her first lecture, scheduled for 27 April at the Odd Fellows Hall.

The next six weeks in Toronto were busy with lecturing and making ambitious plans for autumn tours in the West. Her first talk seemed an encouraging beginning. She raised $64.50 for Spanish refugees, and her message was delivered not only to those who attended but also through extensive newspaper accounts. Spain, she said, had been betrayed by Stalin, but equally by England, France, and the other democracies, and she issued distinct and dire warnings of what would inevitably follow from this failure to oppose fascist dictators bravely. The Spanish people had been defeated, she continued, but not conquered. Perhaps the most positive aspect of the lecture, she reported in a letter, was "the relief I felt for the first few years in speaking". She had been fearful at every word in England, but in Toronto "had no such fears, and my voice rang out free and strong as in the olden days".[9]

More lectures in English and Yiddish followed, along with a brief trip to Windsor in mid-May. Although she reported with disappointment that the visit did not raise enough money to do more than cover expenses, and that communist sympathizers frequently interrupted her speeches, still she was pleased by the coverage in both Windsor and Detroit newspapers. The articles were exactly the type of propaganda she was looking for, in that they detailed her attitude toward Spain and her hope for a continuation of the revolutionary spirit and work she had found there. Her position on warfare—opposition to war but support of revolution, even in the face of fascism—was well stated, and she sent the articles to many friends in the United States. Newspapers now provided an even more attentive forum for her views than they had during her previous Toronto stays, probably for a variety of reasons. There was her renewed prominence due to the Spanish Civil War and also the increasing threat of war and the now undeniable relevance of her long-enunciated analysis of Stalin, Mussolini, and Hitler. There was also perhaps a certain familiarity she enjoyed as an established figure on the Canadian scene. Just as in 1926, the Toronto *Daily Star* interviewed her fresh off the train and ran a long story the following day, 22 April, reminding citizens of her history with the city:

> Emma Goldman, heading into her 70th year, still talking anarchy in her deep, throaty voice, her home still in her suitcase, arrived in Toronto last night, this time to fight a battle for Spanish refugees. Grey hair peeping from under her hat, a grim smile still arriving on her features exactly at the moment photographers' bulbs flashed, Emma seemed to have changed not a whit since last she was in Toronto fighting battles for birth control.

The unbylined story describes her getting off the train "in her soft felt hat and neat ulster, umbrella in hand, spectacles perched above rosy cheeks, [looking] like anyone's kindly grandmother".[10]

Goldman immediately sounded her theme of Spain's betrayal by Stalin, by communists allied to or in line with Russia, and by the non-fascist nations. Not the real communists "but the kind Russia produces" were responsible for the collapse of the Spanish Republic, together with intervention by fascist dictators and lack of help from democracies. Real communists, she stated, are not "extremists" and, further, there were "no communists in Russia", just "opportunists". In Spain, she said, communists "claimed to belong in the anti-Fascist front, but they only wanted to impose their own dictatorship [and] undermined everything the people did".[11] The behaviour of the Spanish anarchists stood in vivid contrast to that of the communists as an example of true devotion to freedom. Spain had been the story of the Russian Revolution all over again, the seizure and destruction of a true people's revolution by tyrannical Bolshevism. The ideas she enunciated to Canadian journalists are further defined by a letter she wrote from Toronto to Rudolf Rocker in May 1939:

> I hold that nothing that our comrades omitted to do to bring their actions in harmony with their ideas was so important and from a historic point of view so significant as their determination not to impose dictatorship on the Spanish people. This will weigh in the balance against any mistakes they may have made. For it is the first time in a social struggle that a group of people had the power for a dictatorship and yet refused to use it for that purpose. Thus, all these so-called practical people now say that the Spaniards have gained nothing because the other side ruled by means of a

dictatorship. But I feel certain that Posterity will evaluate this one determined and consistent step on part of the CNT-FAI, in the highest degree.[12]

The Toronto *Evening Telegram* well understood her main message. "Stalin Was Real Judas In Spain" ran the headline above its 28 April six-col-
umn story on her first English lecture, in which she not only exposed Stalin's role in the war but also continued to excoriate and cajole the German
public, comparing it unfavourably to the Spanish. By turns, she condemned
the Germans as pawns of their dictators and tried to rouse them and the
Italians against these "puppets [who] if the people would only shake themselves ... would fall off". To her audience at the Odd Fellows Temple she
proclaimed, "The Spaniards are a proud people and are still fighting for
their own freedom. They're not Germans who bow before the sight of brass
buttons." She related the non-intervention of the democracies to their fear
that their economic holdings in Spain would fall into communist hands.
Stalin, conversely, once he woke up to his opportunity three months after
the war had begun, schemed not to aid the people or defeat Franco but only
to establish a communist stronghold in Madrid. Britain's prime minister,
Neville Chamberlain, she termed "the spokesman for the Bank of England"
which "naturally preferred Franco to the Loyalists".[13]

When Goldman delivered this same message in Windsor on 19 May, the
meeting was rendered interesting by more than her incisive rhetoric and
arguments, her facts and eye-witness accounts. Heading its 20 May story
"Terms Reds 'Betrayers' ... Communists Irked", the Windsor *Star* reported
that Goldman had lectured in the city's Dom Polskie Hall with "a strong-
arm squad of 'wobblies' on hand to quell Communist-provoked disorder".
Members of Detroit Branch 440 of the Metal Machine Union, affiliated with
the Industrial Workers of the World, had voted to send a twelve-man del-
egation to Goldman's meeting to prevent communist disruptions. "We
wobblies try to help the Anarchists", explained the branch secretary, Ralph
Verlaine. The men had been "ready to go into action and throw them out if
they got rough".[14] Goldman's remarks heated emotions in the hall, provoking a battle of cheers and jeers in the audience of 350, and violence threatened when a Windsor veteran of the Spanish Civil War, Bert Levy, rose to
challenge one of Goldman's remarks. Released from hospital only the previous week after treatment of battle wounds, Levy objected emphatically to
a question, designed to taunt Goldman's hecklers, put to her by one Alan
Clark, a Detroiter sporting the red IWW button in his lapel: "How is it that
the Communists come back from the Spanish war so healthy they can get
up and talk, when the Anarcho-Syndicalists are all shot to hell?"

"Keep your yap shut", shouted Levy, "or you'll get your teeth knocked down your throat."

When Levy, claiming to speak for the International Brigades, expressed heated resentment at Goldman's statements and pointed to "the number of Spanish war victims who lost limbs or eyesight", he was assailed by boo- ing. But Goldman appealed for freedom of speech, the threat of blows faded, and Levy was allowed a parting shot: "I suggest this friend of yours, Miss Goldman, go to the hospitals in Toronto and see men without legs, or arms, or eyes."[15]

Goldman was not daunted by the difficulty of conveying the necessary distinctions between Russian and allied Bolshevik-style communists on one hand and various types of true communists (e.g., anarchists, or com- mon people longing for freedom to establish a communal way of life) on the other, or the difference between actual Stalinists and the many idealists who subscribed themselves under the banner of Russian-led international communism, in honest unawareness of its duplicity and tyranny. Despite the subtleties and passions involved, she hammered Stalin and his role in Spain on every occasion. "The Spanish people came to hate the Commu- nists and Communism even more than they hated Fascism, for they knew Fascism for what it was. The Communist regime was the great deception, the great illusion." She often brought into her lectures not only large his- torical facts or assertions but also details that had been witnessed and documented but did not thereby escape being controversial. Revealing that Stalin had sent obsolete First World War tanks, machine guns, and rifles, she was on one occasion challenged by an International Brigades veteran who had used sound Soviet equipment. Often, she responded, Soviet-allied international units and groups received decent equipment from Russia; but the Spanish people, never. Moreover, she stated, Russian interference had made sure that even relief aid, such as milk, was prevented from reach- ing Catalonia. "The real Judas Iscariot is Stalin", Goldman proclaimed, "and he will have to answer for his destructive work in the anti-Fascist struggle."[16] In the event, of course, it was not Stalin but rather the Russian people once again who had to answer with their suffering.

On 6 May, before the Windsor trip, she had moved from her first, tempo- rary residence with Esther Laddon to her own apartment in a house at 295 Vaughan Road, where various sympathizers lived in independent yet semi- communal style. Her downstairs neighbours were the Dutch anarchists Tom and Dien Meelis, among her closest and most faithful companions. The Meelises did much of Goldman's housework for her, and she delighted in "living in my own place",[17] particularly because she could have friends and family from the United States to visit. Many people did stay with her at the house—Powers Hapgood, Minna Lowensohn, Rachele Sinclair, Rose Pesotta, Harry Kelly, her brother Moe, and others—but two invitees, Ben Reitman and Leon Malmed, never came. Despite pleasures and successes, by the end of May she was discouraged again with prospects for staying in Canada. Early hopes that she might be able to cross the border to see Stella, still in hospital, were disappointed, and lecture crowds were small in Toronto. She found that the anarchist and radical community had grown still older and more cautious, that in fact parts of it had become successful, conservative, and perhaps worst of all, capitalistic; this bothered her particularly with regard to former colleagues who were Jewish. "Whether because of the lickspittle patriotism of the average Canadian whether Jew or Gentile or whether the weather was getting too warm", she wrote to Milly Rocker, "the last three weeks were a flop." Although she found some hope in the group (her friend Dorothy Rogers was now secretary and Attilio Bortolotti continued to be enthusiastic), the members were mostly unemployed and showed little spirit. She was beginning to think that she might just have to go back to Europe or to England. "It will all depend on whether I can make a tour of the west. For, it is certainly not worth while to have made an expensive trip just for Toronto, not only has this city not advanced but it has grown more conservative and most of the people as well as the Jewish comrades with them."[18] That any other place, including England, could have been more worthwhile, was pure mood and conjecture, of course. Her continuous oscillation on this point shows a no-way-out desperation akin to that of a bee in a bottle. Her impatience with Toronto was a subset of her frustration with the lack of interest in the suffering and injustice dealt to Spain, a disregard due largely, ironically, to preoccupation with the threat of which she herself had long been warning, that posed by Hitler and Mussolini. Other North Atlantic countries now feared their time to fight the dictators was coming, and this deepened the climate of reaction. Goldman already had planned, given previous experience in Toronto, to cease lecturing at the end of May and resume in the autumn; but she had wished for larger audiences. Nevertheless, she must be judged successful during 1939 in Canada. An accounting she made in January 1940 shows that, during the spring and autumn, lectures in Toronto, Windsor, and Winnipeg, plus other events she organized and donations she solicited, raised $532.34 for the Spanish refugees—a substantial sum at that time, when Goldman was living on about $1,200 a year. At her most lucrative meeting, the one in Windsor at which violence was narrowly averted, a Windsor *Star* reporter was impressed with her fundraising prowess, writing that "the audience came through nobly when 'Red' Emma, once called the most dangerous woman in America, issued a stirring appeal for aid for Spanish war refugees. No less that $86 in bills and $17.50 in silver poured to the aging woman who spoke with authority of international affairs."[19]

Goldman spent her seventieth birthday in Toronto. Tributes poured in from round the world, telegrams of praise for her long commitment, her energy, her determination. She especially prized one that arrived a little before the date, in which Mariano Vazquez of the CNT, commenting on behalf of the Spanish libertarian movement, praised her "whole life consecrated to service and the liberation of the people" and called her "our spiritual mother" whose example of "sacrifice, austerity, and constancy" he pledged to follow. On the very morning of her birthday, however, she learned from Paris that Vazquez was dead, drowned in a swimming accident during a holiday weekend. She wrote the Rockers, "I simply feel paralyzed. I do not know how I can face the little affair the comrades have arranged. For Mariano was like my own child of my own flesh and blood."[20]

The shock of Vazquez' death added to the gloom that Berkman's 1936 suicide had brought to her birthday, an occasion which for years she had taken special delight in celebrating. She had written to Ben Reitman that "it is no feast to me any longer". She went to the garden party hosted by Esther Laddon in her honour, but wrote afterward that she was "ill all day and had to hold to myself at the affair not to break down." She told the Rockers, "Alas, it was not given me to pass this day without a shadow, a double shadow this year." In her assessment, Vazquez had not been equal to Berkman in intellectual power but had been similar in spirit; and though he was given to bureaucratic methods and a tendency to compromise with governments, yet he had been pure and tirelessly dedicated in freedom's cause. He had "fanatical organizational ways [that] made him bureaucratic with people and overbearant [sic][but] this does not do away with the fact that Mariano was the most tireless worker in the CNT, religiously consecrated to the struggle, always on the height of hope and optimism of the victory of our cause. I could not help but love him though I was often driven to impatience and despair with him. And now he is no more and the Spanish movement has sustained an irreparable loss."[21]

The seventieth birthday event itself, despite the pain she was concealing, impressed her as an unusual success. She received many gifts of money, so many that it was difficult to find time for all the thank-you letters she wrote in response. Moreover there had been a spirit of togetherness at the banquet, "a real harmony", which contrasted with the customary tension she often noticed now in Toronto gatherings. In addition to many tributes received from abroad (forty-five cables and gifts of almost $900), she was liberally honoured by her Toronto associates. Maurice Langbord, she wrote to a friend, had read a beautiful "Jewish" (that is, Yiddish) poem, this being one of the few times in the 1939–40 period in which she makes specific mention of any of those who had been so important to her in 1926–28 residence in the city. She was in touch with them but had grown tired of their quarreling and inactivity. The birthday event had been a respite, a pattern of better things that, she wrote to Leon Malmed, she wished would persist, although she realized that "friction between the groups"[22] made this unlikely.

She was especially pleased with the results of another birthday celebration for her that had been held in Los Angeles. Her friends C.V. and Sadie Cook had presented to the gathering there a folder of "quotations from the Toronto, Windsor, and Detroit papers on my visit to Windsor during May. Also my message to the comrades in America and Canada and a photograph of myself which makes me appear rather young for a lady of seventy; also a definition of Anarchism." Labeled a "70th Birthday Commemorative Edition", the folder opened with a page containing several elements: a large and flattering portrait photograph, the headline and opening paragraph of a 19 May Detroit *Times* interview, "Emma Goldman, 70, Holds Fast to Anarchy"; a list of her publications including all five books and two recent pamphlets, "The Place of the Individual in Society" and "Trotsky Protests Too Much"; and her definition of anarchism. The portfolio included the entire text of the extensive essay/pamphlet on the place of the individual in society, and lengthy, flattering, detailed articles, all dating to May 1939, from the Toronto *Daily Star* and the *Evening Telegram*, the Windsor *Star*, and the *Times* and the *News* of Detroit. At the beginning of her first book, *Anarchism and Other Essays*, more than thirty years earlier, Goldman had defined anarchism. Through the years she had elaborated and honed the definition, until it reached the condensed precision and completeness of a credal statement. This late summary of belief was what the Los Angeles comrades published; it ran as follows:

ANARCHISM: Libertarianism as opposed to Authoritarianism.

The ideal of equal freedom for all in opposition to invasive rule by violence or force, whether exercised by individuals, groups, or governments.

A world philosophy of a new social order, proposed for broadscale practical application, whereby equal freedom for all is unrestricted by invasive man-made laws.

A theory that rulership exercised by one set of men over others is the result of invasive compulsion, on the basis that Might makes Right, which is wrong, wasteful, harmful and needless.[23]

Notably, this definition shows that, having for three decades experienced and maturely considered the ideas and performance of various forms of liberalized and democratic government, she had concluded that there still remained only anarchism on the side of freedom versus (sometimes concealed) "Might" serving its own interests. Furthermore, she had realized that anarchism must recognize that coercion comes not only from governments. And, as the last two paragraphs show, she was more convinced than ever that non-coercive communitarianism was practical and that freedom could never be slowly doled out and taught to the people by authorities but had to be seized whole and practiced by each and all. Finally, in the teeth of the continual argument that her cause anarchism was a beautiful and impossible idealism at best, she insisted that anarchism alone was a truly realistic set of social-political values, that the hierarchal system defined by law, enforced by coercion and inculturation, and insisted on by supposedly practical people was in fact unnecessary. Coercion and thought-control were wrong because they allowed some to limit arbitrarily the action and self-development of others, which in turn made such methods wasteful and harmful by preventing the full exercise of each person's abilities. In a prefatory statement she sent from Toronto for the folder, "To Comrades and Friends on the North American Continent", she remarked:

I can say honestly I am more convinced than in August, 1889, of the logic and justice of our ideal. True, we are passing through a period of the blackest reaction in every country. The Fascists, the so-called democracies, and even "the worker's fatherland" are competing with each other to further forge the chains of economic and political slavery and to destroy the individual altogether. By this very scramble for Power, the State in every country has proven its utter inability to meet the needs of the people and to maintain even a modicum of freedom and well-being.[24]

Copies of the folder were in great demand and she herself ordered many for use in fundraising.

Responding to H.M. Caiserman's birthday wishes, she described her work, remembered friends in Montreal, lamented the highly reactionary conditions which made it impossible for her to appear there, praised his commitment, and revealed that the support she received on her birthday had given her an idea for a fundraising event free from the painful memory of Berkman's death. She would call on her friends to join with her in celebrating the fiftieth anniversary of her commitment to the anarchist movement, which she dated to 15 August 1889, the day she arrived in New York City from Rochester "with just $5 in my pocket and my sewing machine which was sent express, which was to give me a living", the day she met Sasha Berkman and Johann Most. She told Caiserman that, as a result of her idea, plans were already under way for a celebration in Toronto, but that she hoped her admirers would also gather in other cities across North America and contribute to a new Emma Goldman Fund for Spanish Refugees. "To save my comrades and friends the trouble of putting up a tablet or monument on my grave, I intended to ask them to help me create a permanent Emma Goldman Spanish Re-Patriation Testimonial."[25] This theme, that she wanted a living monument rather than an elaborate tomb, resounded through many of her letters during the next few months.

Summer 1939 had begun with Goldman's worries about the wisdom of staying in Canada and her dread of friends' enthusiasm over her upcoming seventieth birthday. These anxieties metamorphosed into excitement about the new project. While work went on, however, she was burdened repeatedly by fresh cares. Emmy Eckstein died. Nellie Harris, Frank's widow, wrote her with the news. Goldman had been estranged from Eckstein for some time, despite continuing to help support her, as Berkman had requested. After discovering that Eckstein's new lover was supporting her as well, Goldman became angry. All the old antagonism about Eckstein, that she was a hypochondriac who had groundlessly resented and even hated Goldman, burst out anew on word of the younger woman's death. Goldman wrote to Fitzi Fitzgerald that Eckstein had "marched into the arms of death [hating] me with deadly hatred and dragged me through the mire". Still, Goldman concluded, "I hope she is at peace".[26]

She was also worried about Stella, still confined to hospital. She often wrote asking for more news than she was getting, and at the same time inquired yet again into the possibility of entering the US. She reported to her friends that overtures to allow her to travel were always accompanied by demands that she betray someone. Currently, a Congressional committee had floated a proposal, she said, that it might support her readmission in return for what she could reveal about communists. Despite her hatred of them, redoubled now by the "judas part"[27] they had played in Spain, she could not work with the government to spy on them. She was also troubled by infighting, which she noted was almost constant among anarchists everywhere, and which sometimes involved her. Vero (Vernon) Richards, who had taken over some of her work in England for the Spanish refugees, complained about her methods, Goldman reported to her British friend, the radical and author Ethel Mannin, in a 25 July letter. She claimed that Richards' charges, which included calling Goldman a dictator, had undermined her work for Spain. Richards wrote Goldman at the beginning of August: "All matters of importance connected with the movement must be focused on to your person. Thus through the Spanish war all contact with the Spanish comrades was through you and we learnt what you wanted us to learn." Goldman replied with a mixture of self-justification and hopes for Richards' work. She was a veteran, she said, one who had "gone through the test of fire and has come out unscathed", and therefore had the right to take the lead. To Richards' criticism that her self-promotion in sending around her folder revealed that she was "a very vain person", she replied poignantly, "Call it vanity if you want, I call it ordinary human longing for kindred spirits. . . ."[28] Conversely, there were English anarchists, such as the prickly Albert Meltzer, a lifelong foe of Richards and his *Freedom* group, who owed their intellectual and political being to Goldman's visits there.

Spain was also on her mind as the possible subject for a new book that her friend, US journalist Don Levine, was urging her to write. The project appealed to her should the tour of Western Canada fall through. Yet she was weighed down with anxiety owing to previous frustration with books and the fact that much of the material she would need had not been translated from Spanish. By summer's end, she told Levine that she did not want to write "in the void"—the void of limited information, of widespread indifference to the issue, of loneliness created by Berkman's absence. But the writing was not definitively shelved until after she had proposed it to a number of publishers and had been rejected. "Poor bleeding Spain," she wrote. "It is indeed forgotten. And yet I feel that it will have a comeback much sooner than the people of other countries. I cling to this hope with every fibre of my being."[29]

The Stalin-Hitler mutual nonaggression pact was announced to the world in August. On the day it was made public, Goldman attended an anarchist picnic for 600 persons in an open field at the corner of Jane Street and Wilson Avenue. Combining anti-fascist protest and entertainment, Attilio Bortolotti made puppets of Hitler, Mussolini, and Stalin as dart-targets for the picnic-goers, arousing the ire of communists in attendance. That evening, Goldman and Bortolotti were together listening to the radio when news of the pact was broadcast.

The Stalin-Hitler alliance meant not only that a major line of defence for the Spanish refugees was gone (Goldman began to worry that Hitler might bomb refugee camps in southern France) but also that a vital check on Hitler's hopes for conquest, perhaps the last check, had been removed. Goldman began to explore in her letters whether, in the event of war, she could support armed resistance to Germany, as, after all, she had in some measure done in sharing the anarchists' struggle in Spain. From Maximilian Olay she received a response outlining an anarchist stance towards the war which came to be her own: "I will not lift a finger to help anybody to obstruct the prosecution of the war, because I don't see how we personally or ideologically can gain anything from having the 'democracies' defeated by Hitler, and on the other hand, I do feel if Hitler is defeated we are at least allowed to live and sometimes even to propagate our ideas."[30]

Not, of course, realizing how future events—Hitler's betrayal of the pact and invasion of Russia—would once again reverse allegiances, Goldman took a certain grim satisfaction in the fact that Stalin's action, so clearly confirming her long-enunciated view of him, now forced great numbers of those who had ignored her to adopt views identical to her own. "Yes", she wrote to Rose Pesotta, "the Pact between Stalin and Hitler would make the great forerunners of the Russian Revolution turn in their grave. I doubt whether the miserable communist gang in America will change one iota in their lickspittle devotion to their master. . . . It will nevertheless be interesting to see if many of them will continue to call everybody to arms in defence of Soviet Russia and against racism now that Soviet Russia has made it so easy for Hitler to grab all he can, and to continue to exterminate Jews, Communists, and all other of his political opponents." To Milly Rocker she commented, "Stalin's pact has vindicated us beyond our own imaginations. . . . Meanwhile the bloody dance has begun and all its evil consequences will follow. Here the press announced that the police have the names and addresses of all radicals and will proceed in due time. . . ."[31]

After a brief late-August holiday in Muskoka, Goldman returned to a Toronto that seemed under increasing constraint. She felt "gagged and helpless" as one plan after another for helping Spain failed. The outbreak of war in Europe at the beginning of September (Hitler invaded Poland on 1 September, Great Britain and France declared war against Germany on 3 September) cast the Spanish cause still deeper in the shade. She did have the satisfaction of attending a mid-month joint meeting of the Socialist Verbund (Union) and the Arbeiter Ring and hearing "speaker after speaker say the same things about Soviet Russia I have been saying for 17 years and for which I was condemned by them and everybody else. Now they spoke of the betrayal of the international proletariat and the Jews. It is a bit too late I fear, but then, better late than never." She added: "About the War—How I wish I had been wrong."[32]

Her western tour, she feared, would have to be cancelled due to lack of interest, since preoccupation over the war now obscured all else. A lecture scheduled for mid-September in Toronto was not held. Although a speech on the Hitler-Stalin pact at the Odd Fellows Hall on 19 September was attended by 500, she was forced to admit that the major summer project— the series of Memorial Fund dinners to mark her fiftieth anniversary in the anarchist movement and raise funds for Spanish refugee relief—was not working. The Toronto meeting, set originally for 22 September and rescheduled to the thirtieth because it conflicted with Rosh Hashanah, seemed shouldered into a corner by Canada's entry into the war. Nonetheless, a hundred people attended and $130 was raised for Spanish relief. Goldman soldiered on, contacting a New York friend to arrange a similar event there in mid-December.

12

The Last Cause

The declaration of war against Germany and the other Axis powers changed the character of Emma Goldman's life in Canada irrevocably. All at once, the country where she was making her home was at war with the totalitarian powers she had long warned against, in a Canadian campaign that went all the way back to her devastating analyses of Lenin, Stalin, and Mussolini in 1926. In 1939, her comrades had met the growing threat from Naziism and fascism, and then the declaration of war itself, with protests. "We made some beautiful demonstrations against fascism", recalled Attilio Bortolotti. The Toronto anarchists "organized demonstrations and street meetings at which I, Ahrne [Thorne], and Dorothy Rogers spoke, and were attacked by mounted police." They staged demonstrations at Queen and Dovercourt, and later at Lippincott and Bloor, blocking Bloor "for an hour one night".[1]

When the war began, however, the foresight of the anarchists was not rewarded. Goldman was not exalted as one of the very few who had been right about the danger Hitler represented. On the contrary, she was if anything more marginalized than ever, isolated within the small ethnic and anarchist communities, which tended to be viewed with suspicion by a country now univocally patriotic. Bortolotti was squeezed from both sides, threatened by fascists and patriots alike. "As soon as the war broke out . . . the fascists in Windsor and Toronto denounced me. . . . The authorities kept me under continuous surveillance, and they now tried in earnest to deport me."[2] On 28 September parliament passed into law a new War Measures Act giving law enforcement sweeping powers against potentially seditious actions, speech, and publication. Four anarchists were charged almost immediately when, on 4 October, a combined team of Toronto and Royal Canadian Mounted Police raided the house at 847 Gladstone Avenue in what was then the industrial northwest section of the city. Toronto Sergeant of Detectives William Nursey and Detective Dan Mann arrested Bortolotti, Ruggero Benvenuti, Ernesto Gava, and a man calling himself Jose Marcos Joaquin. A fifth, Vittorio Valopi, who was never identified in contemporary press reports, was also found in the house but was released after questioning. In addition, police removed from the house what the prosecutor later referred to as a "truckload" of books, pamphlets, and other items, including a poster opposing Italy's invasion of Ethiopia, two broken revolvers, and a small hand printing press. The one piece of literature known to have been seized that might possibly have come from the press was a flimsy four-page newsprint leaflet, "Manifesto of the Provisional Conference against Capitalist War". This document called for a "labor boycott to prevent the production and shipment of all goods destined for Fascist Italy," scarcely a treasonous idea, although the principles upon which it was founded did include sentiments such as: "Decrepit capitalism must as a life and death necessity plunge humanity into periodic wars for the redivision of the world. The only way to end wars is by the overthrow of Capitalism and the establishment of a Working Class Society." The *Globe* reported the raid the following day, mentioning the seizure of the revolvers but not of the literature, and revealed that the men "were taken to different police stations after being fingerprinted and photographed at headquarters". The paper commented, without offering any source, that "No sympathy was expressed in Italian circles"[3] for the four. The men were charged with possession of radical literature under sub-section (c) of Section 39a of the War Measures Act, which prohibited the printing or circulation of literature containing material, "false or otherwise", that might cause disaffection from the government or the war effort or "which would or might be prejudicial to the safety of the State or the efficient prosecution of the war". On account of the revolvers, Bortolotti, a tool-and-die maker who had been given them, he claimed, to repair, was additionally charged with illegal possession of weapons. When, the next day, the men were brought into court, they were remanded—without a hearing, bail or counsel—until 12 October, when a formal bill of particulars was brought against them.

Goldman's involvement with their cause began at once. On 7 October, she wrote to the prominent labour and civil rights lawyer Jacob Lawrence (J.L.) Cohen, to entreat him to take the case. She flattered Cohen on his political knowledge and integrity, and asked him to convey an enclosed letter to Bortolotti to "help him in this decision to cooperate with you in his defense should you definitely decide to represent him".[4] Within three days she was writing to Cohen about her fundraising to cover his fees.

The letter Cohen carried for Goldman to Bortolotti in jail was a study in rhetoric meant to soothe the fiery, impulsive, and perhaps somewhat naive activist into cooperating with a legal defence rather than simply spewing defiance. "I know without seeing you", she wrote, "that you would like to go into court and tell your accusers exactly what you think of them and so called democratic methods." But, she said, his case could be important to all Canada as "a test case of civil rights and civil liberties", and thus could be of value to Bortolotti's own anti-fascist struggle. She agreed with him that "in the deeper sense no such animal [civil liberty] exists under democracies any more than under dictatorships yet everything in life is relative. There is such a thing as some liberties or none at all." She urged on him "the value of a defense exposing the annihilation of all civil liberties in the war law",[5] presenting it as a way of fighting in Canada the same battle that anarchists were fighting against the governments of Italy, Germany, and Russia.

Attilio (since there was no English equivalent of Attilio, he often used Arturo or Arthur) Bortolotti, who emerged as the principal defendant in the case, spoke Friulian as well as Italian, and especially after Mussolini's 1922 march on Rome was fond of drawing the distinction between the two nationalities, saying he was not an Italian and had been brought up in a different tongue. Born in 1903 in Codroipo, in Udine, he came to Canada in July 1920, age 17. At the time of his trial, his parents were both deceased, though his mother lived through the 1920s, long enough to be harassed in her home, an elderly and ailing woman, by the Fascisti on account of news they had received from Canadian fascists of Bortolotti's effective anti-Mussolini activities. Two of his four brothers also were living in North America, Umberto in Windsor and William in Detroit. Bortolotti himself had worked in the Windsor-Detroit area from 1920 to 1929. Starting in 1922, when Mussolini seized power, Bortolotti was a vocal anti-fascist. He crossed to Detroit to participate in Il Gruppo "I Refrattari" there, and in Windsor took part in the almost weekly performances and dances that anarchists held to raise a few dollars to send overseas. At Bortolotti's trial, J.L. Cohen described some of his client's protest activities. In late 1926, Bortolotti broke up a meeting of 1,100 persons at the ballroom of Windsor's Prince Edward Hotel where the famous aeronaut Umberto Nobile was speaking as part of his North American tour to bolster Fascism's reputation abroad by, as Cohen put it in a defence document, "the somewhat specious means of identifying Nobile's accomplishments as an explorer with the fascist regime per se". When a photograph of Mussolini was flashed on a screen accompanying Nobile's eulogy of Il Duce, Bortolotti rose and began shouting, "Down with this murderer of the Italian workers", provoking approving reactions from the audience, who prevented Nobile making any further reference to the dictator. Bortolotti recalled rushing to the stage at a challenge from a Fascist speaker, loudly proclaiming the Fascists to be "a bunch of killers, liars" and tearing a picture of an Italian king from the wall. In the resulting melee the "fascists retreated into a corner", he said, and to the sound of approaching police sirens his brother and other comrades called to him, "Tilio, let's go. . . . Let's go to Detroit and go to the opera and see *Rigoletto* tonight."[6]

In retaliation for Bortolotti's constant interference, Windsor fascists made it increasingly difficult for him to find work in the city after 1922. An example of the type of trouble he encountered is an incident in which he broke up a fascist meeting at which one Luigi Merlo, a former boss of his and a man with some power to affect his employment opportunities, was chair. Similarly, Bortolotti ran afoul of other fascists with prominence in the local Italian-Canadian community and connections to local authorities. As a result, Bortolotti crossed to Detroit in 1926 to find work with his brother William in the building trades, becoming a mason, although he apparently moved back and forth, labouring in both cities. Later, Bortolotti joined Ford Motors and there acquired his tool-and-die making skills. In Detroit on at least two occasions Bortolotti had to avoid immigration authorities who came to his work place, alerted, he believed, by Windsor fascists, who still monitored his doings because he continued to harass them.

When in 1929 he was arrested in Detroit for distributing literature to Fisher Body Plant workers on the second anniversary of the execution of Sacco and Vanzetti, Bortolotti was dismissed from his job at Ford. He jumped bail and secretly reentered Canada, using the name Albert Berthelot (author of an anarchist free-love tract, *L'Amore libero*, which, along with Goldman's essays, Bortolotti admired as embodying his own theory of instinctive free love). In skipping bail, he stated at his 1940 trial, he had been motivated by the fact that the Windsor fascists had alerted US and Canadian authorities to his probably illegal residences and international crossings, though he denied this. In fact, after his arrest for distributing his Sacco and Vanzetti literature at Fisher, a Detroit judge already had ordered him deported to Italy, acting without any information supplied by Canadian enemies. As he waited for the deportation order to be executed, Detroit anarchists raised his bail of $3,000 and retained Jacob Margolis, a Pittsburgh anarchist lawyer. As soon as Bortolotti was released, he was advised, in the words of one colleague, "Tilio, your life is worth more than $3,000. Go back to Canada and get lost." One of his brothers spirited him across the border in a truck.

Back in Windsor, Bortolotti did not exactly lie low. In September 1929, when the acting Italian vice-counsel at Toronto announced a Windsor meeting at which males over twenty who had not yet served in the Italian military could register for Mussolini's army, Bortolotti circulated written protests and in a personal demonstration galvanized anti-fascist audience members to the point that the diplomat "left the scene bedraggled and bespattered to the boos and shouts of the Italian workers". Bortolotti recalled shouting *"Abasso il fascismo! Morte a Mussolini!"* during the vice-counsel's speech, and afterwards spitting on him as he left the Catholic school where the meeting was held, making his jacket "white with spit"[7] before he reached a waiting police car. But Bortolotti did not seek employment in Windsor (where, he claimed to immigration authorities after his 1939 arrest, he always had maintained a residence while working in the Detroit area during the 1920s) but rather moved immediately to Toronto later in September 1929, finding a job as a machinist and resuming his anti-fascist agitation.

Bortolotti returned to Windsor in June 1938, when the Windsor Trade and Labour Council charged publicly that an Italian-language school, operating in rooms provided by the Windsor separate school board, was being used to disseminate pro-fascist propaganda and that the teacher involved, an employee of the Italian consulate in Detroit, was a fascist agent. The accusation was disputed, and the council engaged Bortolotti to try to substantiate its claims. On 10 September 1938, the Windsor *Star* reported that "Arthur Bortolotti of Toronto, imported by the Windsor Trades and Labour Council to further its purge of fascist activities in Windsor, last night branded Luigi Meconi, a member of the city's Italian colony, as an official member of the National Fascist Party. He charged that the Meconi-sponsored Dante Allighieri Society is in reality a Fascist propaganda school, sponsored by the Italian government. . . . He backed up all his claims with an amazing array of evidence", which the newspaper detailed. "Bortolotti produced a copy of a Toronto fascist newspaper with a picture of Meconi on the front page. The caption under the photograph was 'Sezione Fascista a Windsor' (Fascist Section established in Windsor). The note following read: 'The Secretary of the Toronto Fascist Organization, Massimo Jacopo Magi, has announced the formation of a Fascist section in Windsor, Ontario, the direction of which has been entrusted to Mr. Luigi Meconi.'"[8] As a result of Bortolotti's investigation and public presentation, the offending teacher was denied access to the Italian school. From that point forward, however, Bortolotti began to receive frequent death threats and challenges to his residency status, which he had never regularized.

Goldman did not record the exact circumstances of her first meeting with Bortolotti; she may have known of him before Simkin arranged their first face-to-face meeting at the Langbords' home. Bortolotti's lawyer at his 1929 Detroit trial, Jacob Margolis, was a friend of Goldman's and Berkman's. She and Bortolotti had come to know and highly value each other through the anarchist group that Goldman had formed in 1934–35 and of which he was an active member, indeed a sort of co-organizer, since some of the non-Jewish members were old anarchist contacts of his in Toronto. She praised him in 8 and 9 October letters to Rose Pesotta and Marcelino Garcia of New York both as a writer for the Italian-language anarchist newspaper in New York, L'Adunata, and as a fundraiser for it. "Actually he it was who raised hundreds of dollars whenever the paper needed financial support", she wrote to Garcia. During her last Canadian residence, in 1939–40, she and Bortolotti were especially close. One visitor recalled that he "acted as a kind of chauffeur, driving her everywhere".[9]

Goldman knew that the arrest of the Italians was part of wartime sur-veillance and a possible planned crackdown on all anarchists, including herself. Her secretary, Millie Desser, recalled that at this time, "after the war started, there was a burning session in our [the Dessers'] basement to get rid of the 'seditious literature'. I remember that furnace going in August [sic—probably September]! All the archives and papers were burned. . . . The police were barging in on all known anarchists. They raided Bortolotti's house. They never did get to us, though Dad [Joe Desser] was expecting them." Goldman also saw the raid at Gladstone Avenue as part of an ongo-ing campaign against Bortolotti by fascists and fascist sympathizers, and for strategic reasons she chose to emphasize this. To James Heney, secretary of the IWW in Port Arthur, Ontario, she wrote that "the Fascists are back of the raid and arrest. They had it in for our Italian friends for some time because of their anti-Fascist activities."[10]

Her commitment tempted her to public protest, but she feared that her name might actually prejudice her friends' cause in some circles and also threaten her Canadian residence. She wrote to Nick DiDomenico, who be-came the chief fundraiser for Bortolotti's case among New York and New Jersey Italians, that she had wanted to write something for the US press but feared to do so. "If my name will appear in our press or in the Liberal papers there is a possibility that this may cost me my stay in Canada." Deportation to England would "spell suicide" for her, and she feared that "war panic"[11] in Canada might prompt action against her if she took a public role. But she did a great deal in private. She arranged for the defence by J.L. Cohen. She convinced Bortolotti that he should approach the trial not as an opportunity for protest but rather as a case to win for the sake of returning to his anti-fascist work. She led the campaign in Canada and the US to raise money for Cohen's fees. She wrote extensively to friends and colleagues in Europe, the US, and Canada; letters went out to Herbert Read, Rose Pesotta, and many other prominent individuals. In addition, she sent material to newspapers and to radical and liberal magazines in Canada and the US, asking, however, that it be used without her name; such material became the basis of several influential pieces. She wrote to DiDomenico that she would not even hold back from more public action if the moment came when it seemed necessary.

Goldman postponed her planned trip to Winnipeg until December in order to stay in Toronto and devote her entire attention to the cause. Between mid-October and the 2 November trial, she was working to raise Cohen's $1,500 fee and within a few weeks had collected $400, most of it in small amounts donated by individuals and labour groups in the US. She was disappointed in Canadian contributions, commenting that Toronto was largely unresponsive, its Italian community being generous but lacking funds. In a 31 October letter to Milly Rocker, she criticized Toronto Jews for not doing more. "The boys are Italians so why should Jews worry? I cannot understand such narrow nationalism. . . . In this city our middle class comrades owners of houses and factories contributed exactly $2. . . . The Italians are unemployed and poverty stricken yet they raised $200 in this city. So you see that the Jews are all scared stiff and afraid to do anything for our men."[12] Much of the money raised also came from the Spanish liberation groups around the US, such as Chicago's Group Liberi. Goldman also asked these organizations to begin local campaigns for her new cause.

For Goldman the war meant that individual freedom was more at risk than ever in the country where she resided, and she saw the proof of this erosion of freedom in the prosecution of Bortolotti and the others. She wrote to Rose Pesotta, "It seems the authorities intend to railroad our people whose only offense is that they had Anarchist literature in the house. But we intend to move everyone to prevent this. For this reason we intend to make quite a case of it on the grounds that the war law under which they were arrested completely destroyed all civil rights."[13] This was one of her main concerns now: it was the same idea she had urged on Bortolotti in asking him to endure a legal defence that violated his anarchist principles. The irony that anti-fascists should be targeted under a law enacted as a part of Canada's war effort against fascists was not lost on Goldman. She kept stressing Bortolotti's record as an opponent of fascism: that would be his best defence, she argued. The question was whether Canada would be better able now to make distinctions among its radical residents of different stamps, or whether Bortolotti, as Goldman feared, would be condemned and deported to certain death.

Goldman hoped for the best from Cohen's defence. She wrote to Sidney Solomon in New York: "We have engaged a man whom I have known for a number [of] years who has the necessary social vision and the fighting spirit to look after the cases." Cohen had come to Canada at age 10 with his family; his father, a factory worker, died when the future lawyer was 13, Cohen leaving school to support the family. Still, Cohen matriculated from high school at 16 through night studies, and completed his law degree four years later; he had to wait seven months, until he turned 21, to be admitted to the bar. He first became prominent in 1937 for working out a settlement with Ontario Premier Mitchell Hepburn in the United Automobile Workers strike against General Motors in Oshawa. By 1939, he had already acted as legal counsel for many industrial unions and defended many left-wing leaders and organizations, and was to continue to do so through the 1940s, compiling a record of thirty appearances before the Ontario Labour Court without losing a case. Of himself, he once said that he "championed all the wrong people in all the right things".[14]

The four defendants returned to court on 12 October. The accusations against them were presented in full the following week. The basic charge against each was that in September and October 1939 he had printed and circulated literature "false or otherwise which would or might be prejudicial to the safety of the State or the efficient prosecution of the War, contrary to Section 39-A, Subsection C of the Defence of Canada Regulations". Two other major counts accused each man of printing and circulating literature possibly prejudicial to "recruiting, training, discipline or administration of any of His Majesty's forces", and printing and circulating literature "likely to cause dissatisfaction to His Majesty or to interfere with the success of His Majesty's Forces or the forces of any allied or associated power, or to prejudice His Majesty's relations with foreign powers". In addition, each was charged with the "*attempt* to print and circulate" [emphasis added] the said materials. Bortolotti faced the extra charge that "on the 4th day of October 1939 at the City of Toronto you unlawfully did, being an alien, have in your possession offensive weapons, to wit: two Revolvers, without having a permit".[15] With complete charges now presented, the men were finally permitted to enter their not guilty pleas. Bail for Benvenuti and Gava was set at $10,000 (later reduced to $5,000). Bortolotti and Marcos Joaquin, however, were denied bail because of questions about their immigration status.

Cohen already had demanded that the prosecutor, Assistant Crown At-torney Norman Borins, provide particulars of the original single charge; now he called for particulars of all the new ones, too, especially regarding the literature that was going to be introduced in evidence. This led to a lengthy dispute over how the publications seized in the raid would be produced. Borins vigorously resisted Cohen's request, stating that *all* printed matters seized constituted the case, that the accused knew what they had had in their possession, and that defence counsel could examine the material and make copies or extracts if he wished. The Crown also objected that cataloguing everything seized would delay the trial beyond the urgency demanded by wartime conditions. Borins even objected, fool-ishly, to being asked for particulars of the distribution charges on the grounds that the Crown had no knowledge of how the materials had been distrib-uted.

Insisting that the Crown must detail its case on the record, Cohen refuted each point. For instance, he reminded the court that the material had been removed after the men had been arrested, so that they had no knowledge of what had been seized. He argued that without particulars of the publica-tions' offending language, there was no evidence of wrongdoing by his clients. He pointed out the impossibility of preparing "a defense against a complete library of millions of words"[16] and declined responsibility for inspecting the material to ascertain what the Crown's case might be. Fi-nally, he said, the Crown's announced desire for speed ill became a pros-ecution that had taken three weeks to determine charges and receive a plea.

After this hearing, which took place 19 October, Cohen requested com-plete and defined particulars, including "the act or acts . . . it is alleged constitutes an 'attempt' to commit"[17] the offences alleged. The case had been called for one week later, 26 October, but when that date arrived and the particulars still had not been submitted, Borins said that he could not ready them in a week. Annoyed, the court ordered them furnished by Mon-day 30 October, and the case was advanced to Thursday 2 November. Cohen had no choice but to accept this arrangement, which would furnish him with specific allegations only three days before the trial.

At the trial, Cohen's groundwork in casting doubt on the prosecution's procedures and evidence paid off. Cohen pointed out that the Crown still had provided only "somewhat abbreviated lists of alleged material contra-vening the provisions of the Regulations. With the exception of some post-ers alleged to have been in the possession of Bortolotti, all the listed mate-rial represented standard theoretical and discursive works on Anarchism either in English or Italian."[18] No particulars at all of the other charges had been furnished. Despite introducing many materials not listed in the particulars, the Crown was unable to provide any proof of printing, distribution, or circulation of the seized works, nor to show that any of the exhibits contravened the War Measures Act. Among the works entered in evidence were Berkman's *The ABC of Anarchism*, Kropotkin's memoirs, Rudolf Rocker's *Anarcho-Syndicalism: Theory and Practice*, and *Poetry and Anarchism* by Herbert Read.

The Crown even called as a witness Goldman's friend Dorothy Rogers, who, Borins stated, "had for a time acted as Secretary of a general Libertarian group". Cohen described this tactic as an attempt to confuse the issue simply by associating the defendants with one more vaguely unfamiliar and suspicious-sounding activity. He moved for discharge of the prisoners on grounds that "not even a shadow of a prima facie case had been made out".[19] The motion was granted and all charges under the War Measures Act were dismissed. This meant that Gava and Benvenuti were set free, Marcos Joaquin remained in custody for immigration charges pending, and Bortolotti was held both due to immigration questions and his upcoming trial on the weapons charge. Exultant at the result, Goldman wrote to the *Freie Arbeiter Stimme* on 2 November, "The authorities will think twice before they will raid a house, arrest people and take away a truck load of a library."[20]

On Monday, 6 November, Bortolotti was exonerated on the charges of possessing illegal firearms. The guns seized had not been in working condition, as Cohen forced the Crown's police and RCMP witnesses to admit under cross-examination, and the court accepted Bortolotti's statement that he had had them only to repair them for their owners. The prosecution made one further disastrous mistake. Although it had doubtless cooperated with police in alerting the Department of Immigration to irregularities in Bortolotti's status, nevertheless it presented no testimony concerning his residency; since it had included the phrase "being an alien" in the weapons charge, the failure to address this point was in itself enough to deflate the Crown's case, which was dismissed on Cohen's motion.

Bortolotti was now transferred to the custody of immigration authorities and was kept, like Marcos Joaquin, in Toronto's Don Jail, although by now he had been held for more than five weeks without bail. In the "oral history" he gave to *Kick It Over* magazine in 1986, Bortolotti vividly remembered the moment when the exultation of his exoneration turned to the agony of continued incarceration:

The lawyer Cohen came and said, "Hello Art," and put an arm around me and we were walking down the hall and at the door I was told, "Art Berthelot, you're under arrest, we're from the immigration department." So the lawyer says, "What's the charge?" "Entering Canada without our permission . . . ." So they brought me in and I stayed in the Don Jail in Toronto until January fourteenth, 1940.[21]

Goldman did not pause to glory in the judicial victory for which she had fought so hard, but moved quickly to take up the new cause of saving Bortolotti from deportation. She wrote to the *Nation* and the *New Republic* to explain the threat: "Arthur Bortolotti only changes his jailers and now finds himself under the jurisdiction of the immigration authorities who are apparently keen on disposing him. Like many other foreign libertarians who had believed that the world is their country, entirely oblivious to the possibility of what war will usher into the world, Arthur is now likely to pay heavily for his naive faith."[22]

In most of her appeals, Goldman omitted references to Jose Marcos Joaquin, whose situation was quite different from Bortolotti's, although no less perilous if he were to be deported. He was not, in fact, as his passport claimed, a Cuban, but rather an Italian by birth. His name was Agostino Confalonieri, and he had come to Canada in a distinctly illegal manner after fighting on the Republican side in the Spanish Civil War. Goldman feared that he might not command the same sympathetic interest that Bortolotti enjoyed among North Americans, but she arranged for Cohen to represent both men before immigration authorities.

Meanwhile she agonized over the difficulty of meeting Cohen's fee and did not scruple to let him know this. On 10 November she told him that "raising the fund has been the hardest thing I have done in many years"[23] of collecting tens of thousands of dollars for various causes and defences. She gave him an account of the sources (Ontario and US anarchists, Spanish Civil War refugees, Italians) of the $1,000 she had paid him and enclosed an additional $150. At the same time, she prodded him to take a trip to New York City (which he eventually did) to drum up material and moral support. She provided introductions to various influential and potentially helpful persons, such as her old friend Roger Baldwin of the American Civil Liberties Union, and various New York-area labour leaders.

While she was fundraising, she also explored whether her Port Arthur friend, James Heney of the IWW, could help her make a more extended western trip than that which she had postponed to attend to Bortolotti's trial, perhaps a tour as far as the Pacific coast. In the end that much-discussed plan never materialized, but she did leave Toronto for a month in

Winnipeg on 27 November, hoping that this trip would give her opportunities for fundraising on Bortolotti's behalf. In Goldman's absence, Dorothy Rogers directed the campaign in Toronto, and Cohen also helped Goldman with her efforts to raise awareness and funds for Bortolotti's immigration case. On 29 November, the lawyer wrote to A.A. Heaps and J.S. Woodsworth in Winnipeg, both MPs, informing them that Goldman "has now taken advantage of a request to undertake a speaking engagement in Winnipeg so that she can discuss the matter with you intimately with a view to seeing what can be done to save this man"[24] from deportation.

Goldman stayed at the Royal Alexandra Hotel in Winnipeg. Expenses were met by "two friends who are not comrades but sympathize with my ideals". Her public appearances were followed closely by the press and by the RCMP. Agents attending the meetings always noted the ethnic (that is, Jewish) character of the audiences. She lectured in Yiddish at the Hebrew Sick Benefit Hall on 1 and 10 December. Her English-language lectures, sponsored by the Arbeiter Ring, began on 3 December, when more than 600 persons came to the Starland Theatre to hear her speak on "The Farce of Stalin's Democracy and Peace". An RCMP agent reported, "Her whole address was an avalanche of condemnation of Stalin and his predecessor Lenin"; $54 was collected at the door. On 6 December, she spoke at Manor Hall, at the rear of the Manor Hotel, to an audience of eighty to ninety persons on the topic "The Betrayal of Spain by the Democracies and Soviet Russia", linking Stalin's abandonment of the Spanish Republic to his pact with Hitler and the partitioning of Poland. She wrote to Bortolotti, "Winnipeg is very fertile ground for our ideas. The comrades want me back for a few months and I should have remained if it were not for my grandchildren in trouble." Later, from Toronto, she wrote members of the IWW in Winnipeg that in the future she would "make your city my headquarters for a while"[25] in hopes of campaigning into the far west.

As she had planned, the trip in Winnipeg included much work for Bortolotti, including attempts to form a western Canadian support committee. She worried about him constantly. His mental and physical condition were declining in confinement. She was concerned about Confalonieri too: "Please J.L.," she wrote to Cohen from Winnipeg, "see the boys as often as you can. You have no idea what your visits mean to them. I can appreciate it more since I saw Arthur[']s tortured face last Tuesday [21 November]. He tried hard to smile but it brought out his inner state more forcibly."[26] Whether due to Goldman's motherly prompting or his own good offices, Cohen did visit the two prisoners at least three times in her absence.

One of the first people Goldman saw in Winnipeg was J.S. Woodsworth, veteran of the Winnipeg General Strike as well as a founder of the CCF, and Canada's first socialist MP. On arriving at the Royal Alexandra, she found the letters of introduction and the legal statement of facts in the Bortolotti case, which Cohen had agreed to provide her, waiting under her name, and decided to see Woodsworth at once. A mutual friend arranged for him to come to the hotel, and immediately after this meeting, on the afternoon of 30 November, both Goldman and Woodsworth wrote to Cohen. Goldman found Woodsworth "very interested . . . but not with the same interest and warmth as our Rev. friend," referring to the Rev Salem Bland of Toronto. For his part, Woodsworth wrote: "To-day Miss Emma Goldman outlined to me personally the cases in which you are interested [and] it would appear that this is really a case of persecution and that with the wartime sentiment prevailing coupled with the very wide provisions of the War Measures Act we cannot get very far unless instructions are issued from the higher authorities."[27]

Woodsworth was aware that Cohen would be in Ottawa the following Monday, 4 December, and directed him to call upon the CCF's secretary, David Lewis, and its national chair, M.J. Coldwell. He suggested that "more might be accomplished than by the use of purely legal means"[28] if Lewis and Coldwell were to visit the deputy or acting Immigration minister and other officials. Woodsworth was the first to recommend that Cohen (who already had decided on the same course) contact top immigration officials, an approach which eventually proved useful, but Woodsworth himself did not take a hand directly. Perhaps this was because he was now mainly a figurehead in his party. Or one might look to his published works, in which he makes no secret of his negative views of immigrant groups from central and southern Europe. He did, however, invite Goldman to dine with him and Mrs Woodsworth at their home on 4 December.

While Goldman was in Winnipeg, the immigration case against Confalonieri was heard, and he was ordered deported. Like other Italian fighters for the Spanish Republic, he dared not return to Fascist Italy. He was one of many being assisted by anarchists internationally to find places of residence in the face of then-universal suspicion of radicals among European and North American governments. Bortolotti's case, already hurt by his association with Confalonieri, was now further complicated by Confalonieri's revelation, under questioning, that Bortolotti had met him on his arrival in Montreal and driven him to Toronto, although Confalonieri's transit visa under the false name of Marcos Joaquin permitted him to land for only one day. This statement tended to prove, although not directly admitted by either man, that Bortolotti had been part of an anarchist network finding ways to bring into Canada Spanish Civil War refugees who lacked proper papers. Canadian authorities likely suspected Goldman, too, of involvement in this ring. The news about Bortolotti's ties to Confalonieri "prejudiced the case"[29] pending against Bortolotti, Cohen reported to Goldman. The two of them planned an appeal of Confalonieri's deportation. In the meantime, Cohen asked Goldman to return to Toronto as soon as possible.

Goldman continued to worry about the money she was trying to raise. In addition to the $1,500 for the original trial, Cohen was charging $1,500 for the immigration cases. By 7 December, she had raised only $1,200 towards this $3,000, and only $26 of this had come from Winnipeg. She wrote Cohen:

> Believe me I feel utterly miserable and worried all the time how to raise money for you. I think I have not done badly. Yet I know that you are not pleased else you would not remind me so often. . . . Now be a good boy and do not fly off the handle. Nothing is further from me than to hurt you in the least. But I am frightfully weary of the struggle, and tired, tired beyond words.[30]

Her last English lecture was at the Jewish Women's Cultural Club on 9 December, and her last Yiddish lecture the following day at the Hebrew Sick Benefit Hall. When she left for Toronto on 12 December, she was determined first of all to get Bortolotti out of jail, but she was also full of thoughts about future trips to Winnipeg and farther west. She never was able to act on these plans; in fact, she never returned to the lecture stage again.

13

Gagged and Fettered

Goldman returned to Toronto indignant that the Immigration department had not set bail for Bortolotti, but Cohen warned her on 14 December to curb her insistence that he should demand it. She was being misled by her own US experience. There she had been able to require bail, he explained, because of the due process provision of the Constitution, for which no equivalent existed in Canada. "In immigration matters here," he wrote, "the question of bail is entirely a discretionary act within the administrative department",[1] and bail already had been denied to Bortolotti. (In fact, Cohen was in error, for during Goldman's day in the United States the cases of undesirable aliens detained on grounds related to residency and citizenship were handled as administrative matters by immigration authorities, and due process under law was thus skirted.)

Cohen had decided that fighting Immigration on two fronts at once would be a poor tactic. Confalonieri's deportation enquiry had to be completed before he could reapply pressure for Bortolotti's release. "I am now in negotiation with the Department on that subject as well as upon the whole situation, and if I cannot prevail upon them to arrange bail, it is idle for those in correspondence with you to ask 'why something concrete has not been done'", he wrote testily, quoting back to her the complaint she claimed to be hearing from sympathizers. Cohen also expressed surprise that she thought she could raise bail when she was having trouble coming up with his $1,500 fee; it was fine with him, he wrote, that she planned to "clean up the balance of the original fee by the 25th",[2] indicating that the question of the second $1,500, for the immigration matters, still lay in the future.

Through an Ottawa associate, Cohen was continuing negotiations with J.S. Fraser of Immigration, and these talks could be prejudiced by any public display on her part, as both of them realized. By 21 December, Goldman was reporting to Nick DiDomenico that Cohen, "one of the shrewdest men I have met with tremendous tact and judgment", had the previous day been in Ottawa and gained government consent for bail. The amount set was daunting: $5,000 cash. Yet she was elated because "I feel confident and so does J.L. Cohen that if we succeed in bailing Arthur it would have a very great effect on the chances of his remaining in Canada". Her plan for getting the $5,000, since "there is no such money among the comrades in this city and I know of no one outside of our ranks",[3] was to ask several people to offer property they owned as guarantees against loans.

Goldman was frustrated at the beginning of the year, in the midst of her campaigning, to have her mail held up for several days. She sent Cohen to investigate and reported to friends in a letter dated 6 January that the post office "powers that be" had told the lawyer that Emma Goldman's mail was not being held but that "E.G. Colton" was under surveillance because of cheques that had been mailed to her. She began asking correspondents to send letters in double envelopes addressed to such friends as Dorothy Rogers, who also often carried her outgoing letters to Buffalo and Detroit, or to Millie Desser, Sadie Langbord, and Dien Meelis. "It is like living in a totalitarian country", she commented, "to be so cut off and so helpless as one is here. It makes me feel I ought to go back to England where there is still a breath of freedom. At least I learn that anti war propaganda can still be carried on and meetings held. Here one is gagged and fettered."[4]

Cohen had an associate, the Ottawa lawyer A.H. Lieff, visit the Post Office Department and the Board of Censors, both of which denied there was an order to hold Goldman's mail. Finally, an interview with the RCMP's superintendent of intelligence services, Ernest William Bavin, evoked a promise to have the letters released, though not an admission that they were being held. After this, Goldman's mail arrived for two or three days and then stopped again. Once more Lieff returned to the post office and was told the mail was not being held. "The Department", he wrote to Cohen, "knows all about the situation and they even know that some of this money [being sent to Goldman for Bortolotti and other causes] will be used to pay your fees." Cohen shot back that it was "idle" for the authorities to issue their assurance: "The mail is definitely being held up. . . . [T]here has now been a period of ten days in which she had received no mail of any sort." He said that the authorities had previously been "putting us off by allowing a few letters to come through".[5] Lieff again returned to the Post Office Department, and again was told there was no hold; he was given irrelevant explanations based on delays of European mail pending censorship. So the matter continued throughout January and February.

At this time the mail was crucial not only for Goldman's fundraising efforts but also for her publicity campaign on Bortolotti's behalf. A typical example of her procedure to gain and exploit publicity is the reception, in early January, by John Walter of the CCF of a recent article on Bortolotti. It had appeared in the *Nation*, one of several US publications to which Goldman had been sending regular accounts of the case, although always with the request that the material not be attributed to her. It is likely that Goldman herself arranged for the piece to be posted to Walter, since it came from Goldman's friend, Clara Fredericks of New York, who was helping to run the international Bortolotti defence effort. On 8 January, Walter wrote to a prominent CCF member of Parliament, W.D. Euler, briefly outlining the case along the lines given in the article, then adding: "When the war broke out, the black elements saw their chance. It is reasonably certain they were back of his arrest . . . will you in your influential position, spare a little of your time to induce the authorities in charge, to do the humane thing instead of the technical one."[6] After hearing from Walter, Euler pressed Immigration regarding bail for Bortolotti, only to discover that it had already been granted a short time earlier. On 9 January Goldman sent Nick DiDomenico details of how she had raised the necessary sum, which, through Cohen's efforts, had been reduced to $4,000. Detroit anarchists had contributed $1,631 American and $50 Canadian. Three Italian-Canadians had donated a combined $2,000, one of these, a Toronto businessman named Attilio Lorenzette, giving half. Goldman was disappointed that the Toronto labour organization, the Amalgamated Clothing Workers, "had done nothing"[7] for Bortolotti. On 10 January, the Toronto *Daily Star* reported Bortolotti's release to "his counsel, J.L. Cohen, and a couple of friends, including Emma Goldman, the internationally known anarchist". The paper commented: "Presumably because of the interest taken in the case by Emma Goldman the incarceration of Bortolotti attracted wide interest here and in the United States."[8]

Bortolotti's health had suffered in prison, where he had lost twelve pounds and was now "a very sick man", Goldman said. "I had to put him to bed at my place and give him the necessary immediate treatment." While she was nursing him, Goldman sent warm words of praise for her patient to Fitzi Fitzgerald, secretary of the international Bortolotti defence effort, calling him "a sort of younger Sasha, not as profound and able a man but of the same fine nature and large spirit".[9] A few days later, Bortolotti had improved enough to move to Ruggero Benvenuti's new residence at 137 Brandon Avenue. From 17 January on, he was attended there by Goldman's doctor, Dr Maurice A. Pollock. On 24 January, Pollock certified Bortolotti's illness to get his immigration enquiry delayed "for a week or two to give him time to recuperate".[10] Pollock reported that Bortolotti had consistently run a temperature ranging up to 104 degrees and showed a depleted white blood cell count and other symptoms indicating that he was not yet sufficiently recovered to leave the house. The hearing was postponed until 13 February.

In the meantime Cohen circulated a document entitled "The Case of Arthur Bortolotti", which solicited support by, in effect, outlining his planned defence. This document closely resembled the earlier "letters" Goldman had already sent to the *Nation* and the *New Republic* (which focused on the then-ongoing War Measures Act case) and the "statement of facts" on the immigration case, which Cohen had been sending to potential supporters in December and which Goldman had delivered to J.S. Woodsworth and others in Winnipeg. The February 1940 version, rewritten to address Bortolotti's immigration problems more succinctly and powerfully, became a basis of a new five-page Goldman letter on the deportation case, addressed to such periodicals as the *Canadian Forum*.

The busy preparation of these documents indicates Cohen believed that, on technical grounds, the immigration case was lost; in fact, he had probably felt so by December, while Goldman was beginning her Winnipeg trip. Clearly he had come to that conclusion by early December, perhaps as a result of the way in which Confalonieri had implicated Bortolotti: only public opinion, political pressure, and direct appeal to ranking politicians and bureaucrats could save Bortolotti from being deported. This was exactly the point that J.S. Woodsworth made a little later, after meeting with Goldman in Winnipeg.

Drafts of the various forms of the document show that Cohen and Goldman collaborated in producing it and varied it for different uses. Besides the complete versions of December and February, there are briefer ones: for instance, a summary which was the textual part of a never-used petition to be sent to the Mines and Resources minister, Thomas A. Crerar, under whose portfolio Immigration fell. Cohen and Goldman helped each other considerably in the writing: she gave concision, shape, and fire to his often diffuse prose; he brought her sometimes extravagant rhetoric into harmony with the needed tone of sober and mature exposition, and of course added the legal knowledge. One draft, a three-page "Statement re Attilio (Arthur) Bortolotti", in describing the dismissal of the criminal charges, bursts into recognizably Goldmanesque strains: "The magistrate . . . declared it was the most preposterous thing that had ever been brought before him." The court transcription reflects no such remark, and the statement was removed from all versions of their document. Some drafts contain legally irrelevant points, which she must have felt were powerful but which were eliminated. For example: "But for this occurrence [Bortolotti's story to immigration officials that a landlady had thrown away his completed citizenship application] he would, no doubt, be a naturalized citizen today."[11]

A draft of the version intended for the *Canadian Forum*, which Goldman must have written before 10 January, since it has Bortolotti still in jail, summarizes her view with the vividness of quickly spoken feelings. It was probably dictated to Cohen's secretary:

> The defence . . . had exposed the preposterous action of the police under cover of the War Measures Regulations by which police acquire the right to invade people's homes, confiscate their libraries and keep them in jail for weeks without reasonable bail, no matter how innocent they are subsequently proven to be. To check such a course was certainly a triumph for the civil liberties which the War Measures Regulations, Section 39 (a) is intended to abrogate. . . . [D]espite these successes, or perhaps even because of them, Bortolotti . . . is still held a prisoner and this time is threatened with [a] proceeding [deportation] which, undoubtedly, would involve his death. Bortolotti while active in Anti-Fascist work incurred the fierce animosity not only of Fascists within the Italian group [in Canada], but of some police authorities who at that time were thought to be too friendly towards some Fascist group holding public meetings. Determined, evidently, to revenge themselves on Bortolotti, and not having succeeded through Court proceedings, the attack is now being made through the immigration authorities.[12]

The trail is long cold, but one may still try to assess whether Bortolotti in fact was the object of secret official persecution. He himself firmly believed that his troubles sprang from effective action by Canadian fascists, especially those in Windsor, and most especially from the resentment of their leader, Louis Meconi. In Bortolotti's view, Meconi had a sympathetic ear, and perhaps even connections, inside the Toronto police and the Immigration department. Cohen, too, in his various accounts of the case, presented the probability that elements within the police were fascist-inclined and hostile to Bortolotti, a view shared by several other Bortolotti supporters, including Rev Salem Bland and various members of the CCF, such as J.S. Woodsworth and John Walter. At a late date in the case (May 1940), Bland described his beliefs to Thomas A. Crerar: "There is evidence that somewhere in the police organization of Toronto there has been a good deal of sympathy with both the Italian and the French Canadian Fascists, and it is certain that the officer charged with special authority to look after 'leftists' seems to be afflicted with a kind of monomania in regard to such. . . . Some police . . . are vindictive. Having once regarded a man as their quarry, they continue to pursue him."[13]

What was this evidence that Bland and others referred to but did not cite? In the absence of any right of discovery, no evidence from the Toronto police, RCMP, Immigration, or any other government body was obtainable by Bortolotti's friends. The evidence, then, must have been the testimony of Bortolotti supported by inferences from events, such as the fact that his house was raided, with no reasonable cause, virtually as soon as passage of the sweeping War Measures Act made it possible that previously non-criminal activity might be enough to imprison him. Such inferences are supported by a few additional facts, chiefly those developed by Harry S. Bennett, a Detroit lawyer retained by Cohen to investigate Bortolotti's police record in that city. Bennett wrote to Cohen that police files revealed how "in 1926 certain information came to [the Detroit police] with reference to Attilio Bortolotti which caused the authorities to look for Mr. Bortolotti. This information was in connection with one Louie Maconio. . . . There is information to the effect that in October 1939, the department was informed that Mr. Bortolotti was in jail in Toronto."[14] Despite its vague phrasing, Bennett's letter makes clear several points. About the time of Bortolotti's early anti-fascist activities in Windsor, Meconi and perhaps other inform-ers alerted Detroit police to the anarchist's presence in the United States as a possibly illegal alien. Thirteen years later, a person or persons who must have been aware of the earlier information made a point of adding to the Detroit file the fact of Bortolotti's 1939 legal difficulties in Canada. A motive for this last action might have been to head off the possibility of Bortolotti's finding safety in the US following any Canadian guilty verdict or expul-sion order. That such a pattern of persistent informing against Bortolotti would have been repeated in Canada, at least with police forces if not with other authorities, is perfectly reasonable. The fact that immigration au-thorities seem to have known of Bortolotti's potential residency violations virtually the moment he was arrested also suggests that informers were at work, either communicating directly with the ministry or prompting police to do so.

In short, a fascist origin and basis to the 1939 arrest and prosecution of Bortolotti seems highly likely. But were any Canadian officials in the case motivated by fascist sympathies or connections? Possibly, members of the Toronto police, RCMP, or Immigration, or of all three, acted for this reason.

It is also possible, however, that the case unfolded from simple over-zealousness on the part of the Toronto police and RCMP. From such a beginning, the scrupulous pursuit of all legal violations encountered in investigating Bortolotti, first by police and later by Immigration, coupled perhaps with a bit of the official vindictiveness mentioned by Salem Bland, could explain the Bortolotti affair. This, the possibility that most find a reasonable and relatively reassuring explanation as regards the safety of civil liberties in official hands, is precisely the most chilling one from an anarchist standpoint, for it demonstrates how injustice is done by ordinary people, who believe they act from neutral or positive motives of performing their job and aiding their nation.

The legal problems of Agostino Confalonieri finally came to seem almost insoluble. On 25 January, James Malcolm of Immigration informed Cohen that fingerprint records from the Paris police proved that the prisoner, still claiming to be Marcos Joaquin, was in fact named Confalonieri, and established that, far from being a native Cuban brought up from childhood in Spain as he claimed, he had been born in Monza, Italy, on 10 January 1909. Despite this evidence, Confalonieri kept denying adamantly that this was his name, that he was an Italian, that he had ever been to Monza or that he had been arrested in and expelled from France. Malcolm informed Cohen that the Department of Immigration was now taking steps to deport Confalonieri to Italy.

Bortolotti's 13 February immigration examination also ended badly. The proceeding was held in Malcolm's office, Room 245 of the Dominion Public Building at Bay and Front streets, under an order of the Mines and Resources minister signed by A. L. Jolliffe, Immigration commissioner, and dated 22 January. This document gave the ministry's official charge, that Bortolotti "entered Canada by eluding examination, thereby contravening s.s. 7 of Section 33 of the Immigration Act".[15] The official record gave his name as "Attilio Bortolotti, alias Albert Berthelot".

According to the department, Bortolotti had left Genoa 22 June 1920 on the *Duca D'Aosta* and entered at New York, where he had been held at Ellis Island for five or six days while Canadian immigration authorities investigated his claim that his brother Umberto lived in Windsor. On confirmation, Bortolotti had been allowed to enter Canada, arriving sometime between 6 and 10 July 1920 and taking up residence in Windsor. He told Malcolm that he had applied for naturalization in 1925, but this turned out to mean that he had acquired application papers which were lost when, he claimed, his landlady had thrown them away while cleaning. The authorities had also discovered that in 1926 Bortolotti began to work for his other brother, William, a builder and masonry contractor who lived in Detroit and took jobs both there and in Windsor.

Bortolotti denied he had ever had legal difficulties in the United States, and at first tried to maintain that he had returned to Canada permanently in 1928. But Malcolm produced documents from the Ford Motor Company in Dearborn proving Bortolotti had worked there from 5 July 1928 to 30 August 1929 and had been dismissed after his arrest by Detroit police for distributing Sacco and Vanzetti literature. He was forced to admit that friends had paid his bond so that he could escape his plight by jumping bail and crossing illegally to Windsor the first week of September 1929. Asked by Malcolm what country he was a citizen of, Bortolotti could reply only, "I don't know whether I am a citizen of Italy or not. I was born there." Malcolm concluded that on or about 30 August 1929, not having acquired Canadian citizenship or domicile, he had entered at Windsor by eluding examination: "I hereby order his deportation to the place whence he came, United States of America, or the country of his birth and citizenship—Italy."[16]

This result was a cruel disappointment to Goldman, after all her work. She dispatched Cohen to Ottawa to begin an appeal on Bortolotti's behalf. She emphasized in fundraising letters that Bortolotti's offence was a minor one. For instance, in writing to ask Nick DiDomenico on 15 February for an immediate loan of $1,000 in the anti-deportation effort, she mentioned that she was working "day and night to rouse interest in the cruel outrage to send A[ttilio] out just because in his twenty years domicile in Canada he was absent a short period". In the documents they were preparing, Cohen's and Goldman's attack on the immigration charges presented Bortolotti's violations of immigration law as no more than technicalities, stating that police information had been supplied by Canadian fascists for vindictive reasons, and adding that the police themselves were vengeful and perhaps pro-fascist. To these points Goldman added an obvious and absolute distinction virtually unknown to Canadian journalism and officialdom: the difference between Marxist communism and anarchism. "It would appear that certain police officials have believed quite erroneously, that because Mr. Bortolotti is an ardent anti-fascist he is a Communist. Nothing could be farther from the truth. He is not in sympathy with the totalitarian ideas and methods of Communism". She felt this clarification was necessary to ground her argument, already cited, that police authorities friendly "towards some Fascist group holding public meetings [attempted to] revenge themselves on Bortolotti"[17] first through a criminal trial and, that having failed, through immigration proceedings.

In the days immediately following the decision to deport Bortolotti, Goldman emphasized to her correspondents the need to act quickly, before the order could be executed. She told them of the new "statement of facts" on which she was hard at work. She was engaged in local, face-to-face activities, as well, for she reported that she had been promised publicity for Bortolotti's cause in the Toronto *Daily Star*. On 17 February she wrote again to Nick DiDomenico, and her papers contain letters mailed to her on that same date, including one from her old lover, Ben Reitman, wishing her "many more healthy, happy useful years".[18]

14

Unfitted for the Easy Way

On the evening of 17 February 1940, Goldman suffered a severe cerebral hemorrhage. She was with several people at the time of the attack, including those with whom she shared the house at 295 Vaughan Road, Dorothy Rogers and Dien and Tom Meelis. They were getting ready for the weekly meeting of her anarchist group, which gathered regularly in Goldman's rooms for political and intellectual discussion. Dien Meelis wrote to Leon Malmed soon afterward: "Emma had been active all day, dictating letters in the afternoon, and after supper even helping with the dishes. About 8 o'clock she came downstairs and had been talking and laughing with us for little more than half an hour when suddenly, without a sound, she slumped down in her chair."[1] At first her companions thought she had only fainted, but her right side had been entirely paralyzed and she was taken to Toronto General Hospital within the hour.

Bortolotti, in his interview given to *Kick It Over*, recalled the day of Goldman's collapse:

> Then one Friday or Saturday night I was out picking up sympathizers and comrades in my car to have a little chat. It was the seventeenth of February, the anniversary of the burning at the stake of Giordano Bruno. . . . Anyway I picked up Jack and Sylvia Fitzgerald at the corner of Bathurst [Street] and Dundas [Street West]. As they got in, Jack says, 'Come fast. Emma got a stroke. . . .' I got to Vaughan, and there she was trying to pull her skirt down over her knees. Just imagine Emma, she didn't give a damn about whether she showed the . . . sexual organs. But naturally part of her mind of her youth was commanding her, with the arm that wasn't affected by the stroke, to pull down the skirt so as not to show her knees.[2]

Ahrne Thorne, who was also present, had a similar memory: "I just looked at her—she was fully conscious, she knew that she was powerless. She was lying on the stretcher, and with her right hand, I remember she pulled down the hem of the skirt that was uncovering her knee. . . . When somebody writes about her fairly young years and her sexual adventures, I remember that chaste, innocent gesture."[3]

A constant theme among Goldman's friends was the cruelty that someone so active had to endure the mental agony of paralysis. Immediately on hearing the news, Fitzi Fitzgerald wrote to J.L. Cohen, "I'm broken hearted about Emma—she's sister, brother and almost mother to me—somehow never thought that a 'bullet had been made that would hit her'—I realize she will be 71 in June—but so much energy and vitality and aliveness—how could this happen??? I know she has been so exercised about the cases up there—it seems that she has given her life to them! . . . [A]nd if she is to be left helpless it will be much better if she goes quickly—she would want it so. How could Emma stand not being active!!" In March, Stella Ballantine, who spent much time with the patient, wrote to Ben Reitman that "Emma is unable to speak as yet. . . . She weeps a great deal and seems fully aware of her helpless condition."[4] Goldman spent six weeks in Toronto General Hospital. Her physician, Dr Maurice Pollock, called in Dr Herbert Detweiler, a prominent specialist, who began treating Goldman for diabetes as well. Some strength gradually returned to her stricken right side, and at times she attempted to respond to those with her, especially on topics connected with anarchist activities. Still she was unable to move, unable to speak, unable to sleep. The skilled nurse who had maintained so many nightime vigils now was afflicted with insomnia, which provoked some of the crying her companions witnessed in these days.

Dorothy Rogers and Millie Desser formed a committee to raise money for Goldman's medical expenses. Desser wrote to a Winnipeg friend, "We need hardly tell you that Emma Goldman never laid away any funds—there were always too many others in need." The first committee was succeeded by another, Friends of Emma Goldman, which continued the fundraising for her care and backed Harry Weinberger's now redoubled efforts to have her readmitted to the United States. This group's members included many of Goldman's longtime friends in the US, such as Weinberger, Roger Baldwin, Harry Kelly, Freda Kirchwey, Fitzi Fitzgerald, and the novelist Evelyn Scott, as well as prominent admirers such as the novelist Fannie Hurst, the philosopher John Dewey, and the Broadway playwright George S. Kaufman. The chair, John Haynes Holmes, wrote Goldman that the committee "will stand by you and see you through this illness. Also, we shall not be content until we get you back in this country."[5]

The committee's humanitarian efforts encountered a roadblock in Canadian officialdom's continuing suspicion of the notorious anarchist, even in her present state. Once again her mail, including the money being sent for her care, was held up. Again Cohen protested through his Ottawa associate, Abe Lieff, explaining that, "word has been received of a considerable number of checks which have been forwarded and addressed either to Dorothy Rogers of 295 Vaughan Road who was the companion of Emma Goldman" or to Goldman's niece Stella at the same address. Mail was not being delivered any longer to either woman, "and with the considerable expenses involved this is precipitating a serious situation. Now, surely, it is possible for the authorities whether censorship or mounted police, or otherwise, to avoid interfering with mail at this address having regard to the fact that Miss Goldman is in a paralysed condition, helpless at the hospital."[6] Although there is no record of an official response, the protestations may have been successful this time, for the funds from the committee and other well-wishers did arrive to pay Goldman's expenses; perhaps, though, a means other than the post was found to get the money into Canada.

Throughout Goldman's illness, Cohen was forced to fight on many fronts: fundraising, attacking the mail stoppage, desperately seeking a country other than Italy that would accept Confalonieri while fighting Immigration for delays in his deportation, legally appealing Bortolotti's deportation order, rallying support and publicity for him and making personal representations on his behalf. During March and April he worked with organizations as diverse as the United Church of Canada and Solidaridad Internacional Antifascista (SIA), the CCF and the Windsor and District Trades and Labour Council. A 26 February 1940 Toronto *Daily Star* editorial (doubtless the publicity Goldman referred to having arranged in her 17 February letter) gave national attention to Bortolotti's plight.

Arthur Bortolotti . . . has become known here as a man violently opposed to fascism. Canadian Fascists are said to have threatened him with their vengeance because of his anti-Fascist activities. If he were in Italy, the least he could expect would be imprisonment. Already, following one of his anti-Fascist crusades in Canada, his home in Italy has been raided and ransacked, and his sick mother (since dead) was raised out of her bed. . . . It is alleged that Canadian Fascists furnished the information on which his residence in Toronto was raided last October. . . . The Minister at Ottawa will no doubt go into the merits of the deportation order thoroughly. In doing so, he will naturally consider the whole picture—not merely the technical offence which Bortolotti committed at the border 10 years ago.[7]

Bortolotti's plight was also publicized by the March issue of the *Canadian Forum*, which noted in its "Civil Liberties" column that "Arthur Bartolotti [*sic*], Italian libertarian, was ordered deported to Italy by the immigration court because during his 20 years residence in this country he worked for a time in Detroit. Notice of appeal has been filed."[8]

On 1 March, the government announced its intention to deport Bortolotti to Italy. Reaction was immediate. The Prince Edward-Lennox Liberal Association, representing the Liberal Party in the Windsor area, sent Prime Minister Mackenzie King a cable calling the action an "unseemly concession to a foreign power and denial of refuge to political refugees". On 2 March, the Windsor *Star* ran two long pieces, side by side, reviewing the case pro and con, calling Bortolotti "the former Windsor resident who brought about the suppression of Fascist teachings to city school children" in 1938. The paper quoted a sister of Bortolotti's, Mrs Carlo Rossini, of Windsor: "It would be better if they sent him to his death. He would only be tortured over there. The only trouble with Arthur is that he is too outspoken. If he thinks something wrong he tells everyone so, regardless of the trouble it may cause." A Windsor *Star* writer, Norman M. MacLeod, reported the official side of the question: "The immigration authorities state that Bortolotti's case results from a drive in which the department is engaged to round up foreigners who have taken up their residence in Canada illegally . . . a particularly important phase of government war work. . . . Government officials will not say from which source Bortolotti's case came." MacLeod quoted immigration officials as saying that Bortolotti's breaches were not mere technicalities, that he was unequivocally guilty under the law, and that the department would not be "stampeded" into turning the anarchist over to the Italian Fascisti "but neither is it going to give him sanctuary in Canada by any agitation drummed up" by his supporters. Officials claimed they were "not satisfied" that he was a disinterested champion of democracy and in danger if returned to Italy. Bortolotti could not be deported, however, until the appeal Cohen had filed with the minister had been decided. In late March he made a personal representation to the minister as a broad stream of protest and persuasion flowed to the government from "various sections of the country",[9] according to the *Star*.

Goldman's condition improved slightly, but her doctors judged that further hospital care could do nothing more for her. She was taken to her Vaughan Road apartment in late March, where she received a weekly massage and was attended by two nurses constantly on call. Dorothy Rogers reported to Stella, who had returned to New York, that Goldman was able to read letters on her own now and clearly could understand what was said to her. But she still could not speak or write. Thus there is no record in her papers of her reaction to the news on 29 April that the director of the immigration branch of Mines and Resources, F.C. Blair, had decided that Bortolotti could "remain in Canada indefinitely conditional on his good behaviour". The bond that Goldman had raised so laboriously was to be refunded immediately. The two-paragraph letter underscored that Crerar was not accepting the appeal of the deportation order but rather was suspending its execution on the grounds that Bortolotti's life would be in danger in Italy. The ministry's intent, Blair took pains to claim, was to avoid where possible a deportation that "would return a person to a country where his life would be in danger"; Bortolotti, he stated, was thus not being "singled out for special consideration"[10] under pressure of the large outpouring of support.

Bortolotti could stay in Canada, but his freedom of speech was curtailed by the probability that he would remain under surveillance. It was Rev Salem Bland who responded to Crerar on behalf of Bortolotti's supporters, writing that the decision was a relief "to those of us who have come to like and respect him [Bortolotti] very much, though recognizing that he has allowed his peculiarly strong sense of justice and love of freedom to lead him to extreme views on some points". He continued that such views of Bortolotti's were "purely theoretical. He hates all violence, all use of force, is a most thorough-going pacifist—hence is incapable of really making trouble." Apparently referring to certain documentary evidence against Bortolotti that the Bortolotti side knew had been sent to the ministry, Bland argued that "[t]hose sentences which naturally strike one as extravagant are translations into English by Fascists. . . . He condemns those translations as marked by inaccuracies."[11]

Bland also carried forward the free-speech campaign, which had been part of Cohen's battery of arguments and which, for Goldman, had been near the heart of the matter. Expressing misgivings about the form of the reprieve, the clergyman pointed out that a citizen, or even an alien, who had no deportation order suspended over him could not be penalized for any utterance unless it were found unlawful in a court proceeding. Bland feared that immigration authorities, on "the mere assurance of the police that he was making trouble", might put Bortolotti's deportation order into effect. "It would be an additional kindness, therefore, which would be greatly appreciated, if your Office could give assurance that the suspended order will not be carried out unless unlawful conduct was established".[12]

One of the most moving glimpses preserved from Goldman's last weeks involves the unfortunate Agostino Confalonieri. As she lay paralyzed, Cohen turned to Latin America to find a country that would accept him so that he would not be sent to Italy. While complex and frustrating negotiations dragged on with Chile and Mexico, he was forced to beg Immigration for extension after extension of the expulsion date. Finally Mexico agreed to admit him. Success seemed assured, but then unexpectedly the United States refused Confalonieri a transit visa. On 3 April, Cohen obtained one further and final week's extension and was searching frantically for a way to pull strings in Washington to obtain the needed permission for the deportee to cross US territory. Bortolotti finally solved the problem by arranging to deliver Confalonieri at the Canadian border to some "smugglers" he knew who could get the man to Mexico. He recalled that when he offered this solution to Cohen, the lawyer shouted: "'You're telling me that'. . . . And he became violent for a moment. I said, 'Hey, come on Cohen, you're not that stupid. What other ways are there?' 'Find me another way.' He says, 'Don't mention it to me again.'"[13]

The date of this conversation, and de facto decision, must have been some time after 3 April. On the eve of his friend's departure, Bortolotti brought Confalonieri to say goodbye to Goldman.

> I brought him there that afternoon because in the evening I had to be near Niagara Falls to hand him over to the smugglers. . . . Dorothy bent over her and she said, "Look, Joachim is going to Mexico; they finally gave him consent to go." You could see she almost had a smile. Then she got excited and she started to point with one finger towards her study. At that moment we didn't know what the hell. I was on one side of the bed and Dorothy the other. Joachim was beside there too. We didn't know what the hell to see. Finally I said, "Could it be that she wants something from the study?" So Dorothy said, "Could it be a file?" So she came out with her letters file, she had A, B, C, D. She brought it near to Emma. Emma looked and looked, no, no, no. So . . . I brought it back and picked the other one. The fourth or fifth file she said yes. Dorothy opened up and there was a letter.[14]

The file turned out to contain a letter from an Argentinian anarchist exiled in Mexico, and hence a contact and an address that she could offer to Confalonieri to ease his entry into a strange land. The smuggling, which sheds an astonishing light on both Bortolotti's compassion and boldness, not to say recklessness, was a success. On 12 April, Confalonieri cabled Cohen that he had arrived in Mexico City, and on 14 April wrote in poor French to thank him. On 30 April, his deportation was concluded when the British consul in the Mexican capital confirmed the anarchist's presence there in a letter to A.L. Jolliffe of Immigration.

During April and May, Goldman's companions at the Vaughan Road house communicated constantly with a variety of old friends and acquaintances who sent best wishes and donations, plans and suggestions: Rose Pesotta, Leon Malmed, John Cowper Powys, Aldous Huxley, Harry Kelly, and many others. Doctors continued to make hopeful prognoses, but on 2 May Dorothy Rogers reported to Rose Pesotta that a worrisome change had come over Goldman. Then, on 6 May, Goldman suffered a slight hemorrhage and became withdrawn. Even the name of her beloved brother, Moe, did not evoke a response from her. Moe and his wife were now notified and came to be at her side. "It is a tragic condition", Rogers wrote, "for such a one as Emma Goldman to find herself in and we who love her suffer with her while trying to keep up a pretense of cheerfulness for her sake." Summoned again from New York, Stella Ballantine arrived on 11 May and found her aunt crying: "Emma definitely recognized me this morning. She wept bitterly and only a few minutes ago as I stood by her bedside she said the first two understandable words. . . ." These were "Stella" and "Sasha" (the nickname of Alexander Berkman). Dorothy Rogers wrote to Rose Pesotta that Goldman was worse: "the breathing center . . . is now not functioning well at all". Her doctors now believed that "even if Emma recovered somewhat she would never be able to leave her bed."[15] About a day after Stella Ballantine's arrival, Goldman lapsed into thirty hours of unconsciousness and on 14 May died without waking, with Stella and Moe at her side.

On the evening of her death the Toronto *Daily Star*, which had followed her Canadian activities so closely over the years, wrote, "No woman of her generation was more widely known or lived more fully than Emma Goldman." The wonder of her longevity in the cause of freedom impressed those who had seen her in action during her final months in Canada. "At 70 years of age she was still fighting for her ideals when death came. Since last May she had gone on a speaking tour across Canada to raise money for Spanish refugees in camps in France." The newspaper quoted Goldman herself on her arrival in Toronto, "I would never take the easy way. I think if I have had any experience at all it is that I am temperamentally unfitted for what you would call the easy way. No, I'm still going on."[16]

Many tributes arrived at Vaughan Road. Rudolf and Milly Rocker lamented "the loss of a clarion voice for all that is worthwhile in humanity", and a cable from Frank González of the SIA mourned "our old friend Emma, challenger of all injustice throughout the world, the Spanish workers will always keep fresh in their hearts [her] love to our people".[17]

Goldman's body was taken to H. Benjamin and Son Funeral Home, 508–

510 Spadina Avenue. The *Daily Star* reported that a small service was planned for 15 May, "not a religious one, but rather just a gathering of her friends".[18] Salem Bland delivered the eulogy, generously praising Goldman in terms of his own concerns with the "social Gospel", the attempt to redirect Christianity from its emphasis on private morality towards social justice. "A sword might well be laid on the coffin of this brave woman", Bland said, "for she . . . was a brave soldier in the war of the liberation. I count it an honor to be permitted to pay a brief tribute to this brave woman. Naturally I in some respects was far from being in agreement with her views or endorsing all her conduct, but I count it a privilege to have known her and I deeply respect her. I fancy no man or woman of her day had a keener sense of justice or a more passionate love of liberty. I think Jesus would have claimed her as one of the sheep not of the regular fold. Maybe she would not have accepted all my Christianity, but . . . I would say she was deeply and intensely Christian in her love of justice, her passion for liberty, her devotion to the underdog." Bland would not, he said, like to live in the anarchist world "without police or courts" but felt quite sure that Goldman's "ultimate goal is the goal of Christianity, that those who walk in the spirit of Christ—'against such there is no law'. As far as I knew them, I think the central principles she held, the principles by which she lived were these." Stating "I do not feel it strange that she was not attracted by much of Christianity, because the big Christian Churches have never been as devoted to justice and liberty and the cause of the oppressed as they should have been", Bland concluded by picturing "the surprise Emma has already experienced—after the stormiest career any woman of our day has had" at being welcomed into "the other world. Gates of pearl were open—angelic guard of honor to receive her, trumpets sounding . . . welcoming her to . . . a home where she might have a long rest, no fear of [a] police visit with an order to move on."[19]

Permission having been received at last from the US government for Emma Goldman's readmission, her body was then shipped to Chicago. At a 17 May ceremony, she was interred in Waldheim Cemetery, where the men who had inspired her, the anarchists executed for the Haymarket riot, are also buried. Her grave was placed near that of Voltairine de Cleyre and other comrades. Belatedly, on 11 September 1940, a Royal Canadian Mounted Police official submitted a report recording Goldman's death and the fact that her body had been buried in Chicago. On 21 September this information was forwarded to the RCMP commissioner headed by the notation, "Case Concluded".[20]

Notes and Acknowledgements

Acknowledgements

There are many people and institutions to thank for important assistance in the writing of *The World's Most Dangerous Woman*. George Fetherling proposed the project to us and carefully nurtured it throughout its growth to a finished book. Roseanne Carrara contributed crucial research expertise and creative insight in the investigation of Emma Goldman's three major periods of residence in Canada as they were chronicled in her private papers. Victoria College in the University of Toronto provided a grant that enabled Albert Moritz to visit archives in Canada, which was especially valuable in enabling extended work in the Jacob Lawrence Cohen Papers at the National Archives of Canada, Ottawa. At the recommendation of Second Story Feminist Press, the Ontario Arts Council awarded Albert Moritz an OAC Writers' Reserve Grant. Betty Ballantine generously gave permission to publish material from the writings of Emma Goldman and from the letters of Stella Ballantine. Amelia Olay Kaplan was kind enough to allow the use of a letter written by Maximilian Olay. Mieke IJzermans, information officer of the International Institute of Social History, conveyed to us all the invaluable wisdom and courtesy of that most open of institutions. Janet Rosen, archives director of the Canadian Jewish Congress, guided us to many items relating to Goldman's Canadian friendships. Professor Canadace Falk and her staff at the University of California-Berkeley have immeasurably advanced Goldman studies by their production of the *Emma Goldman Papers*. We received helpful counsel on details of Goldman's activity in Toronto from Rosemary Donegan, author of *Spadina Avenue*, and from Coleman Romalis, director and writer of *The Anarchist Guest* (2000), a documentary film on Goldman's life in the city. Many librarians contributed greatly to the project by locating materials, answering questions, and directing us to copyright holders; especially helpful were Sylvia McDowell of the Schlesinger Library, Julie Herrada of the University of Michigan, Patricia K. Bakunas of the University of Illinois at Chicago, Wayne Furman of the New York Public Library, Mike Bott of Reading University, and Fred Bauman of the Library of Congress. The following libraries and archives granted permission to quote from sources in their holdings: Houghton Library, Harvard University; University Library, University of Illinois at Chicago; Harlan Hatcher Graduate Library, University of Michigan; New York Public Library; Tamiment Library, New York University; Princeton University Library; Reading University Library; Schlesinger Library, Radcliffe Institute, Harvard University; Archives of American Art, Smithsonian Institution Library; Hoover Institution Archives, Stanford University; United Church of Canada/Victoria University Archives; and Yale University Library. We have attempted to locate and gain permission from the copyright holders of all materials used; if any oversight is detected, we would appreciate learning of it so that it may be rectified in a future edition.

Notes

Abbreviations

AB	Alexander Berkman
EG	Emma Goldman
EGP	*Emma Goldman Papers*
LM	Leon Malmed
LML	*Living My Life*
ME	*Mother Earth*
MGP	Malmed-Goldman Papers, Schlesinger Library, Radcliffe Institute, Harvard University
RtF	*Road to Freedom*

Chapter 1: A Veritable Fury Unchained

1 James Lemon, *Toronto Since 1918: An Illustrated History* (Toronto: James Lorimer & Company, Publishers, 1985), 57.
2 Emma Goldman, *Living My Life*, 2 vols. (1931; reprint, New York: Dover Publications, 1970), 69.
3 Ibid., 148.
4 EG and Max Baginsky, "A Sentimental Journey.—Police Protection", *Mother Earth*, April 1906.
5 Montreal *Gazette*, 17 February 1908. *La Presse*, 2 May 1906. EG, "On the Road",

ME, April 1907.

6 EG, "On the Road", *ME*, May 1907. *LML*, 398. Cited in part by A.J. Arnold, "Anarchist Had Critics on All Sides", Winnipeg *Tribune*, 10 April 1975. Cf. also Martin Zeilig, "Emma Goldman in Winnipeg", *Manitoba History* (Spring 1993): 23–27.

7 EG, "On the Road", *ME*, May 1907.

8 Ibid.

9 Cited by A.J. Arnold, in "Anarchist Had Critics on All Sides".

10 Ibid.

11 Calgary *Daily Herald*, 17 June 1907.

12 *LML*, 411.

13 EG, "The Joys of Touring", *ME*, February 1908. *La Croix*, 29 February 1908 and 18 March 1908. Montreal *Star*, 22 February 1908. Emma Goldman File, unattributed manuscript, identified as "probably" notes by David Rome, Canadian Jewish Archives, Montreal.

14 Toronto *Evening Telegram*, 19 February 1908.

15 London *Free Press*, 21 February 1908.

16 Richard Drinnon, *Rebel in Paradise* (Chicago: University of Chicago Press, 1961), 138.

17 Walter E. Carr to John H. Clark, 9 April 1908, in Candace Falk, Ronald J. Zboray, and Alice Hall, eds., *The Emma Goldman Papers: A Microfilm Edition* (Alexandria, Va.: Chadwyck-Healey Inc., 1990), reel 56. Winnipeg *Telegram*, 8 April 1908.

18 J.H. Ashdown to Frank Oliver, 8 April 1908, P.A.C., Immigration Branch documents, file 800111, cited by D. Avery, "Continental European Workers in Canada, 1896–1919", *Revue canadienne de sociologie et anthropologie* 12, no. 1 (1975): 59.

19 Walter E. Carr to John H. Clark, 9 April 1908, *EGP*, reel 56.

20 Winnipeg *Tribune*, 1 April 1908.

21 Winnipeg *Tribune*, 3 April 1908. Winnipeg *Telegram*, 4 April 1908.

22 Walter E. Carr to John H. Clark, 9 April 1908, *EGP*, reel 56.

23 Ibid.

24 Winnipeg *Tribune*, 8 April 1908.

25 Winnipeg *Telegram*, 9 April 1908. Winnipeg *Telegram*, 10 April 1908.

26 Dorothy Livesay, *Right Hand, Left Hand: A True Life of the Thirties: Paris, Toronto, Montreal, The West and Vancouver. Love, Politics, The Depression, and Feminism* (Erin, Ontario: Press Porcepic, 1977), 31.

27 *LML*, 422; New York *Herald*, 9 April 1908, cited by Drinnon, in *Rebel in Paradise*, 113.

28 Winnipeg *Tribune*, 24 November 1908.

29 Winnipeg *Tribune*, 1 December 1908. Winnipeg *Tribune*, 2 December 1908.
30 EG, "En Route", *ME*, December 1908.
31 Winnipeg *Tribune*, 2 December 1908. EG, "En Route", *ME*, December 1908.
32 EG, "The Joys of Touring", *ME*, January 1909.
33 *LML*, 469.

Chapter 2: Inseparably Allied with the Future

1 *LML*, 974.
 2 EG to Ben Capes, 23 June 1925, *EGP*, reel 15.
 3 James Colton to Alexander Berkman, 22 July 1925, cited by Drinnon, in *Rebel in Paradise*, 257.
 4 EG to Max Nettlau, 8 July 1925, *EGP*, reel 15.
 5 EG to Stella Ballantine, 30 June 1925, *EGP*, reel 15: from the Emma Goldman Papers, Manuscripts and Archives Division, The New York Public Library, Astor, Lenox and Tilden Foundations.
 6 EG to Harry Weinberger, 3 July 1925, *EGP*, reel 15: from the Harry Weinberger Papers, Manuscripts and Archives, Yale University Library.
 7 EG to Angelica Balabanoff, 15 August 1925, *EGP*, reel 15. EG to Harry Weinberger, 29 September 1925, *EGP*, reel 15. EG to AB, 9 November 1925, *EGP*, reel 15. EG to G.P. Wiksell, 8 December 1925, *EGP*, reel 15.
 8 EG to AB, 20 December 1925, *EGP*, reel 15.
 9 EG to Joseph Ishill, 10 September 1926, *EGP*, reel 16: from the Houghton Library, Harvard University, shelf mark bMS Am 1614 (54).
10 Michael Cohn to EG, 26 May 1926, *EGP*, reel 16. EG to Ben Reitman, 15 April 1926, *EGP*, reel 15: from the Ben Reitman Papers, University Library, University of Illinois at Chicago.
11 Ted Switz to EG, ? October 1925, *EGP*, reel 15. Warren K. Billings to EG, 19 January 1926, *EGP*, reel 15.
12 EG to Leon Malmed, 21 September 1923, *EGP*, reel 13: from the Malmed-Goldman Papers, Schlesinger Library, Radcliffe Institute, Harvard University.
13 EG to W.S. Van Valkenburg, 16 June 1925, *EGP*, reel 15: from the Labadie Collection, Special Collections Library, University of Michigan.
14 EG to LM, 19 January 1926, 25 February 1926, *EGP*, reel 15: MGP.
15 EG to LM, 25 February 1926, *EGP*, reel 15: MGP.
16 EG to LM, 19 January 1926, *EGP*, reel 15: MGP. EG to William C. Owen, 22 June 1926, *EGP*, reel 16.
17 EG to LM, 19 January 1926, *EGP*, reel 15: MGP.
18 EG, "Was My Life Worth Living?", *Harper's* 170 (December 1934): 54.
19 EG to H.L. Mencken, 23 March 1926, *EGP*, reel 15.

20 EG to Frances and Jerome Blum, 31 March 1926, *EGP*, reel 15: from the Jerome Blum Papers, Archives of American Art, Smithsonian Institution.

21 Michael Cohn to EG, 23 April 1926, *EGP*, reel 15. Michael Cohn to EG, 10 May 1926, *EGP*, reel 16.

22 EG to Lady Astor, 18 May 1926, *EGP*, reel 16.

23 *LML*, 983.

24 EG to Ellen Kennan, 6 September 1926, *EGP*, reel 16. EG to Frances Blum, 27 June 1926, *EGP*, reel 16: from the Jerome Blum Papers, Archives of American Art, Smithsonian Institution. EG to Harry Weinberger, 3 June 1926, *EGP*, reel 16: from the Harry Weinberger Papers, Manuscripts and Archives, Yale University Library.

25 EG to LM, 24 May 1926, *EGP*, reel 16: MGP.

26 EG to LM, 7 August 1926, *EGP*, reel 16: MGP.

27 Ibid.

28 EG to Ben Capes, 11 August 1926, *EGP*, reel 16. EG to Joe Desser, 11 August 1926, *EGP*, reel 16: MGP.

29 EG to Michael Cohn, 14 August 1926, *EGP*, reel 16.

30 Michael Cohn to EG, 1 September 1926, *EGP*, reel 16.

31 EG to Michael Cohn, 14 September 1926, *EGP*, reel 16.

32 Ibid.

33 EG to LM, 5 September 1926, 14 September 1926, *EGP*, reel 16: MGP.

34 Theodore Dreiser to EG, 29 September 1926, *EGP*, reel 16.

Chapter 3: If Only I Had Known It Would Be So Easy

1 EG to LM, 15 October 1926, *EGP*, reel 16: MGP.

2 EG, "Patience and Postage", *Road to Freedom*, January 1927.

3 Stamford *Advocate*, 12 November 1926.

4 EG to Don Levine, 24 October 1926, *EGP*, reel 16.

5 EG to LM, 26 September 1926, 31 October 1926, *EGP*, reel 16: MGP.

6 Lena Shlakman, cited by Paul Avrich, in *Anarchist Voices: An Oral History of Anarchism in America* (Princeton, N.J.: Princeton University Press, 1995), 327.

7 Ibid.

8 Bernard Figler and David Rome, *Hannaniah Meir Caiserman: A Biography* (Montreal: Northern Printing and Lithographic Co., 1962), 121–22. Israel Medres, cited by David Rome, "On Our Forerunners—At Work", *Canadian Jewish Archives*, n.s. 10 (1978): 109-11.

9 Kenneth McNaught, *The Pelican History of Canada*, rev. ed. (Middlesex, England: Penguin Books, 1982), 223.

10 Ralph Melville, "Permanent Emigration and Temporary Transnational Migration: Jewish, Polish and Russian Emigration from Tsarist Russia, 1861-

1914", in *Overseas Migration from East-Central and Southeastern Europe 1880-1940,* Julianna Puskás ed. (Budapest: Akadémiai Kiadó, 1990), 138.

11 Rosemary Donegan, *Spadina Avenue* (Toronto: Douglas & McIntyre, 1985), 16.

12 EG, "Patience and Postage," *RtF,* January 1927. EG to LM, 2 November 1926, *EGP,* reel 16: MGP.

13 W.S. Van Valkenburg, "Emma Goldman Speaks Again!", *RtF,* December 1926. Montreal *Star,* 20 October 1926. Montreal *Star,* 1 November 1926. Montreal *Gazette,* 1 November 1926. Montreal *Star,* 1 November 1926.

14 Montreal *Gazette,* 1 November 1926.

15 EG to LM, 11 November 1926, *EGP,* reel 16: MGP. EG to Arthur Leonard Ross, 26 May 1927, reel 18: from the Emma Goldman Papers, Tamiment Library, New York University.

16 Montreal *Gazette,* 1 November 1926.

17 EG to LM, 2 November 1926, *EGP,* reel 16: MGP.

18 EG to LM, 8 November 1926, 17 November 1926, 18 November 1926, 19 November 1926, *EGP,* reel 16: MGP.

19 EG to LM, 8 November 1926, *EGP,* reel 16: MGP.

20 EG to LM, 7 November 1926, *EGP,* reel 16.

21 EG to LM, 11 November 1926, *EGP,* reel 16: MGP.

22 EG to LM, 22 November 1926, *EGP,* reel 16: MGP.

23 EG to LM, 18 November 1926, *EGP,* reel 16: MGP.

24 Fred Jacobs to EG, 4 November 1926, *EGP,* reel 16. Fred Jacobs to EG, 10 November 1926, *EGP,* reel 16.

25 EG to Ben Reitman, 20 November 1926, *EGP,* reel 16: from the Ben Reitman Papers, University Library, University of Illinois at Chicago.

Chapter 4: Toronto, Autumn and Winter 1926–27

1 EG to LM, 27 November 1926, *EGP,* reel 16: MGP. EG, "Patience and Postage", *RtF,* March 1927. EG to LM, 27 November 1926, *EGP,* reel 16: MGP.

2 Toronto *Daily Star,* 27 November 1926. Toronto *Evening Telegram,* 1 December 1926.

3 Toronto *Daily Star,* 27 November 1926.

4 EG to LM, 27 November 1926, *EGP,* reel 16: MGP.

5 EG, "Patience and Postage", *RtF,* March 1927.

6 EG, "Patience and Postage", *RtF,* April 1927.

7 Julius Seltzer, cited by Avrich, in *Anarchist Voices,* 329–30.

8 EG to LM, 28 November 1926, *EGP,* reel 16: MGP.

9 EG to LM, 30 November 1926, 3 December 1926, *EGP,* reel 16: MGP.

10 EG to LM, 11 December 1926, 10 December 1926, *EGP,* reel 16: MGP.

11 EG to LM, 13 December 1926, 15 December 1926, *EGP*, reel 16: MGP.

12 EG to LM, 12 December 1926, *EGP*, reel 16: MGP.

13 EG to LM, 17 December 1926, *EGP*, reel 16: MGP.

14 Toronto *Daily Star*, 30 November 1926. *Mail and Empire*, 1 December 1926.

15 Toronto *Daily Star*, 4 December 1926.

16 Toronto *Daily Star*, 6 December 1926.

17 Toronto *Daily Star*, 15 December 1926.

18 EG to Ellen Kennan, 18 December 1926, *EGP*, reel 16.

19 EG to AB, 15 December 1926, *EGP*, reel 26. EG to Ellen Kennan, 18 December 1926, *EGP*, reel 16. EG to AB, 22 December 1926, *EGP*, reel 16.

20 EG to AB, 22 December 1926, *EGP*, reel 16. EG to LM, 22 December 1926, *EGP*, reel 16: MGP.

21 Toronto *Daily Star*, 15 January 1927.

22 EG to LM, 28 November 1926, 18 November 1926, *EGP*, reel 16: MGP.

23 EG to AB, 27 December 1926, *EGP*, reel 16.

24 EG, "Patience and Postage," *RtF*, March 1927.

25 Frederick Griffin, "Toronto's Anarchist Guest", Toronto *Star Weekly*, 31 December 1926.

26 EG to LM, 7 January 1927, *EGP*, reel 17: MGP.

27 EG, "Patience and Postage", *RtF*, April 1927. EG to LM, 5 January 1927, *EGP*, reel 17: MGP.

28 EG to Doris Zhook, 17 January 1927, *EGP*, reel 17: from the Emma Goldman Papers, Tamiment Library, New York University.

29 EG to LM, 7 January 1927, 8 January 1927, *EGP*, reel 17: MGP.

30 EG to LM, 20 January 1927, *EGP*, reel 17: MGP.

Chapter 5: Winnipeg and Edmonton, 1927

1 *Free Press*, 28 January 1927. *Tribune*, 27 January 1927.

2 EG to LM, 27 March 1927, 27 December 1926, 17 February 1927, 20 February 1927, *EGP*, reel 17: MGP.

3 EG to Joseph Ishill, 1 March 1927, *EGP*, reel 17: from the Houghton Library, Harvard University, shelf mark bMS Am 1614 (54).

4 RCMP Report, 9 March 1927, *EGP*, reel 66.

5 *Free Press*, 31 January 1927. Toronto *Daily Star*, 4 February 1927.

6 *Free Press*, 28 January 1927. *Telegram*, 2 February 1927.

7 EG to AB, 4 April 1927, *EGP*, reel 18. EG to Ben Capes, 28 March 1927, *EGP*, reel 17.

8 *LML*, 989.

9 *Journal*, 4 March 1927. *Bulletin*, 4 March 1927.

10 *Bulletin*, 5 March 1927.

11 *Bulletin*, 14 March 1927.

12 *Journal*, 15 March 1927. *Journal*, 14 March 1927.

13 EG to Lena Margolis, 21 March 1927, *EGP*, reel 17.

14 EG, "Patience and Postage", *RtF*, April 1927.

15 EG to Harry Weinberger, 3 November 1926, *EGP*, reel 16: from the Harry Weinberger Papers, Manuscripts and Archives, Yale University Library. William Fraser to EG, 27 December 1926, *EGP*, reel 16. EG to Thomas H. Bell, 31 December 1926, *EGP*, reel 16.

16 Henry Lynch to EG, 25 January 1927, *EGP*, reel 17. EG to Henry Lynch, 5 February 1927, *EGP*, reel 17. Frank Girard and Ben Perry, *The Socialist Labor Party 1876–1991: A Short History* (Philadelphia: Livra Books, 1991), 52. Henry Lynch to EG, 19 February 1927, *EGP*, reel 17.

17 EG to Joseph Cohen, 7 March 1927, *EGP*, reel 17.

18 *Weekly People*, 9 April 1927.

19 Don Levine to EG, 15 December 1926, *EGP*, reel 16.

20 W.S. Van Valkenburg to EG, 8 April 1927, *EGP*, reel 18: from the Labadie Collection, Special Collections Library, University of Michigan.

21 EG to Don Levine, 15 April 1927, *EGP*, reel 18.

22 EG, "Our Propaganda: Patience and Postage Stamps", *RtF*, June 1927.

23 AB to EG, 24 February 1927, *EGP*, reel 17.

Chapter 6: Spring and Summer 1927

1 Buffalo *Evening News*, 28 March 1927. New York *World*, 10 April 1927.

2 Toronto *Daily Star*, 16 March 1927.

3 Ibid.

4 Ibid. Toronto *Daily Star*, 15 March 1927.

5 *Globe*, 16 March 1927.

6 EG to AB, 17 May 1927, *EGP*, reel 18. W.A. Cameron, cited in New York *World*, 10 April 1927. Toronto *Daily Star*, 21 March 1927.

7 New York *World*, 10 April 1927.

8 Ibid.

9 Toronto *Daily Star*, 4 April 1927.

10 Ibid. *Mail and Empire*, 4 April 1927.

11 Toronto *Daily Star*, 4 April 1927.

12 *Mail and Empire*, 4 April 1927.

13 Ibid.

14 EG to AB, 4 April 1927, *EGP*, reel 18. *Mail and Empire*, 4 April 1927. EG, "Patience and Poststamps Some Times Have Their Rewards", draft article, ? March 1928, *EGP*, reel 51. EG to LM, 3 April 1927, *EGP*, reel 18: MGP.

15 EG to AB, 11 April 1927, *EGP*, reel 18.

16 *Globe*, 12 March 1927. Toronto *Daily Star*, 4 April 1927.

17 Toronto *Daily Star*, 28 April 1927.

18 Ibid.

19 EG, "Patience and Poststamps Some Times Have Their Rewards". *Mail and Empire*, 7 May 1927.

20 EG to LM, 10 May 1927, *EGP*, reel 18: MGP. EG to AB, 18 June 1927, *EGP*, reel 18.

21 W.S. Van Valkenburg to EG, 3 May 1927, *EGP*, reel 18. EG to AB, 31 January 1927, *EGP*, reel 17. EG to W.S. Van Valkenburg, 16 June 1927, *EGP*, reel 18.

22 *LML*, 990.

23 EG to W.S. Van Valkenburg, 14 May 1927, *EGP*, reel 18. W.S. Van Valkenburg to EG, 11 July 1927, *EGP*, reel 18. EG to Sacco and Vanzetti, 19 July 1927, *EGP*, reel 18; EG to LM, 4 August 1927, *EGP*, reel 18; EG to LM, 6 August 1927, *EGP*, reel 18; MGP.

24 *Mail and Empire*, 19 August 1927. Freda Diamond, cited by Avrich, in *Anarchist Voices*, 54.

25 EG to LM, 1 September 1927, *EGP*, reel 19: MGP. RCMP Agent #30, Report to "O" Division, Western Ontario District, 2 September 1927, *EGP*, reel 66. EG, "Patience and Poststamps Some Times Have Their Rewards". EG to Evelyn Scott, 3 September 1927, *EGP*, reel 19.

26 Ora Robbins, cited by Avrich, in *Anarchist Voices*, 76.

Chapter 7: Reliving Her Life

1 Toronto *Daily Star*, 26 October 1927.

2 Toronto *Daily Star*, 9 November 1927.

3 Ibid. Toronto *Daily Star*, 16 November 1927.

4 Toronto *Daily Star*, 9 November 1927.

5 Toronto *Daily Star*, 28 October 1927.

6 Toronto *Daily Star*, 11 November 1927.

7 Toronto *Daily Star*, 18 November 1927.

8 Livesay, *Right Hand, Left Hand*, 31.

9 Dorothy Livesay, *Journey with My Selves: A Memoir 1909-1963* (Vancouver and Toronto: Douglas & McIntyre, 1993), 66.

10 Ibid.

11 EG to AB, 3 October 1927, *EGP*, reel 19.

12 Joseph Ishill to EG, 2 November 1927, *EGP*, reel 19. AB to EG, 7 December 1927, *EGP*, reel 19.

13 EG to AB, 23 December 1927, *EGP*, reel 19. EG to Sadie Robins, 1 December 1927, *EGP*, reel 19.

14 EG, "Patience and Poststamps Some Times Have Their Rewards".

15 Ibid.

16 EG to Joseph Ishill, 14 February 1928, *EGP*, reel 19: from the Houghton Library, Harvard University, shelf mark bMS Am 1614 (54).

17 EG, "Patience and Poststamps Some Times Have Their Rewards".

18 AB to EG, 19 November 1928, *EGP*, reel 20.

19 Arthur Leonard Ross to EG, 28 December 1928, *EGP*, reel 20. EG to Arthur Leonard Ross, 13 January 1929, *EGP*, reel 20.

20 EG to AB, 14 May 1929, *EGP*, reel 21.

21 EG to AB, 3 July 1928, *EGP*, reel 20. AB to EG, 28 November 1928, *EGP*, reel 20. EG to AB, 23 November 1928 *EGP*, reel 20. AB to EG, 28 November 1928, *EGP*, reel 20. AB, unpublished diary, 30 November 1928, cited by Alice Wexler, *Emma Goldman in Exile: From the Russian Revolution to the Spanish Civil War* (Boston: Beacon Press, 1989), 135.

22 AB, diary, 19 January 1929, cited by Wexler, in *Emma Goldman in Exile*, 135. Drinnon, *Rebel in Paradise*, 268. EG to AB, 20 February 1929, *EGP*, reel 20.

23 EG to Arthur Leonard Ross, 2 September 1929, *EGP*, reel 21. EG to AB, 20 February 1929, *EGP*, reel 20.

24 EG to Milly Rocker, 6 March 1930, *EGP*, reel 22. EG to Henry Alsberg, 27 June 1930, *EGP*, reel 23.

25 EG to Arthur Leonard Ross, 29 April 1930, *EGP*, reel 23.

26 AB to EG, 22 December 1931, *EGP*, reel 25.

27 EG to LM, 27 November 1931, *EGP*, reel 25: MGP.

28 New York *Sun*, 20 November 1931. *New Republic*, 30 December 1931. *New Yorker*, 23 November 1931. Baltimore *Evening Sun*, 14 November 1931. *Time*, 9 November 1931.

29 EG to Mary Leavitt, 2 November 1932, *EGP*, reel 27. EG to Michael Cohn, 22 December 1931, *EGP*, reel 25. EG to AB, 18 November 1931, *EGP*, reel 25.

Chapter 8: Clinging to the Chance of Canada

1 AB to Fitzi Fitzgerald, 11 November 1932, cited by Drinnon, in *Rebel in Paradise*, 299.

2 EG to Ellen Kennan, 19 September 1932, *EGP*, reel 27. EG to AB, 21 January 1932, *EGP*, reel 26.

3 Windsor *Star*, 3 March 1933.

4 EG to Lenore Frederickson, 23 October 1933, *EGP*, reel 29. EG to Rudolf Rocker, 7 November 1933, *EGP*, reel 29. EG to Rudolf and Milly Rocker, 18 October 1933, *EGP*, reel 29.

5 EG to Mabel Crouch, 7 November 1933, *EGP*, reel 29.

6 EG to Milly Rocker, 20 November 1933, *EGP*, reel 29.

7 EG to Ben Capes, 9 December 1933, *EGP*, reel 29.

8   EG to AB, 18 December 1933, *EGP*, reel 29.

9   Ibid. EG to Harry Weinberger, 20 December 1933, *EGP*, reel 29.

10 Toronto *Daily Star*, 20 December 1933.

11 EG, "The Tragedy of the Political Exiles", *Nation* 139 (10 October 1934): 401–02. Toronto *Daily Star*, 20 December 1933.

12 Toronto *Daily Star*, 20 December 1933.

13 EG to Roger Baldwin, 22 December 1933, *EGP*, reel 29.

14 EG to AB, 31 December 1933, *EGP*, reel 29.

15 EG to Arthur Leonard Ross, 30 December 1933, *EGP*, reel 29.

16 EG to AB, 3 January 1934, *EGP*, reel 29.

17 EG to Milly and Rudolf Rocker, 2 January 1934, *EGP*, reel 29. Roger Baldwin to EG, 5 January 1934, *EGP*, reel 29. EG to Stella Ballantine, 7 January 1934, *EGP*, reel 29.

18 EG to AB, 10 January 1934, *EGP*, reel 29.

19 EG to Roger Baldwin, 10 January 1934, *EGP*, reel 29.

20 EG to Arthur Leonard Ross, 18 January 1934, *EGP*, reel 29. EG to Thomas Bell, 19 January 1934, *EGP*, reel 29.

21 EG to Milly Rocker, 29 January 1934, *EGP*, reel 29.

22 Toronto *Daily Star*, 18 January 1934.

23 Attilio Bortolotti, cited by Avrich, in *Anarchist Voices*, 184.

24 Attilio Bortolotti, "Guardian of the Dream: A [*sic*] Oral History with Art Berthelot", *Kick It Over*, no. 17 (Winter 1986/87): 1. Bortolotti, cited by Avrich, in *Anarchist Voices*, 185. Bortolotti, "Guardian of the Dream", 1.

25 EG to Milly Rocker, 29 January 1934, *EGP*, reel 29. EG to Arthur Leonard Ross, 18 January 1934, *EGP*, reel 29. EG to Milly Rocker, 29 January 1934, *EGP*, reel 29.

Chapter 9: To Vesuvius and Back

1   New York *Sun*, 8 February 1934.

2   Ibid. EG, cited by Drinnon, in *Rebel in Paradise*, 278. EG to AB, 23 March 1934, *EGP*, reel 30.

3   EG to Arthur Leonard Ross, 9 April 1934, *EGP*, reel 31. James Pond, cited by Drinnon, in *Rebel in Paradise*, 344.

4   Heywood Broun, "It Seems to Me by Heywood Broun", column syndicated to Scripps-Howard newspapers, January 1934.

5   Ibid. EG to C.V. Cook, 2 April 1934, *EGP*, reel 31.

6   Montreal *Gazette*, 2 May 1934.

7   EG to Henrietta Posner, 15 May 1934, *EGP*, reel 31. EG to AB, 12 May 1934, *EGP*, reel 31. EG to Rudolf Rocker, 4 May 1931, *EGP*, reel 31.

8   EG to Henrietta Posner, 15 May 1934, *EGP*, reel 31. Montreal *Gazette*, 16 May

1934.

9 Montreal *Daily Star*, 2 May 1934. *La Presse*, 4 May 1934.

10 EG to Frank Heiner, 18 May 1934, *EGP*, reel 31. EG to Frank Heiner, 6 May 1934, *EGP*, reel 31.

11 EG to Frank Heiner, 22 May 1934, *EGP*, reel 31. Toronto *Daily Star*, 29 May 1934. Toronto *Daily Star*, 23 May 1934. Albert de Jong to EG, 30 May 1934, *EGP*, reel 31.

12 Hye Bossin, "A Rebel Speaks", *Jewish Standard*, 29 June 1934, 6, 14.

13 Charles Angoff to EG, 2 July 1934, *EGP*, reel 31. George R. Leighton to EG, 9 July 1934, *EGP*, reel 31. EG to Stella Ballantine, 14 July 1934, *EGP*, reel 31.

14 EG to Albert de Jong, 17 July 1934, *EGP*, reel 31. EG to Stella Ballantine, 27 July 1934, *EGP*, reel 31. EG to Emmy Eckstein, 30 July 1934, *EGP*, reel 31.

15 EG to Albert de Jong, 17 July 1934, *EGP*, reel 31. EG to Frank Heiner, 21 July 1934, *EGP*, reel 31.

16 EG to Frank Heiner, 1 June 1934, *EGP*, reel 31. EG to Frank Heiner, 27 June 1934, *EGP*, reel 31.

17 EG to Mary Heiner, 23 June 1934, *EGP*, reel 31.

18 Mary Heiner to EG, 10 August 1934, *EGP*, reel 32.

19 EG to AB, 30 August 1934, *EGP*, reel 32.

20 Ibid.

Chapter 10: We Cling to an Ideal No One Wants

1 EG to Frank Heiner, 5 September 1934, *EGP*, reel 32.

2 EG to Frank Heiner, 9 September 1934, *EGP*, reel 32.

3 AB to EG, 6 September 1934, *EGP*, reel 32.

4 EG to Stella Ballantine, 25 October 1934, *EGP*, reel 32.

5 EG to Frank Heiner, 2 November 1934, *EGP*, reel 33. EG to Frank Heiner, 24 October 1934, *EGP*, reel 32.

6 Bortolotti, "Guardian of the Dream", 1.

7 Montreal *Gazette*, 13 November 1934.

8 EG to Emmy Eckstein, 9 December 1934, *EGP*, reel 33.

9 EG to Roger Baldwin, 17 November 1934, *EGP*, reel 33: from Volume 690, American Civil Liberties Union Archives, Seeley G. Mudd Manuscript Library, Princeton University Library. Published with permission of the Princeton University Library.

10 EG to Stella Ballantine, 11 March 1935, *EGP*, reel 34.

11 EG to Ben Reitman, 28 December 1934, *EGP*, reel 33.

12 AB to Michael Cohn, 15 March 1935, cited by Drinnon, in *Rebel in Paradise*, 292.

13 EG to Frank Heiner, 27 March 1935, *EGP*, reel 34. EG to W.S. Van Valkenburg, 28 March 1935, *EGP*, reel 34.

14 EG to Anna Olay, 30 March 1935, *EGP*, reel 34.

15 EG to Milly Rocker, 7 April 1935, EGP, reel 34.

16 EG to Joe Desser, 1 May 1935, *EGP*, reel 34.

17 EG to Dorothy Rogers, 11 May 1935, *EGP*, reel 34.

18 EG, "The Tragedy of the Political Exiles", 401–02.

19 EG, "Was My Life Worth Living?", 53–54.

20 EG, "Was My Life Worth Living?", 55, 57.

21 EG, "The Place of the Individual in Society," *70ᵗʰ Birthday Commemorative Edition* (Los Angeles: Liberation Committee, 1939), 2–4.

22 EG, "The Place of the Individual in Society," 7–14.

23 EG, "Was My Life Worth Living?", 52.

24 EG to Roger Baldwin, 11 April 1935, *EGP*, reel 34.

25 EG to AB, 5 January 1935, *EGP*, reel 33. EG to AB, 17 April 1935, *EGP*, reel 34.

26 AB to Stella Ballantine, 14 August 1935, cited by Richard Drinnon and Anna Maria Drinnon, editors, *Nowhere at Home: Letters from Exile of Emma Goldman and Alexander Berkman* (New York: Schocken Books, 1975), 245.

27 EG to Roger Baldwin, 19 June 1935, *EGP*, reel 34.

28 EG to AB, 19 November 1935, *EGP*, reel 35.

29 EG to AB, 24 January 1936, *EGP*, reel 36. AB to EG, 9 January 1936, *EGP*, reel 36.

30 AB to EG, 21 March 1936, *EGP*, reel 37. EG to AB, 24 March 1936, *EGP*, reel 37.

31 EG to AB, 24 March 1936, *EGP*, reel 37. AB to EG, 23 March 1936, *EGP*, reel 37.

32 EG to Ben Taylor, 11 June 1936, *EGP*, reel 37.

33 EG to Comrades, 12 July 1936, *EGP*, reel 38.

Chapter 11: The Spanish Civil War

1 EG to Stella Ballantine, 22 August 1936, *EGP*, reel 38: from the Emma Goldman Papers, Manuscripts and Archives Division, The New York Public Library, Astor, Lenox and Tilden Foundations.

2 EG, *CNT-AIT-FAI Boletín de Información*, 25 September 1936, cited by Drinnon, in *Rebel in Paradise*, 302.

3 Windsor *Star*, 20 May 1939.

4 Samuel Abramson to H.M. Caiserman, 29 October 1938, Canadian Jewish Congress Archives, Series DA 1.

5 EG to John Cowper Powys, 21 March 1939, *EGP*, reel 46: from the Labadie Collection, Special Collections Library, University of Michigan.

6 EG to Rudolf Rocker, 31 March 1939, *EGP*, reel 46.

7 EG to Hutchins Hapgood, 20 August 1939, *EGP*, reel 46.

8 EG to Dorothy Rogers, 21 March 1939, *EGP*, reel 46. EG to Harry Weinberger, 18 April 1939, *EGP*, reel 46. EG to Liza Kodolfsky, 29 April 1939, *EGP*, reel 46: from the Emma Goldman Papers, Manuscripts and Archives Division, The

New York Public Library, Astor, Lenox and Tilden Foundations.

9 EG to Liza Kodolfsky, 29 April 1939, *EGP*, reel 46: from the Emma Goldman Papers, Manuscripts and Archives Division, The New York Public Library, Astor, Lenox and Tilden Foundations.

10 Toronto *Daily Star*, 22 April 1939.

11 Ibid.

12 EG to Rudolf Rocker, 10 May 1939, *EGP*, reel 46.

13 Toronto *Evening Telegram*, 28 April 1939.

14 Windsor *Star*, 20 May 1939.

15 Ibid.

16 Ibid. Toronto *Evening Telegram*, 28 April 1939.

17 EG to LM, 4 June 1939, *EGP*, reel 46: MGP.

18 EG to Milly Rocker, 31 May 1939, *EGP*, reel 46. EG to LM, 4 June 1939, *EGP*, reel 46: MGP.

19 Windsor *Star*, 20 May 1939.

20 EG to Rudolf and Milly Rocker, 27 June 1939, *EGP*, reel 46. Mariano Vazquez to EG, 12 June 1939, *EGP*, reel 46.

21 EG to Ben Reitman, 6 June 1939, *EGP*, reel 46: from the Ben Reitman Papers, University Library, University of Illinois at Chicago. EG to Rudolf and Milly Rocker, 27 June 1939, *EGP*, reel 46.

22 EG to LM, 2 July 1939, *EGP*, reel 46: MGP. EG to Mark Mratchny, 1 July 1939, *EGP*, reel 46: from the Labadie Collection, Special Collections Library, University of Michigan.

23 *70ᵗʰ Birthday Commemorative Edition*, n.p.

24 EG to Comrades and Friends on the North American Continent, 27 June 1939, in *70ᵗʰ Birthday Commemorative Edition*, n.p.

25 EG to H.M. Caiserman, 26 July 1939, *EGP*, reel 46: from the Canadian Jewish Congress Archives, Series DA 1.

26 EG to Fitzi Fitzgerald, 30 June 1939, *EGP*, reel 46.

27 EG to Fitzi Fitzgerald, 21 May 1939, *EGP*, reel 46.

28 EG to Ethel Mannin, 25 July 1939, *EGP*, reel 46. Vero Richards to EG, 8 August 1939, *EGP*, reel 46. EG to Vero Richards, 29 August 1939, *EGP*, reel 46.

29 EG to Don Levine, 22 September 1939, *EGP*, reel 46. EG to Rudolf Rocker, 7 October 1939, *EGP*, reel 46.

30 Maximilian Olay to EG, ? August 1939, *EGP*, reel 46: from the Labadie Collection, Special Collections Library, University of Michigan. EG to Milly Rocker, 2 September 1939, *EGP*, reel 46.

31 EG to Rose Pesotta, 27 August 1939, *EGP*, reel 46: from the Rose Pesotta Papers, Manuscripts and Archives Division, The New York Public Library, Astor, Lenox and Tilden Foundations. EG to Milly Rocker, 2 September 1939,

EGP, reel 46.

32 EG to Liza Kodolfsky, 12 September 1939, *EGP*, reel 46: from the Emma Goldman Papers, Manuscripts and Archives Division, The New York Public Library, Astor, Lenox and Tilden Foundations.

Chapter 12: The Last Cause

1 Attilio Bortolotti, cited by Ross Munro, "The Black Flag of Anarchism Is Flying Again", *Globe Magazine*, 4 July 1970.

2 Bortolotti, cited by Avrich, in *Anarchist Voices*, 186.

3 *The Globe*, 5 October 1939.

4 EG to J.L. Cohen, 7 October 1939, in Jacob Lawrence Cohen Papers, National Archives of Canada, Volume 14.

5 EG to Attilio Bortolotti, 7 October 1939, JLCP, Volume 14.

6 "The Case of Arthur Bortolotti", draft document prepared by J.L. Cohen and EG, JLCP, Volume 14.

7 Bortolotti, cited by Avrich, in *Anarchist Voices*, 184.

8 Windsor *Star*, 10 September 1938.

9 EG to Marcelino Garcia, 9 October 1939, *EGP*, reel 46: from the Labadie Collection, Special Collections Library, University of Michigan. Audrey Goodfriend, cited by Avrich, in *Anarchist Voices*, 460.

10 Millie Desser, cited by Avrich, in *Anarchist Voices*, 79. EG to James Heney, 17 October 1939, *EGP*, reel 46: from the Labadie Collection, Special Collections Library, University of Michigan.

11 EG to Nick DiDomenico, 19 October 1939, *EGP*, reel 46: from the Labadie Collection, Special Collections Library, University of Michigan.

12 EG to Milly Rocker, 31 October 1939, *EGP*, reel 46.

13 EG to Rose Pesotta, 8 October 1939, *EGP*, reel 46: from the Rose Pesotta Papers, Manuscripts and Archives Division, The New York Public Library, Astor, Lenox and Tilden Foundations.

14 EG to Sidney Solomon, 14 October 1939, EGP, reel 46: from the Labadie Collection, Special Collections Library, University of Michigan. J.L. Cohen obituary, JLCP, Volume 49.

15 "Rex vs. Arthur Bartolliti, Ernest Gava, Ruggero Benvenuti", JLCP, Volume 14.

16 Ibid.

17 Ibid.

18 Ibid.

19 Ibid.

20 EG to *Freie Arbeiter Stimme*, 31 October-2 November 1939, *EGP*, reel 46: from the Labadie Collection, Special Collections Library, University of Michigan.

21 Bortolotti, "Guardian of the Dream", 2.
22 EG to *Nation*, 25 November 1939, *EGP*, reel 46.
23 EG to J.L. Cohen, 10 November 1939, JLCP, Volume 14.
24 J.L. Cohen to A.A. Heaps and to J.S. Woodsworth, 29 November 1939, JLCP, Volume 14.
25 Report by RCMP Agent #302 to RCMP Commissioner, Ottawa, 6 December 1939, *EGP*, reel 66. EG to Attilio Bortolotti, 15 December 1939, JLCP, Volume 14. EG to Bunya and Jasha of IWW, 16 December 1939, *EGP*, reel 46.
26 EG to J.L. Cohen, 30 November 1939, JLCP, Volume 14.
27 EG to J.L. Cohen, 30 November 1939, JLCP, Volume 14. J.S. Woodsworth to J.L. Cohen, 30 November 1939, JLCP, Volume 14.
28 J.S. Woodsworth to J.L. Cohen, 30 November 1939, JLCP, Volume 14.
29 J.L. Cohen to EG, 5 December 1939, JLCP, Volume 14.
30 EG to J.L. Cohen, 9 December 1939, JLCP, Volume 14.

Chapter 13: Gagged and Fettered

1 J.L. Cohen to EG, 14 December 1939, JLCP, Volume 14.
2 Ibid.
3 EG to Nick DiDomenico, 19 December 1939, *EGP*, reel 46: from the Labadie Collection, Special Collections Library, University of Michigan.
4 EG to Comrades and Friends, 6 January 1940, *EGP*, reel 46. EG to Nick DiDomenico, 9 January 1940, *EGP*, reel 46: from the Labadie Collection, Special Collections Library, University of Michigan.
5 A.H. Lieff to J.L. Cohen, 22 January 1940, JLCP, Volume 14. J.L. Cohen to A.H. Lieff, 25 January 1940, JLCP, Volume 14.
6 John Walter to W.D. Euler, 8 January 1940, JLCP, Volume 14.
7 EG to Nick DiDomenico, 9 January 1940, *EGP*, reel 46: from the Labadie Collection, Special Collections Library, University of Michigan.
8 Toronto *Daily Star*, 10 January 1940.
9 EG to Fitzi Fitzgerald, 12 January 1940, *EGP*, reel 46.
10 Dr Maurice A. Pollock, medical report on Attilio Bortolotti, JLCP, Volume 14.
11 "Statement re Attilio (Arthur) Bortolotti", draft document prepared by J.L. Cohen and EG, JLCP, Volume 14.
12 "To: The Editor of The Canadian Forum, Toronto", draft letter to the editor prepared by J.L. Cohen and EG, JLCP, Volume 14.
13 Salem Bland to Thomas A. Crerar, 16 May 1940, JLCP, Volume 14.
14 Harry S. Bennett to J.L. Cohen, February 1940, JLCP, Volume 14.
15 Examination conducted by James L. Malcolm, officer-in-charge at Toronto, on an order of the Minister of Mines and Resources, 22 January 1940, JLCP, Volume 14.

16 Ibid.

17 EG to Nick DiDomenico, 15 February 1940, *EGP*, reel 46: from the Labadie Collection, Special Collections Library, University of Michigan. "Statement re Attilio (Arthur) Bortolotti", JLCP, Volume 14.

18 Ben Reitman to EG, 17 February 1940, *EGP*, reel 46: from the Ben Reitman Papers, University Library, University of Illinois at Chicago.

Chapter 14: Unfitted for the Easy Way

1 Dien Meelis to Leon Malmed, 29 February 1940, *EGP*, reel 46: MGP.

2 Bortolotti, "Guardian of the Dream", 2.

3 Ahrne Thorne, cited by Paul Kennedy, *Emma Goldman: A Life of Anarchy* (Toronto: The Canadian Broadcasting Corporation, 1983), 34.

4 Fitzi Fitzgerald to J.L. Cohen, 19 February 1940, JLCP, Volume 14. Stella Ballantine to Ben Reitman, March 1940, cited by Candace Falk, *Love, Anarchy, and Emma Goldman* (New York: Holt, Rinehart, 1984), 515.

5 Millie Desser to Jacob Silverstein, 24 February 1940, *EGP*, reel 46. John Haynes Holmes to EG, 5 April 1940, *EGP*, reel 46.

6 J.L. Cohen to A.H. Lieff, 5 March 1940, JLCP, Volume 14.

7 Toronto *Daily Star*, 26 February 1940.

8 *Canadian Forum*, March 1940.

9 Windsor *Star*, 2 March 1940.

10 F.C. Blair to J.L. Cohen, 29 April 1940, JLCP, Volume 14.

11 Salem Bland to Thomas Crerar, 16 May 1940, JLCP, Volume 14.

12 Ibid.

13 Bortolotti, "Guardian of the Dream", 2.

14 Ibid.

15 Dorothy Rogers to J.C. Powers, 8 May 1940, *EGP*, reel 46: from the Labadie Collection, Special Collections Library, University of Michigan. Stella Ballantine to Harry Kelly, 11 May 1940, *EGP*, reel 46: from the Labadie Collection, Special Collections Library, University of Michigan. Dorothy Rogers to Rose Pesotta, 11 May 1940, *EGP*, reel 46: from the Rose Pesotta Papers, Manuscripts and Archives Division, The New York Public Library, Astor, Lenox and Tilden Foundations.

16 Toronto *Daily Star*, 14 May 1940.

17 Frank Gonzalez to EG, 14 May 1940, *EGP*, reel 46.

18 Toronto *Daily Star*, 14 May 1940.

19 United Church of Canada/Victoria University Archives, Salem Bland fonds, Salem G. Bland Papers, 86.037C-Box 3, "Tribute to Emma Goldman at her obsequies May 15, 1940".

20 R.J. Smith, RCMP Report, 11 September 1940, forwarded to commissioner, 21 September 1940, *EGP*, reel 66.

Selected Bibliography

Anctil, Pierre. *Les Juifs de Montréal face au Québec de l'entre-deux-guerres. Le rendez-vous manqué*. Québec: Institut Québécois de Recherche sur la Culture, 1988.

Anctil, Pierre and Gary Caldwell, eds. *Juifs et realités juives au Québec*. Québec: Institut Québécois de Recherche sur la Culture, 1984.

Avrich, Paul. *An American Anarchist: The Life of Voltairine de Cleyre*. Princeton, N.J.: Princeton University Press, 1978.

———. *Anarchist Voices: An Oral History of Anarchism in America*. Princeton, N.J.: Princeton University Press, 1995.

———. *Sacco and Vanzetti: The Anarchist Background*. Princeton, N.J.: Princeton University Press, 1991.

———. *The Anarchists in the Russian Revolution*. Ithaca: Cornell University Press, 1973.

———. *The Russian Anarchists*. Princeton, N.J.: Princeton University Press, 1967.

Berkman, Alexander. *The ABC of Anarchism*. 1929. Reprint. London: Freedom Press, 1977.

Betcherman, Lita-Rose. *The Little Band: The Clashes Between the Communists and the Political and Legal Establishment in Canada, 1928-1932*. Ottawa: Deneau, 1982.

———. *The Swastika and the Maple Leaf: Fascist Movements in Canada in the Thirties*. Toronto: Fitzhenry & Whiteside, 1975.

Brown, L. Susan. *The Politics of Individualism: Liberalism, Liberal Feminism and Anarchism*. Montreal: Black Rose Books, 1993.

Chalberg, John. *Emma Goldman: American Individualist*. New York: HarperCollins, 1991.

Cranston, James Herbert. *Ink on My Fingers*. Toronto: Ryerson Press, 1953.

Delisle, Esther. *The Traitor and the Jew: Anti-Semitism and the Delirium of Extremist Right-Wing Nationalism in French Canada from 1929–1939*. Translated by Madeleine Hébert with Claire Rothman and Käthe Roth. Montreal and Toronto: Robert Davies Publishing, 1993.

Dell, Floyd. *Women as World Builders: Studies in Modern Feminism*. Chicago: Forbes & Company, 1913.

Donegan, Rosemary. *Spadina Avenue*. Introduction by Rick Salutin. Toronto: Douglas & McIntyre, 1985.

Drinnon, Richard, and Anna Maria Drinnon, eds. *Nowhere at Home: Letters from Exile of Emma Goldman and Alexander Berkman.* New York: Schocken Books, 1975.

Drinnon, Richard. *Rebel in Paradise.* Chicago: University of Chicago Press, 1961.

Falk, Candace, ed. *Emma Goldman: A Guide to Her Life and Documentary Sources.* Alexandria, Va.: Chadwyck-Healey Inc., 1995.

————. *Love, Anarchy, and Emma Goldman.* New York: Holt, Rinehart, 1984.

Falk, Candace, and Ronald J. Zboray and Alice Hall, eds. *The Emma Goldman Papers: A Microfilm Edition.* Alexandria, Va.: Chadwyck-Healey Inc., 1990.

Figler, Bernard, and David Rome. *Hannaniah Meir Caiserman: A Biography.* Montreal: Northern Printing and Lithographic Co., 1962.

Frazer, Winifred L. *E.G. and E.G.O.: Emma Goldman and "The Iceman Cometh".* Gainesville, Fla.: A University of Florida Book, The University Presses of Florida, University of Florida Humanities Monograph 43, 1974.

Gallagher, Dorothy. *All the Right Enemies: The Life and Murder of Carlo Tresca.* New Brunswick and London: Rutgers, 1988.

Ganguli, B. N. *Emma Goldman: Portrait of a Rebel Woman.* Bombay: Allied, 1979.

Girard, Frank, and Ben Perry. *The Socialist Labor Party 1876-1991: A Short History.* Philadelphia: Livra Books, 1991.

Goldman, Emma. *Anarchism and Other Essays.* 1917. Third revised edition. Reprint, with an introduction by Richard Drinnon. New York: Dover Publications, Inc., 1983.

————. *Living My Life.* 2 vols. 1931. Reprint. New York: Dover Publications, 1970.

————. *My Disillusionment in Russia.* 1922. Reprint. New York: Thomas Y. Crowell, 1970.

————. *The Social Significance of the Modern Drama.* Boston: Richard G. Badger, 1914.

————. *Voltairine de Cleyre.* Berkeley Heights, N.J.: Oriole Press, 1932.

Griffin, Frederick. *Variety Show.* Toronto: Macmillan, 1936.

Harris, Frank. *Contemporary Portraits.* Fourth Series. London: Grant Richards, 1924.

Hart, Arthur Daniel. *The Jew in Canada.* Toronto and Montreal: Jewish Publications Limited, 1926.

Kayfetz, Ben. *Toronto Jewry: An Historical Sketch.* Toronto: Canadian Jewish Congress, Central Region, United Jewish Welfare Fund of Toronto, 1957.

Kennedy, Paul. *Emma Goldman: A Life of Anarchy.* Toronto: The Canadian Broadcasting Corporation, 1983.

Larivière, Claude. *Le premier Mai: fête internationale de travailleurs.* Montréal: Editions coopératives Albert St.-Martin, 1975.

Lemon, James. *Toronto Since 1918: An Illustrated History.* Toronto: James Lorimer & Company, Publishers, and National Museum of Man, National Museums of Canada, 1985.

Livesay, Dorothy. *Right Hand, Left Hand: A True Life of the Thirties: Paris, Toronto, Montreal, The West and Vancouver. Love, Politics, The Depression, and Feminism.*

Erin, Ontario: Press Porcepic, 1977.

———. *Journey with My Selves: A Memoir 1909-1963.* Vancouver and Toronto: Douglas & McIntyre, 1993.

Livesay, J.F.B. *The Making of a Canadian.* Toronto: Ryerson Press, 1947.

Morton, Marian J. *Emma Goldman and the American Left: "Nowhere at Home".* New York: Wayne, 1992.

Nordquist, Joan. *Rosa Luxembourg and Emma Goldman: A Bibliography.* Santa Cruz, California: Reference and Research Services, 1996.

Peirats, Josi. *Emma Goldman, una mujer en la tormenta del siglo.* Barcelona: Laia, 1983.

Robin, Martin. *Shades of Right: Nativist and Fascist Politics in Canada, 1920–1940.* Toronto: University of Toronto Press, 1992.

Shulman, Alix Kates, ed. *Red Emma Speaks: Selected Writings and Speeches by Emma Goldman.* New York: Random House, 1972.

———. *To the Barricades: The Anarchist Life of Emma Goldman.* New York: Thomas Y. Crowell, 1971.

Solomon, Martha. *Emma Goldman.* Boston: Twayne Publishers, 1987.

Speisman, Stephen A. *The Jews of Toronto: A History to 1937.* Toronto: McClelland & Stewart, 1979.

Thompson, Lee Briscoe. *Dorothy Livesay.* Boston: Twayne Publishers, 1987.

Wexler, Alice. *Emma Goldman: An Intimate Life.* New York: Pantheon Books, 1984.

———. *Emma Goldman in Exile: From the Russian Revolution to the Spanish Civil War.* Boston: Beacon Press, 1989.

Woodcock, George. *Anarchism: A History of Libertarian Ideas and Movements.* New York: World Publishing, 1962.

Index